Alfresco 3 Web Services

Build Alfresco applications using Web Services,
WebScripts, and CMIS

Ugo Cei

Piergiorgio Lucidi

BIRMINGHAM - MUMBAI

Alfresco 3 Web Services

First published: August 2010

Production Reference: 1110810

Published by Packt Publishing Ltd.
32 Lincoln Road
Olton
Birmingham, B27 6PA, UK.

ISBN 978-1-849511-52-0

www.packtpub.com

Cover Image by John M. Quick (john.m.quick@gmail.com)

Credits

Authors
Ugo Cei

Piergiorgio Lucidi

Reviewers
Adrián Efrén Jiménez Vega

Amita Bhandari

Acquisition Editor
Steven Wilding

Development Editor
Mayuri Kokate

Technical Editor
Vishal D Wadkar

Copy Editor
Leonard D'silva

Indexer
Hemangini Bari

Editorial Team Leader
Aanchal Kumar

Project Team Leader
Lata Basantani

Project Coordinator
Jovita Pinto

Proofreader
Lesley Harrison

Graphics
Geetanjali Sawant

Production Coordinator
Aparna Bhagat

Cover Work
Aparna Bhagat

About the Authors

Ugo Cei is a solutions delivery manager at Sourcesense, Italy. He has over 20 years of experience in the IT sector. His areas of expertise include web application development, content management systems, database, and search technologies. He has a Ph.D. in Engineering from the University of Pavia, Italy. Ugo is a long-time active contributor to numerous open source projects and a member of the **Apache Software Foundation (ASF)**.

Besides his interest in computer-related matters, Ugo is a passionate photographer. He sometimes dreams of leaving the IT field to pursue his passion full-time, and travel the world with a camera.

I would like to thank the employers at Sourcesense, Italy for introducing me to Alfresco and giving me the opportunity and the time to work on this book.

Piergiorgio Lucidi is an open source product specialist and a certified Alfresco trainer at **Sourcesense**. Sourcesense is a European open source systems integrator providing consultancy, support, and services around key open source technologies. Piergiorgio has worked as a software engineer and developer for six years in the areas of **Enterprise Content Management (ECM)**, system integrations, web and mobile applications. He is an expert in integrating ECM solutions in web and portal applications. He contributes to the Alfresco Community forum regularly supporting both newbies and expert users.

Piergiorgio is a project leader and committer of the JBoss community and contributes to some of the projects around the portal platform. He is a speaker at the conferences dedicated to Java, Spring framework, and open source products and technologies. He is an affiliate partner at Packt Publishing, and writes and publishes book reviews on his website Open4Dev (http://www.open4dev.com/).

I would like to thank my colleague — Jacopo Franzoi for helping us to write the chapter of the book on the Microsoft .NET framework topic.

My special thanks to my colleague — Ugo Cei for giving me the opportunity to write my first book with him. I would like to thank all my team members at Sourcesense for improving and fixing my writing style. I would also like to thank my girlfriend — Barbara, who encouraged me during the making of this book.

About the Reviewers

Adrián Efrén Jiménez Vega works at the **Center** of **Information Technologies** (**CTI**) of the University of the Balearic Islands, in Mallorca (Spain). For four years, he has built and deployed various applications based on Alfresco. Since registering in the Alfresco Spanish forum approximately two years ago, he has dedicated time and openly shared his experience posting more than 600 messages, and contributed many practical solutions and useful hints for members of the community. The 'mini-guides' that he developed are now widely used and referenced among developers in Spain and Spanish speaking countries.

He won the "Alfresco Chumby Awards for Community Achievement" in November 2008. He has also won the "Web Script Developer Challenge" with a Web Script solution to limit the space for users, including e-mail notification. He has also worked as technical reviewer for the book *Alfresco 3 Enterprise Content Management Implementation* (Packt Publishing) in 2009.

I would like to thank all those people who made my participation possible in this project. In particular, my parents (despite the distance), my sister, and my friends at CTI.

Amita Bhandari has hands-on experience in Alfresco CMS, Java, J2EE, object-oriented Architecture, and Design Patterns. Her expertise lies in implementing J2EE technologies (JSP, Servlets, EJB, and MVC Frameworks) to develop Enterprise web applications. She has worked with various design patterns such as Struts, Spring, and Hibernate.

Tranformations of XML files into various formats, advanced workflows, Web Scripts along with experience in server-side configuration, administration, Web Services, and application deployments are really what make her a sought after authority on the subject. She has worked with clients in media and gaming, healthcare, and e-governance. She has experience of training students in Java and advanced Java technologies.

She is a senior consultant at CIGNEX. She holds a Masters in Computer Applications from Rajasthan University, India. She is also the co-author of *Alfresco 3 Enterprise Content Management Implementation*, which was published by Packt Publishing.

I would like to thank all the people who made my participation possible in this project. In particular, my parents, my spouse, my brother, my friends, and especially, Munwar Shariff and Manish Sheladia for their help and contribution.

Table of Contents

Preface

During recent years, we at Sourcesense supported our customers by implementing different system integrations based on open source technology. At Sourcesense, our main goal is to help our customers to choose the best approach for adopting open source.

Sourcesense offers consultancy, integration, high-level support, and training in enterprise-ready open source technologies across four business areas: Enterprise Content Management, Enterprise Search, Business Intelligence, and Application Lifecycle Management. We have offices in four European cities — London, Amsterdam, Rome, and Milan and we are able to offer local, co-developers and near-shoring solutions.

Sourcesense is well regarded in the open source community, contributing to many OS projects through the Apache foundation and JBoss community; we actively look for contributors and committers to hire, and we encourage them to keep contributing to the OS ecosystem. Sourcesense is also one of the exclusive training partner of Alfresco, we are the only one offering official training in the UK, Italy, and Netherlands.

Alfresco 3 is one of the most versatile open source **Enterprise Content Management (ECM)** platforms. This is a real open source alternative to commercial product such as Microsoft SharePoint and EMC Documentum. It is also very well designed and suitable to be customized and extended. The open source adoption allows developers to contribute on the project and that's why you can find more than 240 extensions in the Alfresco Forge.

This book shows you how to build applications on top of Alfresco using all the Web Service interfaces exposed by the product. Alfresco provides services to client applications for manipulating content and for performing additional operations to manage the content lifecycle.

We start discussing about the Web Services API of Alfresco that is based on the SOAP protocol. Then we describe how to extend the REST API of Alfresco using the Web Scripts Framework. Finally, we explain the new specification named **Content Management Interoperability Services (CMIS)**, it is dedicated to improve interoperability between content management systems. Alfresco was one of the first ECM platforms to provide a complete CMIS implementation. We hope that it could be useful for you to learn this new standard and how you can use it with any CMIS-compliant repository.

What this book covers

Chapter 1, Introducing the SOAP Web Services introduces the basic information about Web Services and the specific Alfresco Web Services implementation. It also explains how to set up your development environment before starting to use the Alfresco Web Services API.

Chapter 2, Creating and Modifying Content includes an overview of the **Content Manipulation Language (CML)** of Alfresco. It also describes how to use the CML language for manipulating content using the Alfresco Web Services API. This chapter also teaches you how to search contents in the repository.

Chapter 3, Collaboration and Administration covers operations for collaborative editing. You'll also learn how to manage repository actions, rules, and users.

Chapter 4, A Complete Example describes an example of a bookshop application implemented using the Web Service Client stub provided by Alfresco. This chapter shows you how to implement basic operations to manage users, books, and the cart for orders.

Chapter 5, Using the Alfresco Web Services from .NET teaches you how to use the Alfresco Web Services API from your Microsoft .NET application. It also shows you how to configure your development environment using the open source IDE SharpDevelop.

Chapter 6, Introducing the Web Scripts Framework takes you through an overview of REST concepts and also provides you a step-by-step example to start developing your first Web Script.

Chapter 7, Templating with Freemarker gives the basic concepts about Freemarker discussing about how to build your view template. It also includes an overview about the Alfresco Template Node API and the JSON format.

Chapter 8, Writing a Web Script Controller in JavaScript and Java covers how to implement a Web Script using a JavaScript controller. It describes all the root objects available in the JavaScript API of Alfresco and how to perform basic operations to manage the content. It also shows you how to pass values to the view template. It also explains how to implement Web Scripts in Java, if you need more powerful features for your functionality.

Chapter 9, Putting it All Together shows you a complete example of how to implement a bookshop application using the Web Scripts Framework.

Chapter 10, Overview of CMIS focuses on the **Content Management Interoperability Services (CMIS)** specification. You'll learn the history of this new standard and its main objectives. You'll also learn the available protocol bindings and the CMIS domain model.

Chapter 11, The CMIS AtomPub Binding introduces a section about how to perform basic operations using the REST Binding of CMIS.

Chapter 12, Developing a CMIS Client Using Apache Chemistry explains how to implement a CMIS client using the REST binding. It describes with a complete example how to perform basic operations on contents and how to search contents in the repository using Apache Chemistry.

Chapter 13, The Web Services Binding describes how to implement your client application using the CMIS SOAP binding. This chapter starts showing you how to retrieve all the WSDLs and how to generate your client stub using Apache CXF. It also explains how to perform basic operations on contents using the SOAP binding of CMIS.

Chapter 14, A Complete CMIS Client Application shows you a complete example of a Wiki application that stores contents in a CMIS-compliant repository.

At the end of the book, you will find an *Appendix* about the CMIS query language. In this section, you'll find reference information about how to build queries to search contents using CMIS. Specifically, in this section, you'll learn the CMIS relational view, clauses, operators, and predicates.

What you need for this book

The following is a list of the software that you will need for this book:

- Alfresco Community 3.3
- Eclipse 3.5
- Apache Chemistry (unreleased)

- Google Web Toolkit 2.0.3
- Spring Framework 2.5.6
- Apache CXF 2.2.6
- Microsoft .NET Framework 3.5
- SharpDevelop 3.2

Who this book is for

If you are a web developer who wants to build business applications on top of Alfresco, then this is the book for you. It is intended to be a complete overview to help developers choose a specific API with related method invocations.

Conventions

In this book, you will find a number of styles of text that distinguish between different kinds of information. Here are some examples of these styles, and an explanation of their meaning.

Code words in text are shown as follows: "A CML operation is defined with an XML `complexType` and its `sequence` of properties."

A block of code is set as follows:

```
<soapenv:Body>
<update xmlns="http://www.alfresco.org/ws/service/repository/1.0">
<statements>
<ns1:create xmlns:ns1="http://www.alfresco.org/ws/cml/1.0">
<ns1:id>1</ns1:id>
<ns1:parent>
```

When we wish to draw your attention to a particular part of a code block, the relevant lines or items are set in bold:

```
<soapenv:Body>
<update xmlns="http://www.alfresco.org/ws/service/repository/1.0">
<statements>
<ns1:create xmlns:ns1="http://www.alfresco.org/ws/cml/1.0">
<ns1:id>1</ns1:id>
<ns1:parent>
```

Any command-line input or output is written as follows:

```
curl -v -u admin:admin -X DELETE 'http://localhost:8080/alfresco/service/
books/999-0552997858'
```

New terms and **important words** are shown in bold. Words that you see on the screen, in menus, or dialog boxes for example, appear in the text like this: "Right-click on the **Package Explorer**, and click on **Import...**".

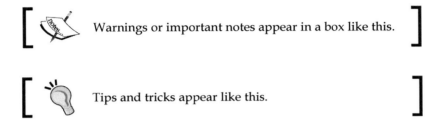

Warnings or important notes appear in a box like this.

Tips and tricks appear like this.

Reader feedback

Feedback from our readers is always welcome. Let us know what you think about this book—what you liked or may have disliked. Reader feedback is important for us to develop titles that you really get the most out of.

To send us general feedback, simply send an e-mail to feedback@packtpub.com, and mention the book title via the subject of your message.

If there is a book that you need and would like to see us publish, please send us a note in the **SUGGEST A TITLE** form on www.packtpub.com or e-mail suggest@packtpub.com.

If there is a topic that you have expertise in and you are interested in either writing or contributing to a book, see our author guide on www.packtpub.com/authors.

Customer support

Now that you are the proud owner of a Packt book, we have a number of things to help you to get the most from your purchase.

Downloading the example code for the book

You can download the example code files for all Packt books you have purchased from your account at http://www.PacktPub.com. If you purchased this book elsewhere, you can visit http://www.PacktPub.com/support and register to have the files e-mailed directly to you.

Errata

Although we have taken every care to ensure the accuracy of our content, mistakes do happen. If you find a mistake in one of our books—maybe a mistake in the text or the code—we would be grateful if you would report this to us. By doing so, you can save other readers from frustration and help us improve subsequent versions of this book. If you find any errata, please report them by visiting http://www.packtpub.com/support, selecting your book, clicking on the **errata submission form** link, and entering the details of your errata. Once your errata are verified, your submission will be accepted and the errata will be uploaded on our website, or added to any list of existing errata, under the Errata section of that title. Any existing errata can be viewed by selecting your title from http://www.packtpub.com/support.

Piracy

Piracy of copyright material on the Internet is an ongoing problem across all media. At Packt, we take the protection of our copyright and licenses very seriously. If you come across any illegal copies of our works, in any form, on the Internet, please provide us with the location address or website name immediately so that we can pursue a remedy.

Please contact us at copyright@packtpub.com with a link to the suspected pirated material.

We appreciate your help in protecting our authors, and our ability to bring you valuable content.

Questions

You can contact us at questions@packtpub.com if you are having a problem with any aspect of the book, and we will do our best to address it.

1
Introducing the SOAP Web Services API

One of the most adopted ways to manipulate content in the enterprise content management world is to use Web Services. In this chapter, you will learn about some aspects of the specification of Web Services. You will also get an overview of Alfresco and an in-depth description of the Alfresco-specific Web Services implementation.

You will learn about the Alfresco software architecture, so that you understand how Alfresco exposes the Web Services API in a better way. You can find many other implementations of Web Services outside this context, but we will focus only on the Alfresco-specific implementation.

So, in this chapter, you will learn the following:

- What Web Services are
- An introduction to the Alfresco software architecture
- An overview of the **Simple Object Access Protocol (SOAP)**
- What the **Web Services Description Language (WSDL)** is
- Which services are exposed by the Alfresco Web Services API
- How to use the Web Service Client provided by Alfresco
- How to set up the development environment using the Alfresco SDK

Web Services

Nowadays, the World Wide Web is being used more and more for making applications that communicate with each other, in addition to the kind of human-computer interaction that was prevalent in the early days.

Whenever an application provides some kind of interface that can be programmatically invoked by another application by sending some command using the HTTP protocol, we say that this is an example of a **Web Service**.

Web Services in Alfresco

The Alfresco repository is a set of Java classes that provide services to client applications for creating, manipulating, searching, and transforming content and for performing a host of additional operations such as checking and managing permissions, executing content-centric business processes, classifying content, and so on.

The publicly accessible entry points that clients can access to perform such operations make up the so-called Alfresco Foundation APIs. This is the lowest layer of APIs that can be used by client code, and all the other APIs, such as JCR and the JavaScript ones, all of the network protocols supported by Alfresco (CIFS, FTP, NFS, WebDAV, IMAP), and the Alfresco Explorer web-based frontend, call this layer in the end. There isn't any feature provided by the Alfresco repository that cannot be exploited using the Foundation APIs. However, the Foundation APIs have two main constraints:

1. The first constraint is that they are implemented as Java libraries. As long as you are developing your client applications using Java, this is not going to be too much of a limiting factor. But calling Java libraries from other languages, though possible in some circumstances, can be cumbersome and difficult.

2. The second constraint is that by using the Foundation APIs, you effectively end up *embedding* the Alfresco repository in your application. This is what the `alfresco.war` package does—it contains the Alfresco Explorer (Web Client) application and that embeds the Alfresco Repository, via the Foundation APIs in turn.

The problem here is that only one application at a time can embed the Alfresco repository. If you try to have two distinct applications embed a copy of Alfresco, both configured to act on the same storage (database, content store, and indexes), and try to run them at the same time, you will end up corrupting the contents of the repository.

If you intend to run the **Alfresco Explorer**, this will be one application embedding the repository, and you will not be able to have another custom application do the same. Therefore, if you want to develop your own custom application on top of Alfresco, using the Foundation APIs, you have no choice but to develop and deploy it as an extension of the explorer or to embed Alfresco inside your application exclusively and give up the explorer.

Web Services provide a way out of this conundrum by exposing the features of the Alfresco Repository through a layer of services that can be invoked remotely over the network by exchanging messages over HTTP. This frees client applications from having to embed Alfresco—there will be only one repository, usually embedded in the Explorer, that also provides network-accessible services for remote clients to call.

These kind of Web Services are also language-agnostic, which means that you are not limited to using Java for implementing your client application, but you are also free to use any language, as long as it provides a way to send and receive messages using the HTTP protocol and is able to parse and generate messages using some well-known format such as XML.

You are also not forced to develop your application as a Web application. Creating a native GUI client, a Flash, or an iPhone application can be a perfectly reasonable choice.

Introducing SOAP

The organizations that oversee the creation of new standards for the Web—most notably the **World Wide Web Consortium (W3C)**–have, since a long time, acknowledged the necessity of defining a set of technologies. This set would favor the interoperability of applications running on different hardware and software architectures and is developed using the most disparate programming languages and platforms.

These technologies are mostly based upon the XML language, which include a protocol called **Simple Object Access Protocol (SOAP)**. This protocol has been defined with the purpose of letting heterogeneous applications, running in a distributed, decentralized environment, exchange structured messages. Providing an extended description of SOAP is beyond the scope of this book, as there are many other printed and online resources covering it in minute detail. A few points, starting with the normative reference issued by the W3C at `http://www.w3.org/TR/soap/` especially, will be presented here, as they are relevant to the Web Services exposed by Alfresco.

SOAP vs. REST

If you have been following the trends and the discussions in the Web Services community, you will, undoubtedly, have heard about this supposedly ongoing war between proponents of SOAP and the new-fangled way of doing Web Services that is usually referred to as **REST**. You might also be justified in thinking that SOAP is somewhat old-fashioned, driven by industry interests, totally designed by committee, and therefore should be avoided as much as possible.

While some of the previous claims have a ring of truth to them, we are not here to tell you that you should never consider SOAP for using Alfresco-provided Web Services. It is still a reasonable technology, especially if your aim is to be able to quickly develop a new client application, as the existing toolkits hide much of the complexity from your code.

Moreover, the most recent version of SOAP, 1.2, is not so much tied to a model of distributed object calling methods on each other as it once was. However, it also pays due reverence to a model based on the exchange of resource representations, which is the underlying concept of REST. It is not entirely unreasonable to think of using SOAP 1.2 to implement a perfectly *RESTful* service.

In the end, the choice is yours, but if you are not interested at all in SOAP-based Alfresco Web Services, you can go straight to *Chapter 6, Introducing the Web Scripts Framework.*

The format of SOAP messages

Applications using SOAP communicate by exchanging one-way XML messages over a communication channel. Typically, but not exclusively, HTTP is used as the transmission protocol. A SOAP message, such as the following, contains one XML document, whose root element is Envelope:

```xml
<?xml version="1.0" encoding="UTF-8"?>

<soapenv:Envelope xmlns:soapenv="http://schemas.xmlsoap.org/soap/
envelope/" xmlns:xsd="http://www.w3.org/2001/XMLSchema" xmlns:
xsi="http://www.w3.org/2001/XMLSchema-instance">

  <soapenv:Header>
    <!-- application specific information -->
  </soapenv:Header>

  <soapenv:Body>
    <yourCustomServiceMethod xmlns="yourCustomServiceNamespace">
    <parameters />
    </yourCustomServiceMethod>
  </soapenv:Body>

</soapenv:Envelope>
```

The Envelope element is the root element of a SOAP message, and it must conform to the following XML Schema:

http://schemas.xmlsoap.org/soap/envelope/

A SOAP Envelope element consists of:

- A Header element (optional)
- A Body element (mandatory)

The Header element is used to communicate information that is not application data, but is used to control the message exchange. For instance, a header can be used to send information about security or transactions. The contents of the Body element can be any valid XML fragment, and it is meant to convey application-specific information from the client to the server.

While the SOAP specification does not impose any type of semantic constraint upon the contents of the body of messages, the original purpose, and still the most common usage of SOAP, is for implementing a **Remote Procedure Call (RPC)** mechanism. When this is the case, such as with most Web Services exposed by Alfresco, the XML message contained in the client request will specify the names of remote procedures and the values of the parameters being passed to those procedures. Likewise, the response returned by the server will contain a representation of the return values from those procedures.

In the following code, you can find an example of calling the getStores method exposed by Alfresco (only the SOAP Body element is shown):

```
<soapenv:Body>
  <getStores xmlns="http://www.alfresco.org/ws/service/
repository/1.0">
  </getStores>
</soapenv:Body>
```

A possible response from the Alfresco server is shown as follows:

```
<soapenv:Body>
  <getStoresResponse
  xmlns="http://www.alfresco.org/ws/service/repository/1.0">
  <return xsi:type="cms:store">
  <!-- returns structured datatypes -->
...
  </return>
  </getStoresResponse>
</soapenv:Body>
```

Note that if you want to implement a different SOAP response message for your service, the response method has the same name of the request method with a suffix `Response`. In this specific sample, we have:

- A `getStores` method as the request method
- A `getStoresResponse` method as the `getStores` response method

If you don't define a different response message for your method invocation, the SOAP protocol will send the same request message with a different timestamp as the default response. It is shown in the following figure:

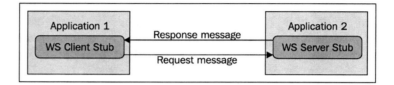

The Web Services Description Language

Another important element in the Web Services protocol stack is the **Web Services Description Language (WSDL)**. This is the language that is used to describe the format of messages exchanged by actors using SOAP.

A server that exposes one or more SOAP-based Web Services should make available, at a documented URL, a set of WSDL documents describing such services. Using the information gathered from consulting the published WSDL documents, clients should be able to generate messages that conform to the formats required by the server in a fully automated way.

For a service that provides an RPC style of invocation, the WSDL will specify the names of the following:

- The **operations** that the service exposes, usually corresponding to the methods on the server
- The request and response messages that, together, realize a method invocation and its response
- The types of the parameters and return values contained in the request and response messages

The types involved in the calls are usually defined with the help of an **XML Schema Declaration (XSD)** document.

In Alfresco, each service exposed through the Web Services API is defined in a separate WSDL file that contains the specifications of all the operations and data types involved.

Using a WSDL document and one of the commonly available Web Services development toolkits, it is possible to automatically generate the so-called **client stub**. A client stub is set of classes and methods that reflects the operations available on the server. It also relieves the client application from having to deal with the complexity of setting up a connection using the relevant transport protocol — for formatting messages according to the SOAP specification and marshalling and un-marshalling native data types to and from XML.

Such toolkits are available from many programming languages, including Java, C#, PHP, and many others. Therefore, it is relatively easy to implement a Web Services client, even without knowing a lot about SOAP, as most of the complexity involved in using it is usually hidden beneath a suitable abstraction layer.

The Alfresco SDK contains, such a client stub which was mostly generated automatically from the relevant WSDLs and that will be used throughout the rest of this chapter and the following few.

Using Alfresco Web Services

Provided you can access an instance of Alfresco running on the server `host` and listening on TCP `port`, you can retrieve all the WSDLs for the Alfresco Web Services by pointing a browser to the URL for each service, as detailed in the following table.

Each service provides a set of operations related by a common purpose, so that you may use only the ones that you are interested in:

Service name	Purpose	URL
`AccessControlService`	Manage permissions	`http://host:port/alfresco/api/AccessControlService?WSDL`
`ActionService`	Execute custom actions and rules	`http://host:port/alfresco/api/ActionService?WSDL`
`AdministrationService`	Manage users and groups	`http://host:port/alfresco/api/AdministrationService?WSDL`

Service name	Purpose	URL
AuthenticationService	Login and access session tickets	http://host:port/alfresco/api/AuthenticationService?WSDL
AuthoringService	Allows collaboration between users	http://host:port/alfresco/api/AuthoringService?WSDL
ContentService	Read and write content	http://host:port/alfresco/api/ContentService?WSDL
ClassificationService	Manage categories	http://host:port/alfresco/api/ClassificationService?WSDL
DictionaryService	Manage content models	http://host:port/alfresco/api/DictionaryService?WSDL
RepositoryService	Navigate, search, and manipulate nodes.	http://host:port/alfresco/api/RepositoryService?WSDL

Besides retrieving the WSDL documents online, using the URLs from the previous table, you can also find copies of the WSDLs as files in the Alfresco source tree. You can download a copy of the Alfresco source from the Subversion repository, as explained in the wiki page at http://wiki.alfresco.com/wiki/Alfresco_SVN_Development_Environment. The WSDL files can be found under root/projects/remote-api/source/wsdl in your copy of the source tree. In this folder, you can also find all the WSDL files related to the Web Services binding of the CMIS implementation of Alfresco that will be described in *Chapter 13, The Web Services Binding*. Another location where you can find a copy of the WSDL documents is inside the Alfresco SDK, in the lib/remote/wsdl folder. Downloading and installing the Alfresco SDK is the subject of the next section.

Using the Alfresco Web Services client SDK

If you are developing a remote application to contact Alfresco using Java, Alfresco provides you with a precompiled Web Services client stub. The client stub allows you to invoke the Alfresco SOAP Web Services from a remote Java application, using a set of Java interfaces.

The code that makes up this client stub is available as part of the Alfresco SDK. You can download the Alfresco SDK from the same location where you can download the rest of Alfresco software. You can always browse the following web page to discover the list of files that can be downloaded for the most recent version of Alfresco Community:

http://wiki.alfresco.com/wiki/Download_Community_Edition.

Click on the **Custom Installs** link and look for a file to download named something like `alfresco-community-sdk-3.3.zip`. Once you have unpacked it, you can load the SDK as a set of projects in the Eclipse IDE, which is explained as follows, or create a project in a different IDE, and add the libraries contained in the SDK as dependencies there.

The client stub code is contained in the `alfresco-web-service-client-3.3.jar`. The interfaces contained therein can be used from your client Java application, as depicted in the following diagram. The purpose of the various interfaces and their intended usage will be the subject of the upcoming chapters.

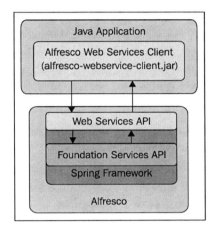

Setting up the Alfresco SDK

To develop your own Web Service client application using the Web Services API of Alfresco, you need to configure your development environment with the Alfresco SDK.

Before starting to develop an application that uses the Alfresco Web Services, you need the following prerequisites:

- Java JDK 1.5 (Sun implementation)
- An IDE application to write your own source code for your application

The most common known IDEs used in the community are Eclipse and NetBeans. In this book, we will use Eclipse for all the examples and screenshots, but you can use any other IDEs.

The steps to set up your development environment using Eclipse IDE are as follows:

1. Download the latest updated version of Java JDK 1.6 from the Sun website.
2. Install Java JDK 1.6.
3. Download the latest version of the Eclipse IDE from `http://eclipse.org`.
4. Install Eclipse IDE.
5. Extract the Alfresco SDK package previously downloaded.
6. Import all the projects from the extracted Alfresco SDK projects from the root folder in your workspace in your IDE, in the following way:
7. Right-click on the **Package Explorer**, and click on **Import....**
8. Expand the **General** folder.
9. Select **Existing Projects into Workspace**, and press the **Next** button
10. Now on the **Select Root Directory** field, you can browse to select the root folder of the extracted Alfresco SDK.
11. Click on the **Finish** button to import all the projects in your Eclipse Workspace.
12. Make sure that the Java compiler compliance level is set at least to 5.0 from **Windows | Preferences | Java | Compiler**.

Now we have imported all the projects provided by the Alfresco SDK in to our workspace.

In order to have Alfresco source code and Java docs configured properly in Eclipse, we need to associate source code packages, related to Alfresco libraries, in the following way:

1. Right-click on the **SDK AlfrescoEmbedded** project.
2. Click on **Properties**.
3. Click on **Java Build Path**.
4. Click on **Libraries**.
5. Expand **alfresco-repository-3.3.jar**.
6. Select **Source attachment**.
7. Click on the **Edit...** button.
8. Click on the **External File...** button.
9. Browse to and select this file: `Alfresco SDK/src/alfresco-repository-src.zip`.
10. Repeat all the previous steps for the following libraries:

Alfresco SDK Project	Library	Source code package
SDK AlfrescoEmbedded	`alfresco-repository-3.3.jar`	`alfresco-repository-src.zip`
SDK AlfrescoEmbedded	`alfresco-core-3.3.jar`	`alfresco-core-src.zip`
SDK AlfrescoEmbedded	`alfresco-remote-api-3.3.jar`	`alfresco-remote-api.zip`
SDK AlfrescoEmbedded	`alfresco-web-client-3.3.jar`	`alfresco-web-client-src.zip`
SDK AlfrescoRemote	`alfresco-web-service-client-3.3.jar`	`alfresco-web-service-client-src.zip`

If you want Javadocs, you also need to associate Javadocs archives:

1. Right-click on the **SDK AlfrescoEmbedded** project.
2. Click **Properties**.
3. Click on **Java Build Path**.
4. Click on **Libraries**.
5. Expand **alfresco-repository-3.3.jar**.
6. Select the **Javadoc** location.
7. Click the **Edit...** button.
8. Click the **Javadoc in archive** button.
9. Click the **External file** button.
10. Click the **Browse...** button for the **Archive path** field.
11. Browse to and select the `Alfresco SDK/doc/alfresco-repository-doc.zip` file.

In the same way as source code packages, repeat all the previous steps for all the following Javadoc archives:

Alfresco SDK project	Library	Archive package
SDK AlfrescoEmbedded	`alfresco-repository-3.3.jar`	`alfresco-repository-doc.zip`
SDK AlfrescoEmbedded	`alfresco-core-3.3.jar`	`alfresco-core-doc.zip`
SDK AlfrescoEmbedded	`alfresco-remote-api-3.3.jar`	`alfresco-remote-api-doc.zip`
SDK AlfrescoEmbedded	`alfresco-web-client-3.3.jar`	`alfresco-web-client-doc.zip`
SDK AlfrescoRemote	`alfresco-web-service-client-3.3.jar`	`alfresco-web-service-client-doc.zip`

The most important projects that we will use in this book are:

- `SDK AlfrescoEmbedded`
- `SDK AlfrescoRemote`

`SDK AlfrescoEmbedded` will be used to show you how to implement a Java-backed Web Script using the Foundation Services API of Alfresco.

`SDK AlfrescoRemote` will be used to show you how to implement your own Web Services client stub in your custom application. In this way, we can invoke remote calls to the repository using the **Content Manipulation Language (CML)**.

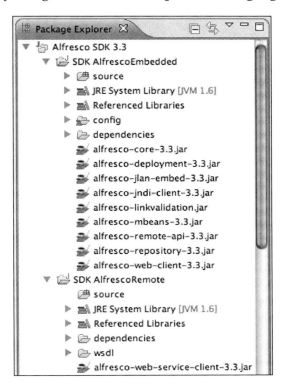

Testing the Web Services client

Once you have set up the SDK in Eclipse, as explained in the previous section, you can run a sample program to verify that it is working correctly. In order to perform this test, make sure that you have installed Alfresco and that it is running. We are going to assume that it is listening for an incoming connection on the host `localhost`, port `8080`.

From within Eclipse, expand the **SDK FirstWebServiceClient** project, and look for the source code file named `FirstWebServiceClient.java`. Right-click on the file, and select **Run As | Java Application**. The program should start up and, after a couple of seconds, print out the following to the console window:

`Content Length: 43`

Now, browse the **Company Home** space using the **Alfresco Explorer** (http://localhost:8080/alfresco) and check that a file has been created there with a name like Web Services sample (*long number here*).

 If your server is not listening on port 8080 of the localhost, which is the default port, you need to modify the file source/alfresco/webserviceclient.properties, contained in the sample, and change the value of the repository.location property according to your server's hostname and port.

Summary

In this chapter, we have given you an overview of Web Services and specifically discussed how the Web Services API is integrated in the Alfresco software architecture. In the second section, we saw an overview of the SOAP protocol and the basics behind the client/server paradigm. Then we introduced the services that are exposed by Alfresco and where you can retrieve all the available WSDL files.

Finally, we discussed how to set up and test your Java development environment using the Alfresco SDK in Eclipse IDE. In this way, you can start to develop your application using all the dependencies described. You also learned how to associate Alfresco source code and Javadocs in Eclipse.

In the next chapter, you will learn how to remotely perform operations in the Alfresco repository using the Web Services API.

2
Creating and Modifying Content

In this chapter, you will learn how to perform operations on nodes using the Alfresco Web Services API. We will start by introducing the **Content Manipulation Language (CML)**, which is the language used to invoke operations against the repository. Then, we will discuss the operations that you can use to manage your content. Specifically, you will learn how to perform the following operations:

- Authenticate users against the Alfresco repository
- Search content on Alfresco
- Create nodes
- Remove nodes
- Move nodes
- Copy nodes
- Manage associations
- Update nodes
- Add and remove aspects on nodes

The Content Manipulation Language (CML)

Alfresco has created the **Content Manipulation Language** (CML) to provide a mechanism to perform multiple statements in the repository using a unique SOAP message. This is an XML-based language defined with an XML Schema available at the following address:

```
http://svn.alfresco.com/repos/alfresco-open-mirror/alfresco/HEAD/
root/projects/remote-api/source/wsdl/cml.xsd.
```

You can also find it in the Alfresco SDK, at this path:
`Alfresco SDK/lib/remote/wsdl/cml.xsd`.

As the CML is based on XML, it can easily be represented in other programming languages. This means that each statement will be declared with an XML snippet that must conform to the XML schema of the CML language. One of the operations that we will start to describe later is the `CMLCreate` operation. This operation allows you to create a new node in the repository, and it is declared in the `cml.xsd` file as a statement, in the following way:

```xml
<xsd:element name="create" maxOccurs="unbounded" minOccurs="0">
    <xsd:complexType>
        <xsd:sequence>
            <xsd:element name="id" type="xsd:string" maxOccurs="1"
minOccurs="0"></xsd:element>
            <xsd:element name="parent" type="cms:ParentReference"
maxOccurs="1" minOccurs="0" nillable="true"></xsd:element>
            <xsd:element name="parent_id" type="xsd:string" maxOccurs="1"
minOccurs="0" nillable="true"></xsd:element>
                <xsd:group ref="cms:ChildAssociation" maxOccurs="1"
minOccurs="0"></xsd:group>
            <xsd:element name="type" type="cms:Name" maxOccurs="1"
minOccurs="0"></xsd:element>
            <xsd:element name="property" type="cms:NamedValue"
maxOccurs="unbounded" minOccurs="0"></xsd:element>
        </xsd:sequence>
    </xsd:complexType>
</xsd:element>
```

A CML operation is defined with an XML `complexType` and its `sequence` of properties. For each request of a `CMLCreate`, the client stub will generate the following XML code to perform the operation:

```xml
<soapenv:Body>
    <update xmlns="http://www.alfresco.org/ws/service/
repository/1.0">
        <statements>
            <ns1:create xmlns:ns1="http://www.alfresco.org/ws/
cml/1.0">
                <ns1:id>1</ns1:id>
                <ns1:parent>
                    <ns2:store xmlns:ns2="http://www.alfresco.org/ws/
model/content/1.0">
                        <ns2:scheme>workspace</ns2:scheme>
                        <ns2:address>SpacesStore</ns2:address>
                    </ns2:store>
                    <ns3:path xmlns:ns3="http://www.alfresco.org/ws/
```

```
model/content/1.0">/app:company_home</ns3:path>
                    <ns4:associationType
xmlns:ns4="http://www.alfresco.org/ws/model/content/1.0">{http://www.
alfresco.org/model/content/1.0}contains
                    </ns4:associationType>
                    <ns5:childName xmlns:ns5="http://www.alfresco.org/
ws/model/content/1.0">{http://www.alfresco.org/model/content/1.0}AWS
                        Book</ns5:childName>
                </ns1:parent>
            <ns1:type>{http://www.alfresco.org/model/content/1.0}content
            </ns1:type>
                    <ns1:property>
                    <ns6:name xmlns:ns6="http://www.alfresco.org/ws/
model/content/1.0">{http://www.alfresco.org/model/content/1.0}name
                    </ns6:name>
                    <ns7:isMultiValue xmlns:ns7="http://www.alfresco.
org/ws/model/content/1.0">false
                    </ns7:isMultiValue>
                    <ns8:value xmlns:ns8="http://www.alfresco.org/ws/
model/content/1.0">AWS Book</ns8:value>
                    </ns1:property>
                    <ns1:property>
                    <ns9:name xmlns:ns9="http://www.alfresco.org/ws/
model/content/1.0">{http://www.alfresco.org/model/content/1.0}title
                    </ns9:name>
                    <ns10:isMultiValue xmlns:ns10="http://www.alfresco.
org/ws/model/content/1.0">false
                    </ns10:isMultiValue>
                    <ns11:value xmlns:ns11="http://www.alfresco.org/ws/
model/content/1.0">AWS Book</ns11:value>
                    </ns1:property>
                    <ns1:property>
                    <ns12:name xmlns:ns12="http://www.alfresco.
org/ws/model/content/1.0">{http://www.alfresco.org/model/content/
1.0}description
                    </ns12:name>
                    <ns13:isMultiValue xmlns:ns13="http://www.alfresco.
org/ws/model/content/1.0">false
                    </ns13:isMultiValue>
                    <ns14:value xmlns:ns14="http://www.alfresco.org/
ws/model/content/1.0">This is a content created with a sample of the
book</ns14:value>
                    </ns1:property>
                </ns1:create>
            </statements>
        </update>
    </soapenv:Body>
```

As you can see, in this sample message, we have a unique operation of type `create`. This operation must conform to the XML Schema of the CML language, as declared in the previous namespace as `http://www.alfresco.org/ws/cml/1.0`.

The `statements` element allows you to encapsulate many CML statements in a unique request message. If you want to create two nodes, then the client stub will generate an array of `CMLCreate` operations in this way:

```
<soapenv:Body>
    <update xmlns="http://www.alfresco.org/ws/service/repository/1.0">
        <statements>
            <ns1:create xmlns:ns1="http://www.alfresco.org/ws/cml/1.0">
                <ns1:id>1</ns1:id>
            </ns1:create>
            <ns15:create xmlns:ns15="http://www.alfresco.org/ws/cml/1.0">
                <ns15:id>2</ns15:id>
            </ns15:create>
        </statements>
    </update>
</soapenv:Body>
```

CML allows you to perform multiple operations defining an array for each type of operation. You can also perform different types of operations in the same request.

 You can find more information about CML at the following URL: `http://wiki.alfresco.com/wiki/CML`.

Setting up the Java classpath

Before starting the implementation of your client, you need to configure your Java project properly. You can follow two main different approaches for this, namely, using the precompiled Alfresco Web Service Client or using a third-party implementation.

Using the precompiled client

If you would like to use the SDK AlfrescoRemote, you can use the precompiled Web Service Client provided by Alfresco. This is the adopted approach for the book. This project must be selected as one of your required projects for your build path. In this way, you are going to use all the dependencies needed for the Alfresco Web Services Client.

We are assuming that you have correctly set up the SDK in Eclipse, as shown in the previous chapter. In order to configure your Java project correctly in Eclipse, you need to follow these steps:

1. Right click on your application module in the **Package Explorer**.
2. Select **Java Build Path | Projects**.
3. Click on the **Add...** button.
4. Choose **SDK AlfrescoRemote** and click on the **OK** button.

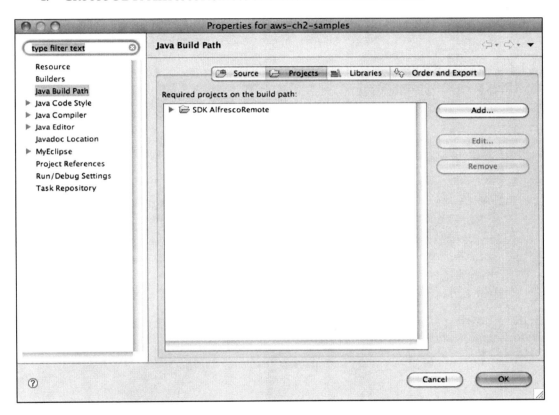

Using third-party frameworks

Alternately, if you don't want to use the precompiled Web Service Client, you can generate your client stub getting all the WSDLs exposed by Alfresco. These are described in the previous chapter. Each WSDL file can be used with any framework dedicated to implement Web Services, for instance, Apache CXF or Apache Axis.

The final artifact of the framework is the client code that you can embed in your project to invoke remote methods using the Alfresco Web Services API. This means that you will have specific dependencies in your Java Build Path without using the SDK AlfrescoRemote project. But all the methods and objects are the same as we described in this chapter.

Authentication

The first step needed for each operation that you want to perform in the repository is an authentication request for a specific user. The authentication process allows you to create a user session in the repository. During this operation, the user credentials are verified to allow a specific user to start executing any operation on contents. In order to manage an authentication request, you need to use a utility class provided by Alfresco named `AuthenticationUtils`.

The methods that are available to manage authentication are as follows:

1. `startSession(String username, String password)`: It is used to start a new user session.
2. `endSession()`: It is used to end the current user session.
3. `getAuthenticationDetails()`: It is used to get the authentication details for the current user session.
4. `setAuthenticationDetails(AuthenticationDetails authenticationDetails)`: It is used to set authentication details for the current session.
5. `getTicket()`: It is used to get the ticket for the current authentication details.

In the following sample, you can see how to create and remove a user session for the default user admin available in Alfresco:

```
AuthenticationUtils.startSession("admin", "admin");
  Try
  {
  // now Admin is authenticated in the repository
  }
  finally {
AuthenticationUtils.endSession();
  }
```

As you can imagine, the Alfresco Web Service Client has a default value for the endpoint address of the service exposed by the repository; that's why you don't find any line of code dedicated to this. The default value defined for the endpoint address is:

```
http://localhost:8080/alfresco/api.
```

However, you can set the endpoint address in two ways—using a properties file or programmatically.

Setting the endpoint address with a properties file

In order to set the endpoint address using a properties file for your client application, you need to create a properties file named webserviceclient.properties in a package named alfresco, and then you need to type its content as follows:
repository.location=http://<IP ADDRESS>:<PORT NUMBER>/alfresco/api.

The Alfresco Web Service Client will override the default value, taking the new one from your classpath, as you can see in the following sample project included with this chapter, which is displayed in the following screenshot:

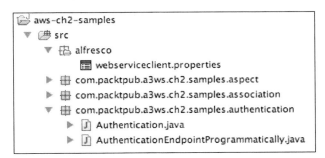

Setting the endpoint address programmatically

If you want to programmatically set the endpoint address, you need to provide the remote location using another utility class named WebServiceFactory.

Before starting a new user session, you need to invoke the static method named setEndpointAddress in the following way:

```
//overriding default endpoint programmatically
String endPointAddress = "http://localhost:8080/alfresco/api";
WebServiceFactory.setEndpointAddress(endPointAddress);
```

```
AuthenticationUtils.startSession("admin", "admin");
try {

// now admin is authenticated in the repository

} finally {
AuthenticationUtils.endSession();
}
```

`WebServiceFactory` allows you to configure your client stub and helps you to get all the services available in Alfresco.

Performing operations on nodes

In order to perform operations on contents, you need to create a specific CML operation object. You have to create a unique CML container object with multiple CML operations using the Repository Service and invoking the `update` method in this way:

```
UpdateResult[] result = WebServiceFactory.getRepositoryService().
update(cml);
```

We are going to see how to perform the following CML operations in the repository:

Operation	Description
CMLCreate	Creates a new node.
CMLAddAspect	Adds an aspect on a node.
CMLRemoveAspect	Removes an aspect from a node.
CMLUpdate	Updates a node.
CMLWriteContent	Writes a byte stream of the file associated with a node.
CMLMove	Moves a node to another space.
CMLCopy	Copies a node.
CMLAddChild	Adds a child to a node (defined with a child-association).
CMLRemoveChild	Removes a child from a node (defined with a child-association).
CMLCreateAssociation	Creates an instance of a peer association from a node to another node.
CMLRemoveAssociation	Removes an instance of a peer association from a node to another node.
CMLDelete	Removes a node.

All these groups of operations are executed exactly in this order by Alfresco. This means that Alfresco starts to perform all the CMLCreate operations, then all the CMLAddAspect operations, and so on. All the operations are sorted only by its own group using the local ID that you have to provide for performing any CML operation.

Creating nodes

In order to create a new node in the repository, you need to create a new CMLCreate object. The following is its constructor:

```
public CMLCreate(
java.lang.String id,
org.alfresco.webservice.types.ParentReference parent,
java.lang.String parent_id,
java.lang.String associationType,
java.lang.String childName,
java.lang.String type,
org.alfresco.webservice.types.NamedValue[] property)
```

A CMLCreate object requires you to set some of the arguments declared in the constructor because some of them are optional. You can find all the details in the following table:

Argument	Description
id	The local ID defined to sort the execution for all the CMLCreate operations.
parent	ParentReference associated to the new child node (optional, if parent_id is defined).
parent_id	Parent UUID (optional, if parent is defined).
associationType	QName of the association (optional, if associationType is defined in the parent reference).
childName	ID for the new specific instance of association (optional, if the childName is defined in the parent reference).
type	QName of the content type.
property	Properties array defined with a NamedValue[].

As you can see, before creating a new CMLCreate object, you need to create a ParentReference object. The container for your new node is as follows:

```
public ParentReference(
org.alfresco.webservice.types.Store store,
java.lang.String uuid,
java.lang.String path,
java.lang.String associationType,
java.lang.String childName)
```

Again, you can create this object in two different ways, because there are some optional arguments that you can omit, which are shown as follows:

- `store`—stores the reference of the store for the involved parent
- `uuid`—stores the UUID of the parent reference (optional, if the `path` is defined)
- `path`—stores the path of the parent reference (optional, if `uuid` is defined)
- `associationType`—stores the QName of the association
- `childName`—stores the ID for the new specific instance of association for the new node

Finally, you can create a new node in the **Company Home**, as shown in the following code:

```
ParentReference parent = new ParentReference(
spacesStore,
null,
"/app:company_home",
Constants.ASSOC_CONTAINS,
"{" + Constants.NAMESPACE_CONTENT_MODEL + "}"+name);

//build properties
NamedValue[] properties = buildCustomProperties(createSampleVo);

//create operation
CMLCreate create = new CMLCreate();
create.setId("1");
create.setParent(parent);
create.setType(Constants.TYPE_CONTENT);
create.setProperty(properties);

//build the CML object
CML cml = new CML();
cml.setCreate(new CMLCreate[]{create});
//perform a complete CML update
UpdateResult[] result = WebServiceFactory.getRepositoryService().
update(cml);
```

The `update` method is **transaction-aware**—this means that Alfresco will execute all the CML operations in a unique transaction. If one of the CML operations throws an exception, then Alfresco will roll back the transaction.

It is suggested to create a `buildCustomProperties` method dedicated to specified content types in Alfresco.

```
private static NamedValue[] buildCustomProperties(String name, String
title, String description) {
    NamedValue[] properties = new NamedValue[3];
    properties[0] = Utils.createNamedValue(Constants.PROP_NAME,
name);
    properties[1] = Utils.createNamedValue(Constants.PROP_TITLE,
title);
    properties[2] = Utils.createNamedValue(Constants.PROP_
DESCRIPTION, description);
    return properties;
}
```

`Utils` is a utility class that helps you to create the `NamedValue` array for the node properties. Note that all the properties in Alfresco must be referred to by a `QName`.

Creating content

In the previous section, you learnt how to create a new node with metadata in the repository. However, if you want to store a file associated with this new node, you need to perform a `CMLWriteContent` operation as follows:

```
public CMLWriteContent(
java.lang.String property,
byte[] content,
org.alfresco.webservice.types.ContentFormat format,
org.alfresco.webservice.types.Predicate where,
java.lang.String where_id)
```

In the previous code, `property` is the specific property dedicated to referring to the content file in the content store of Alfresco. The `content` is the byte stream of the file to be stored.

The `format` argument must be a `ContentFormat` object, and you need to set the MIME type and the `encoding` of the content for indexing. It's important to set the MIME type and the encoding for the content correctly because this allows Lucene to create all the indexes correctly. In this way, you can search and find the content in the repository.

If you set the wrong values in the `ContentFormat` object, Lucene cannot create the indexes for the new content, and this means that this content can't be found in Alfresco.

If you are considering a new file with a text/plain mime type and UTF-8 encoding, you will have to provide a `ContentFormat` instance created in this way:

```
ContentFormat format = new ContentFormat("text/plain", "UTF-8");
```

For the next argument, we find another optional item. This means that you can create a `CMLWriteContent` object in two ways using `where` or `where_id` as follows:

- `where_id` must be a UUID of the involved node

- `where` argument must be a `Predicate` object that allows you to declare all the references involved in the association with the new content, which can be shown as follows:

```
//create the node reference
Reference reference = new Reference();
reference.setStore(spacesStore);
reference.setPath("/app:company_home/cm:"+ISO9075.encode(name));
//create the predicate
Predicate predicate = new Predicate();
predicate.setNodes(new Reference[]{reference});
```

A `Reference` for a node can be created in two ways—using the UUID or using the path:

```
public Reference(
org.alfresco.webservice.types.Store store,
java.lang.String uuid,
java.lang.String path)
```

This means that you can use this constructor with optional arguments that you can set to null value. For instance, you can create a node reference for the **Company Home | Data Dictionary** space, using a UUID taken from the repository as follows:

```
Reference reference =
new Reference(spacesStore, "d43d38c1-02ff-4ae7-a540-651134228747",
null);
```

Or you can use the following path:

```
Reference reference =
new Reference(spacesStore, null, "/app:company_home/app:dictionary");
```

`ISO9075` is an utility class that allows you to encode a string according to the ISO 9075 format. This encoding is mandatory for all the space names when you set the path value because paths in Alfresco are stored using the ISO 9075 format.

Finally, you learned how to provide all the arguments, and you can perform a
CMLWriteContent operation in this way:

```
//write operation
CMLWriteContent writeContent = new CMLWriteContent();
writeContent.setFormat(format);
writeContent.setWhere(predicate);
writeContent.setProperty(Constants.PROP_CONTENT);
writeContent.setContent("This is the content for the new node".
getBytes());
//build the CML object
CML cml = new CML();
cml.setCreate(new CMLCreate[]{create});
cml.setWriteContent(new CMLWriteContent[]{writeContent});
//perform a complete CML update
UpdateResult[] result = WebServiceFactory.getRepositoryService().
update(cml);
```

Creating content using the content service

An alternative way to store a file for a node is using the content service. There are no
particular differences between the previous CMLWriteContent and this. Using the
content service, you have to perform a separate call to the repository after you have
created the related node.

The write method is the involved method, and it is based on the following declaration:

```
public Content write(
final Reference node,
final String property,
final byte[] content,
final ContentFormat format) throws RemoteException, ContentFault
```

Now, you should be able to create all the needed arguments for this method, and so
you can use the write method as follows:

```
//perform a CML update for the node
UpdateResult[] result = WebServiceFactory.getRepositoryService().
update(cml);
//get the new node reference
Reference referenceForContent = result[0].getDestination();
//create content with ContentService
ContentFormat format = new ContentFormat(mimeType, encoding);
```

```
Content content =
WebServiceFactory.getContentService().write(
referenceForContent,
Constants.PROP_CONTENT,
"This is the content for the new node".getBytes(), format);
```

In the previous sample, the result nodes are taken from `UpdateResult` and invoke the `getDestination()` method.

Removing nodes

In order to remove nodes from the repository, you have to create a `CMLDelete` object, setting a `Predicate` with all the node references involved in this operation, as shown in the following snippet:

```
Predicate predicate = new Predicate(
new Reference[]{reference}, spacesStore, null);

//delete content
CMLDelete delete = new CMLDelete();
delete.setWhere(predicate);
//create CML update object
CML cmlRemove = new CML();
cmlRemove.setDelete(new CMLDelete[]{delete});
//perform a CML update to create the node
WebServiceFactory.getRepositoryService().update(cmlRemove);
```

Moving nodes

In the following sample, you will learn how to move nodes from one space to another in the repository. The involved object for this operation is the `CMLMove` object, which can be shown as follows:

```
public CMLMove(
org.alfresco.repo.webservice.types.ParentReference to,
java.lang.String to_id,
java.lang.String associationType,
java.lang.String childName,
org.alfresco.repo.webservice.types.Predicate where,
java.lang.String where_id)
```

Again, in this sample, you can find some optional arguments that you can omit. They are as follows:

- `to` — the target `ParentReference` (optional, if `to_id` is defined)
- `to_id` — the UUID of the parent reference(optional, if `to` is defined)
- `associationType` — the QName of the association involved (optional)
- `childName` — the instance id of the node in the association (optional)
- `where` — the source predicate with all the references to move (optional, if `where_id` is defined)
- `where_id` — the UUID of the source node to move (optional, if `where` is defined)

We want to create two nodes in the **Company Home**, namely, a generic content node and a folder (a space).

1. We are going to create the generic content node as follows:

```
//create a node
CMLCreate create = new CMLCreate();
create.setId("1");
create.setParent(parentForNode);
create.setType(Constants.TYPE_CONTENT);
create.setProperty(properties);
```

2. We are going to create the space as follows:

```
//create a space
CMLCreate createSpace = new CMLCreate();
createSpace.setId("2");
createSpace.setParent(parentForSpace);
createSpace.setType(Constants.TYPE_FOLDER);
createSpace.setProperty(propertiesForSpace);
```

3. We need to package all the CML operations in an unique CML container object as follows:

```
//build the CML object
CML cmlAdd = new CML();
cmlAdd.setCreate(new CMLCreate[]{create, createSpace});
//perform a CML update to create nodes
UpdateResult[] result = WebServiceFactory.getRepositoryService().
update(cmlAdd);
```

4. Finally, we want to move the generic node from **Company Home** to the new subspace as follows:

```
//create a predicate with the first CMLCreate
Reference referenceForNode = result[0].getDestination();
Predicate sourcePredicate =
new Predicate(new Reference[]{referenceForNode}, spacesStore,
null);
//create a reference from the second CMLCreate performed for space
Reference referenceForTargetSpace = result[1].getDestination();
//reference for the target space
ParentReference targetSpace = new ParentReference();
targetSpace.setStore(spacesStore);
targetSpace.setPath(referenceForTargetSpace.getPath());
targetSpace.setAssociationType(Constants.ASSOC_CONTAINS);
targetSpace.setChildName(name);
//move content
CMLMove move = new CMLMove();
move.setWhere(sourcePredicate);
move.setTo(targetSpace);
CML cmlMove = new CML();
cmlMove.setMove(new CMLMove[]{move});
//perform a CML update to create the node
WebServiceFactory.getRepositoryService().update(cmlMove);
```

As you can see in the source code, you need to get all the results from the UpdateResult related to the executed CML operations. We have sorted all the CMLCreate operations by local id; this means that you can retrieve the new node reference of a specific CMLCreate operation:

```
//build the CML object
CML cmlAdd = new CML();
cmlAdd.setCreate(new CMLCreate[]{create, createSpace});

//perform a CML update to create nodes
UpdateResult[] result = WebServiceFactory.getRepositoryService().
update(cmlAdd);


System.out.println("Node created: "+result[0].getDestination().
getPath());
System.out.println("Space created: "+result[1].getDestination().
getPath());
```

Copying nodes

In order to perform a copy for nodes, you need to create a CMLCopy object as follows:

```
public CMLCopy(
org.alfresco.repo.webservice.types.ParentReference to,
java.lang.String to_id,
java.lang.String associationType,
java.lang.String childName,
org.alfresco.repo.webservice.types.Predicate where,
java.lang.String where_id,
java.lang.Boolean children)
```

Take a look at all the following details and only set the required arguments, depending on your specific implementation of your feature:

Argument	Description
to	The target ParentReference (optional, if to_id is defined)
to_id	The UUID of the parent reference (optional, if to is defined)
associationType	The QName of the association involved (optional)
childName	The instance id of the node in the association (optional)
where	The source predicate with all the references to copy (optional, if where_id is defined)
where_id	The UUID of the source node to copy (optional, if where is defined)
children	This boolean value is used to enable the entire copy of all the children of the involved node

In the following sample, you can see how to create a CMLCopy object:

```
//copy content
CMLCopy copy = new CMLCopy();
copy.setWhere(sourcePredicate);
copy.setTo(targetSpace);
CML cmlCopy = new CML();
cmlCopy.setCopy(new CMLCopy[]{copy});
//perform a CML update to move the node
WebServiceFactory.getRepositoryService().update(cmlCopy);
```

Associations

In Alfresco, you can define the following two types of association in your content model:

- peer-association
- child-association

A **peer-association** allows you to define a unidirectional association among nodes. **Unidirectional association** means that you can navigate the association only from a source node to a target node. If you remove one of the nodes involved in a peer-association, the associated node will not be removed.

A **child-association** allows you to define a bidirectional association among a parent node with children nodes. **Bidirectional association** means that you can navigate a child-association from parent nodes to children and from children to parents. The first parent associated to a child is the primary parent; all subsequent parents associated to a node are secondary parents. If you remove the primary parent, all the children will be removed. If you remove one of the secondary parents, all the children will not be removed.

The CML operations that are dedicated to manage associations in the repository are as follows:

- CMLAddChild—adds a child to a node (defined with a child-association)
- CMLRemoveChild—removes a child from a node (defined with a child-association)
- CMLCreateAssociation—creates a peer-association from a source node to a target node
- CMLRemoveAssociation—removes a peer-association from a source node to a target node
- CMLAddChild and CMLRemoveChild can be used only to manage child-associations
- CMLCreateAssociation and CMLRemoveAssociation can be used only to manage peer-associations

As you will see, all the following operations can be created using the same arguments that you learned in the previous CML operation samples.

Adding child nodes

If we want to add new content in a specific space in Alfresco, all the contents that you can see in the Alfresco Explorer must be stored in a space. In order to manage association between nodes inside spaces, Alfresco provides a default child-association named cm:contains. This is the default association that allows you to manage your content using a space. A space in Alfresco is declared as a cm:folder content type.

The first time that you are dropping a new content in a space, Alfresco creates a new instance of cm:contains association between the folder node and the content node.

So this means that every content note has a primary parent. If you want to set more than one parent for each node, then you need to learn about the removing process.

In order to perform a CMLAddChild operation, you can type the following code:

```
//reference for the target space
ParentReference targetSpace = new ParentReference();
targetSpace.setStore(spacesStore);
targetSpace.setPath(referenceForTargetSpace.getPath());
targetSpace.setAssociationType(Constants.ASSOC_CONTAINS);
targetSpace.setChildName(name);


//add child
CMLAddChild addChild = new CMLAddChild();
addChild.setWhere(sourcePredicate);
addChild.setTo(targetSpace);
CML cmlAddChild = new CML();
cmlAddChild.setAddChild(new CMLAddChild[]{addChild});
//perform a CML update to add the node
WebServiceFactory.getRepositoryService().update(cmlAddChild);
```

Removing child nodes

In order to perform a CMLRemoveChild operation, you need to provide the container space (targetSpace) and a predicate for all the nodes that you want to remove. In the related sample, you can learn how to perform this operation:

```
//perform a CML update to add a child node
UpdateResult[] resultAddChild = WebServiceFactory.
getRepositoryService().update(cmlAddChild);
Reference refUpdate = resultAddChild[0].getDestination();
Predicate nodeToRemove =
new Predicate(new Reference[]{refUpdate}, spacesStore, null);
```

```
//remove child
CMLRemoveChild removeChild = new CMLRemoveChild();
removeChild.setFrom(targetSpace);
removeChild.setWhere(nodeToRemove);
CML cmlRemoveChild = new CML();
cmlRemoveChild.setRemoveChild(new CMLRemoveChild[]{removeChild});
//perform a CML update to remove the node WebServiceFactory.
getRepositoryService().update(cmlRemoveChild);
```

Versioning

In order to manage versioning in Alfresco, you can use the CMLUpdate object
to update a node in the repository with new properties.

Updating nodes without versioning

If you need to update a node without creating a new version, you must verify that
the node doesn't have the versionable aspect. For this operation, you need to
provide a predicate for all the nodes involved as follows:

```
String name = "AWS Book - Changed by CMLUpdate "+System.
currentTimeMillis();

createSampleVo.setName(name);
createSampleVo.setTitle(name);
createSampleVo.setDescription("Changed by CMLUpdate "+description);
//update node
CMLUpdate update = new CMLUpdate();
update.setProperty(buildCustomProperties(createSampleVo));
update.setWhere(sourcePredicate);
CML cmlUpdate = new CML();
cmlUpdate.setUpdate(new CMLUpdate[]{update});
//perform a CML update
WebServiceFactory.getRepositoryService().update(cmlUpdate);
```

The result of this operation is that the node will be updated without creating a new
version, but updating the existing one.

Getting the version history

In order to retrieve all the old versions of a node in the repository, you can use the Authoring Service to get the `VersionHistory` related to a specific node in the following way:

```
VersionHistory nodeHistory = WebServiceFactory.getAuthoringService().
getVersionHistory(sourcePredicate.getNodes(0));
for (int i = 0; i < nodeHistory.getVersions().length; i++) {
Version version = nodeHistory.getVersions(i);
System.out.println("version id:" +version.getId().getUuid());
System.out.println("version label:" +version.getLabel());
System.out.println("version created: "+version.getCreated().
getTime());
System.out.println("version creator: "+version.getCreator());
}
```

Aspects

An aspect consists of a group of properties that can be added to and removed from a node on the fly.

Adding aspects

Alfresco cannot manage versioning for you, if you haven't added the `versionable` aspect to the node. You can add it before creating a new version, in the following way:

```
//add versionable aspect to the node
CMLAddAspect aspect = new CMLAddAspect();
aspect.setAspect(Constants.ASPECT_VERSIONABLE);
aspect.setWhere(sourcePredicate);
//update node
CMLUpdate update = new CMLUpdate();
update.setProperty(buildCustomProperties(createSampleVo));
update.setWhere(sourcePredicate);
CML cmlUpdate = new CML();
cmlUpdate.setAddAspect(new CMLAddAspect[]{aspect});
cmlUpdate.setUpdate(new CMLUpdate[]{update});
//perform a CML update
WebServiceFactory.getRepositoryService().update(cmlUpdate);
```

Now, for each update to one of the nodes defined in the `sourcePredicate`, Alfresco will create a new version of the node.

Removing aspects

In the previous section, you learned how to add an aspect to enable versioning for a specific node in the repository. In order to remove an aspect, you can take a look at the CMLRemoveAspect operation as follows:

```
//remove aspect
CMLRemoveAspect removeAspect = new CMLRemoveAspect();
removeAspect.setAspect(Constants.ASPECT_VERSIONABLE);
removeAspect.setWhere(sourcePredicate);
CML cmlRemoveAspect = new CML();
cmlRemoveAspect.setRemoveAspect(new CMLRemoveAspect[]{removeAspect});
//perform a CML update WebServiceFactory.getRepositoryService().
update(cmlRemoveAspect);
```

In this example, we are removing the versionable aspect for a node. This means that now this node doesn't have any old versions associated in its own version history.

Searching the repository

In order to execute a search in the repository, you need to get the Repository Service using the WebServiceFactory:

```
RepositoryServiceSoapBindingStub repositoryService =
WebServiceFactory.getRepositoryService();
```

The Repository Service allows you to invoke the following methods for query purpose:

- query(Store store, Query query, boolean includeMetaData) executes a query in a store
- queryAssociated(Reference node, Association association) gets the associated contents of a node, related to a specific association
- queryChildren(Reference node) gets the contents of the children node
- queryParents(Reference node) gets all the parents of a node

Performing Lucene queries

The query method allows you to execute Lucene queries in the repository. Your queries must be expressed using the Lucene syntax, which is fully described at the following address:

http://wiki.alfresco.com/wiki/Search#Lucene.

This is the declaration of the `query` method:

```
public QueryResult query(
final Store store,
final Query query,
final boolean includeMetaData)
throws RemoteException, RepositoryFault
```

The `store` is a logical section of the repository that contains a group of nodes. A `store` can be referred with a store reference (`StoreRef`) that consists of the store protocol concatenated with the store name. This is the `store` dedicated to the latest version of contents in order to execute a query on the `SpacesStore` in Alfresco. You need to create the following `Store` object:

```
import org.alfresco.webservice.util.Constants;
import org.alfresco.webservice.types.Store;
. . .
. . .
Store spacesStore = new Store(Constants.WORKSPACE_
STORE,"SpacesStore");
```

As you can see in the previous snippet, you need to pay attention on the complete package of the class because many objects of this API have the same name as that of the Foundation API of Alfresco, but these have different packages.

> When you are using the Web Services API of Alfresco, check your objects and make sure that you are referring to the `org.alfresco.webservice` as the root package.

The next step is creating the `Query` object that consists of:

- The language used to search contents
- A query statement

For the Alfresco Web Services API, the only available language is the Lucene query API as the unique search query language.

In order to create a `Query` object, you need to use the following lines:

```
String luceneQuery = "PATH:\"/app:company_home\"";
Query query = new Query(Constants.QUERY_LANG_LUCENE,luceneQuery);
```

`Constants` is a utility class provided by Alfresco to retrieve constants dedicated to store, node, aspects, and properties. In this way, you don't need to take care of specific default namespace or property strings.

The `luceneQuery` contains the Lucene query statement to retrieve nodes in the repository. In this sample, we want to search the **Company Home** space. You can build your own Lucene query using all the Lucene tokens, thus narrowing down your search query as you desire.

Another sample of a Lucene query is as follows:

```
String luceneQuery = "PATH:\"/app:company_home/*\" AND TYPE:\"cm:
content\"";
```

In this second example query, we are searching all the contents inside the **Company Home**, excluding all the sub-spaces.

If you need to search only the sub-spaces, then the Lucene query will be as follows:

```
String luceneQuery = "PATH:\"/app:company_home/*\" AND TYPE:\"cm:
folder\"";
```

Now, we have set all the needed arguments to invoke the `query` method correctly:

```
QueryResult queryResult =
repositoryService.query(spacesStore, query, false);
```

The `QueryResult` object will contain all the information retrieved from the repository. In this specific case, the method returns only a unique result, precisely the node reference of **Company Home**.

You can iterate result nodes retrieving the `ResultSet` object as follows:

```
ResultSet resultSet = queryResult.getResultSet();
```

In order to retrieve all the information for each result, you need to get nodes from the `ResultSetRow` array. In the following snippet, we are creating a new list of value objects needed for our business logic:

```
ResultSetRow[] results = resultSet.getRows();
  //your custom list
    List<CustomResultVO> customResultList = new
    ArrayList<CustomResultVO>();
  //retrieve results from the resultSet
for (ResultSetRow resultRow : results) {
ResultSetRowNode nodeResult = resultRow.getNode();
System.out.println(nodeResult.getId());
System.out.println(nodeResult.getType());
}
```

A `ResultSetRow` allows you to invoke the following methods for each result:

- `getNode()` — returns the `ResultSetRowNode` to retrieve ID, type, and aspects
- `getColumns()` — returns the `NamedValue` array with all the properties for the current node

In the Alfresco Web Services API, you need to use a wrapper for properties named `NamedValue` to retrieve and store properties for nodes. It allows you to invoke the following methods:

- `getName()` returns the `QName` for the current property
- `getValue()` returns the value for the current property
- `getIsMultiValue()` returns true, if the current property is multivalued
- `getValues()` returns all the values for the current multivalued property

In Alfresco, each property, type, or aspect is identified by a qualified name (`QName`). A qualified name consists of two elements: a namespace and a local name. It has the following structure in the repository:

```
{namespace}localname
```

For instance, the `QName` for the default `name` property in Alfresco is:

```
{http://www.alfresco.org/model/content/1.0}name
```

You can run this sample in Eclipse as a Java Application in this way:

1. Right click on `SearchQuery.java` (**Package Explorer**)
2. Then click on **Run As | Java Application**

You should see an output in your console for the first sample Lucene, similar to the following:

```
---- Result ----
Node ID: b1a91ac0-cfe2-48c5-9e44-90e342a59357
Node Type: {http://www.alfresco.org/model/content/1.0}folder
Name: Company Home
Description: The company root space
---- /Result ----
```

Querying associated nodes

The next query method that we are going to see is the `queryAssociated` method. By invoking this method, you can retrieve associated nodes of a specific node. Notice that you have to provide the `association` object to select the right association definition for the content type. You can use this method only for nodes associated with peer associations.

The method declaration is as follows:

```
public QueryResult queryAssociated(
final Reference node,
final Association association)
throws RemoteException, RepositoryFault
```

As you can see, you need to provide two arguments for this method, namely, a reference for the node and the involved association. We are going to describe the new `Association` object.

Association

The second argument for the `queryAssociated` method is an Association object, which can be created by providing an `associationType` (QName) and a direction.

The declaration of an `Association` constructor is as follows:

```
public Association(
java.lang.String associationType,
java.lang.String direction)
```

The `associationType` argument is the QName of the peer association. The `direction` argument allows you to declare which direction of association you want to consider for this query; the possible values are `source` or `target`.

For this example, we will use the `avatar` association that is one of the peer associations defined in the built-in model of Alfresco. This association allows users to store an avatar icon in their profile in the repository. This is the definition of the association that you can find in the `cm:person` type:

```
<association name="cm:avatar">
   <source>
      <role>cm:avatarOf</role>
      <mandatory>false</mandatory>
      <many>false</many>
   </source>
   <target>
```

```
            <class>cm:content</class>
            <role>cm:hasAvatar</role>
            <mandatory>false</mandatory>
            <many>false</many>
        </target>
    </association>
```

This definition will be used to create a new instance of association between a `cm:person` node and a `cm:content` node. The `source` element of the association is mapped to the content type `cm:person` and the `target` element for the image is mapped to the content type `cm:content`. The `many` element value is `false` for both elements. This means that this is a one-to-one association.

In order to add an image for the avatar to the default user of Alfresco, you have to carry out the following steps using the Alfresco Explorer:

1. Browse to any space in the **Company Home**, and click on **Add Content**.
2. Click on the **Browse...** button, select your avatar image, and click on the **OK** button three times.
3. Click on **User Profile**.
4. Click on **Modify** in the **My Details** tab.
5. Browse and select the stored image for the **Avatar** field, and click the **OK** button.

Now, we can start to execute a query for both the directions of the association. The first query retrieves the avatar image (target node) associated to the default user of Alfresco. This means that we have to set a `target` direction for the association as follows:

```
Store spacesStore =
new Store(Constants.WORKSPACE_STORE, "SpacesStore");

String associationType = "{http://www.alfresco.org/model/content/
1.0}avatar";

String direction = "target";
Association association =
new Association(associationType, direction);
Reference reference = new Reference();
reference.setStore(spacesStore);
reference.setPath("/sys:system/sys:people/cm:admin");
QueryResult queryResult =
repositoryService.queryAssociated(reference, association);
```

```
ResultSetRow[] targetNodes = queryResult.getResultSet().getRows();

//retrieve results of all the target nodes
for (ResultSetRow targetNode : targetNodes) {
   ResultSetRowNode targetNodeResult = targetNode.getNode();
   System.out.println("---- Result ----");
   //getting the target node
   System.out.println("-- Target --");
   System.out.println("Node ID: "+targetNodeResult.getId());
System.out.println("Node Type: "+targetNodeResult.getType());

//retrieve properties of the target node
for (NamedValue property : targetNode.getColumns()) {
   if (Constants.PROP_NAME.equals(property.getName())) {
      System.out.println("Name: "+property.getValue());
   } else if(Constants.PROP_DESCRIPTION.equals(property.getName())) {
      System.out.println("Description: "+property.getValue());
   }
}
}

System.out.println("-- /Target --");
```

In the next section, you can see how to retrieve the associated person node (source node) from the avatar image. In this case, we have to set a `source` direction for the association, which is shown as follows:

```
//getting the source node
System.out.println("-- Source --");

String directionSource = "source";
Association associationSource = new Association(associationType,
directionSource);

Reference referenceSource = new Reference();
referenceSource.setStore(spacesStore);
referenceSource.setUuid(targetNode.getNode().getId());

QueryResult queryResultSource =
repositoryService.queryAssociated(referenceSource, associationSource);

//retrieve results of all the source nodes
ResultSetRow[] sourceNodes = queryResultSource.getResultSet().
getRows();
for (ResultSetRow sourceNode : sourceNodes) {
   ResultSetRowNode sourceNodeResult = sourceNode.getNode();
```

```
    System.out.println("Node ID: "+sourceNodeResult.getId());
    System.out.println("Node Type: "+sourceNodeResult.getType());

    //retrieve properties of the source node
    for (NamedValue property : sourceNode.getColumns()) {
      if (Constants.PROP_NAME.equals(property.getName())) {
        System.out.println("Name: "+property.getValue());
    } else if(Constants.PROP_DESCRIPTION.equals(property.getName())) {
      System.out.println("Description: "+property.getValue());
      }
    }
  }

  System.out.println("-- /Source --");
  System.out.println("---- /Result ----");
```

You should see a similar output in your console from Eclipse when you'll run the previous script as a Java Application:

```
---- Result ----
-- Target --
Node ID: c56dc8c3-f2cd-4b0f-8843-9a5d6e3a7214
Node Type: {http://www.alfresco.org/model/content/1.0}content
Name: avatar.jpg
Description:
-- /Target --
-- Source --
Node ID: b59a72a7-359e-437a-9dee-5813860a3446
Node Type: {http://www.alfresco.org/model/content/1.0}person
Name: b59a72a7-359e-437a-9dee-5813860a3446
-- /Source --
---- /Result ----
```

Querying child nodes

The next query method that you can invoke using `repositoryService` is `queryChildren`. This method allows you to retrieve all the child nodes of a parent node. The following is the declaration for this method:

```
public QueryResult queryChildren(final Reference node) throws
RemoteException, RepositoryFault
```

In order to invoke this method, you have to provide a parent reference, for instance, you can test it using the default **Company Home | Data Dictionary** space:

```
Reference reference =
new Reference(spacesStore, null, "/app:company_home/app:dictionary");
```

So now you can invoke a search for child nodes in this way:

```
QueryResult queryResult = repositoryService.queryChildren(reference);
```

If you try to execute the related example as a Java Application in Eclipse, you should see some output similar to the following, in your console:

```
Result:   | Name: Space Templates
Result:   | Name: Presentation Templates
Result:   | Name: Email Templates
Result:   | Name: RSS Templates
Result:   | Name: Saved Searches
Result:   | Name: Scripts
Result:   | Name: Web Scripts
Result:   | Name: Web Scripts Extensions
Result:   | Name: Models
Result:   | Name: Messages
Result:   | Name: Web Client Extension
Result:   | Name: Workflow Definitions
Result:   | Name: Imap Configs
Result:   | Name: Email Actions
Result:   | Name: Transfers
Result:   | Name: Rendering Actions Space
```

As you can verify in the Alfresco Explorer, all the retrieved results are the subspace nodes that are stored in the **Company Home | Data Dictionary** space:

Querying parent nodes

The next query method that you can invoke using `repositoryService` is `queryParents`, which allows you to retrieve all the parent nodes of a child node. It can be declared as follows:

```
public QueryResult queryParents(final Reference node) throws
RemoteException, RepositoryFault
```

For this sample, we can use the same parent reference of the previous method (**Data Dictionary**):

```
Reference reference =
new Reference(spacesStore, null, "/app:company_home/app:dictionary");
```

Then we can invoke the `queryParents()` method in this way:

```
QueryResult queryResult = repositoryService.queryParents(reference);
```

The result for this sample code is that you find the parent reference for **Data Dictionary**, namely, the **Company Home** space.

In Eclipse, you should see the following output when you run the sample as a Java Application in your console:

```
---- Result ----
Node ID: b1a91ac0-cfe2-48c5-9e44-90e342a59357
Node Type: {http://www.alfresco.org/model/content/1.0}folder
Name: Company Home
Description: The company root space
---- /Result ----
```

Summary

This chapter introduced the Content Manipulation Language of Alfresco. In this chapter, you learned:

- The basics behind the CML language and the main goal
- How to authenticate users against the repository
- The basic operations to create, remove, and update nodes in the repository
- How to manage associations using the CML language
- How to manage versioning and aspects

In the next chapter, you will learn how to perform operations to allow user collaboration and repository administration.

3
Collaboration and Administration

In this chapter, you will learn how to:

- Perform check-out and check-in operations
- Manage versioning explicitly
- Manage locking
- Manage classifications and categories
- Manage authorization using permissions and roles
- Manage actions
- Manage rules
- Manage users

You will also learn how to invoke remote calls to perform operations dedicated to:

- Allowing collaborative editing of content among users
- Administering your repository

The first part of this chapter addresses how to manage check-out and check-in operations to allow collaboration among editors. Moreover, it discusses how to explicitly manage locking and versioning. The second part of this chapter is based on how to remotely administer an Alfresco repository, specifically, how to configure classifications, authorization, actions, rules, and users.

Creating collaborative content

In order to manage content editing to allow collaboration among users, Alfresco provides a mechanism based on check-out and check-in operations. To start managing collaboration, you need to get the AuthoringService that allows you to invoke the following methods:

Method	Description
`checkout(Predicate items, ParentReference destination)`	Performs a check-out for a node by creating a working copy
`checkin(Predicate items, NamedValue[] comments, boolean keepCheckedOut)`	Performs a check-in for a node with new properties and content
`cancelCheckout(Predicate items)`	Removes the current check-out for the content
`checkinExternal(Reference node, NamedValue[] comments, boolean keepCheckedOut, ContentFormat format, byte[] content)`	Performs a check-in overriding the current working copies
`CreateVersion(Predicate items, NamedValue[] comments, boolean versionChildren)`	Creates a new version for the node in the version store
`deleteAllVersions(Reference node)`	Removes all the versions for the node in the version store
`revertVersion(Reference node, string versionLabel)`	Restores an old version as the current version of the content
`getVersionHistory(Reference node)`	Returns the version history for the node
`lock(Predicate items, boolean lockChildren, LockTypeEnum lockTypeEnum)`	Locks all the nodes that cannot be modified by other users
`unlock(Predicate items, boolean unlockChildren)`	Unlocks all the nodes
`getLockStatus(Predicate items)`	Returns an array with all the statuses for the nodes

Performing a check-out

A check-out is one of the collaborative operations supported by Alfresco. Whenever a check-out is performed, it means that the repository is:

- locking all the involved nodes to prevent other users from editing
- creating a working copy of all the involved nodes

In this section, you'll learn how to perform check-out by using the Web Services API. This is the same check-out operation that you can execute from the Alfresco Explorer by clicking on **View Details | Check Out** for any content inside **Company Home**.

Using the checkout() method, you can allow collaborative manipulation of content among users. The code can be shown as follows:

```
public CheckoutResult checkout(
final Predicate items,
final ParentReference destination)
throws RemoteException, AuthoringFault
```

The destination argument is optional—you can set a value for this field only if you want to create working copies in another specific space in the repository. In the following example, you can learn how to invoke the checkout() method for a predicate as follows:

```
AuthoringServiceSoapBindingStub authoringService = WebServiceFactory.
getAuthoringService();
Predicate predicate = new Predicate(new Reference[]{result[0].
getDestination()}, spacesStore, null);
CheckoutResult checkOutResult = authoringService.checkout(predicate,
null);
```

CheckOutResult is used to get the response result and allows you to retrieve node references related to all the new working copies created:

```
// Get a reference to the working copy
Reference workingCopyReference = checkOutResult.getWorkingCopies()[0];
```

After a check-out execution, you will find that all the involved nodes are locked and all the working copies are ready for editing. The result in the Alfresco Explorer is as follows:

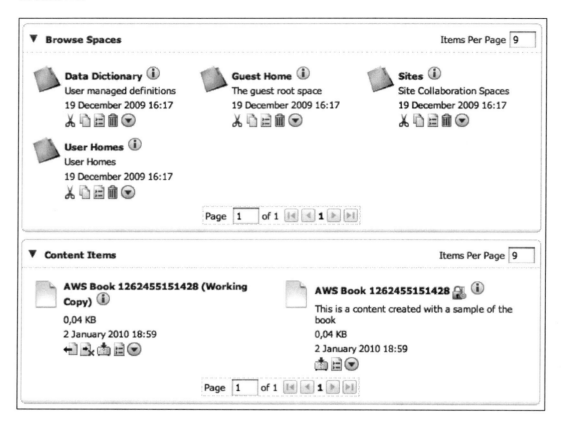

We have locked a new content to allow its collaborative editing. In the next section, you will learn how to perform a check-in operation for the node to update the related content.

Check-in

In the previous section, you learned how to perform a check-out operation. Now you will learn how to update the existing content using the checkin() method. The check-in operation allows you to import and update all the modified working copies to the related locked nodes, maintaining the same node references, so that the editors can modify working copies to update the contents. When they want to update the old content, they can use this check-in feature in your custom application.

Performing a check-in for content means that you are updating all the involved nodes, which you have locked before, using the previous check-out operation.

The `checkin()` method is based on the following declaration:

```
public CheckinResult checkin(
final Predicate items,
final NamedValue[] comments,
final boolean keepCheckedOut)
throws RemoteException, AuthoringFault
```

For this method, `items` must be a predicate of working copies that you want to replace with their related locked nodes (the original nodes). `keepCheckedOut` is a boolean value used to keep (`true`) or remove (`false`) all the previous working copies for the involved nodes. `comments` is an array of notes typed by editors about changes for the content. This field is used only if the nodes have a `versionable` aspect.

Here, you can see how to invoke a check-in operation for a working copy:

```
//Predicate for the existing Working Copy
Predicate workingCopy = new Predicate(
new Reference[]{checkOutResult.getWorkingCopies()[0]}, spacesStore,
null);
//CheckIn
NamedValue[] comments =
new NamedValue[]{Utils.createNamedValue(
"description", "update the content sample")};
CheckinResult checkInResult =
authoringService.checkin(workingCopy, comments, false);
```

`CheckInResult` allows you to get the result to check all the changes on nodes—checked-in nodes and working copies.

Check-in with versioning

As we saw in the previous section, check-in operation allows you to update content using the related working copy. When you are using versioning on nodes and you are performing check-out and check-in operations on these involved nodes, Alfresco will create a new version of the node for each check-in invocation.

The last version of the node reference (updated or checked-in) will always be exactly the same as the first node reference. This means that whenever you update the content, Alfresco maintains the same node reference for the latest version.

Notice that you can see all the notes typed by editors for all the versions dropped in the repository in the **Details View | Version History** panel for a node.

To see the Version History for a node, you have to:

1. Authenticate in the Alfresco Explorer.
2. Click on **Company Home**.
3. Click on **View Details** for a node.
4. At the bottom, inside the property sheet, expand the panel named **Version History**.

If you try to execute the CheckInWithVersioning example, you can see the following information in your Alfresco Explorer:

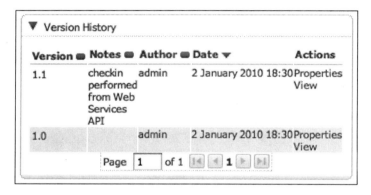

In this example, we have added the versionable aspect on the involved node and then we have performed a check-out and then a check-in operation.

Check-in—importing external content

Sometimes, you may need to perform a check-in operation without using the content that exists in the repository, you may probably be working on this content with an external application, or you may want to let users upload external files. In such specific cases, you can use the check-in external operation. This is the same check-in operation that you can execute from the Alfresco Explorer by clicking on **Details View | Check In** (use a copy uploaded from your computer) for any **checked-out** content inside **Company Home**.

In order to perform a check-in with external content, you need to use the
`checkinExternal()` method as follows:

```
public Reference checkinExternal(
final Reference node,
final NamedValue[] comments,
final boolean keepCheckedOut,
final ContentFormat format,
final byte[] content)
throws RemoteException, AuthoringFault
```

For this method, we need to consider only a single node reference. In addition, we
need to provide the `format` object to set `MIME` type and `encoding` for the content and
finally an array of bytes for the external content.

The following code shows how to invoke the `checkinExternal()` method for a
checked-out node:

```
Predicate workingCopy = new Predicate(new Reference[]{checkOutResult.
getWorkingCopies()[0]}, spacesStore, null);
//Checkin with an external content
String externalContent = "new content for checkin external";
//Format dedicated to this external content
ContentFormat formatForCheckIn = new ContentFormat();
formatForCheckIn.setEncoding("UTF-8");
formatForCheckIn.setMimetype("text/plain");
//Comments
NamedValue[] comments = new NamedValue[]{Utils.createNamedValue(
"description", "checkin performed from Web Services API")};
//Checkin External
Reference checkinExternalResult =
authoringService.checkinExternal(workingCopy.getNodes(0), comments,
false, formatForCheckIn, externalContent.getBytes());
```

As usual, the response allows you to retrieve the involved reference nodes to
perform other operations.

Cancelling a check-out

When you provide check-in and check-out features in your custom application, you
can let users cancel a check-out operation to remove all the modified working copies.
Cancelling a check-out means that you are removing all the working copies, and you
are unlocking all the involved nodes. The code snippet can be shown as follows:

```
public CancelCheckoutResult cancelCheckout(final Predicate items)
throws RemoteException, AuthoringFault
```

The value of items must be a group of working copy references. If they are, then you can type the following lines to invoke this operation:

```
Predicate workingCopy = new Predicate(new Reference[]{checkOutResult.
getWorkingCopies()[0]}, spacesStore, null);
//Cancel Checkout
CancelCheckoutResult cancelCheckOutResult = authoringService.cancelChe
ckout(workingCopy);
```

`CancelCheckoutResult` allows you to check which working copies and which locked nodes have been correctly processed. Specifically, for this operation:

- All the working copies will be removed
- All the involved nodes will be unlocked

Managing versioning explicitly

Alfresco provides a mechanism to manage versioning one of the sub-operations used by check-in and check-out operations in an explicit way.

Creating a new version

In order to create a new version of content, you can invoke the `createVersion()` method:

```
public VersionResult createVersion(
final Predicate items,
final NamedValue[] comments,
final boolean versionChildren)
throws RemoteException, AuthoringFault
```

The value of `versionChildren` must be a boolean, and it is used to enable versioning for all the children of the referenced node. If the value is TRUE, Alfresco will create versions for all the child nodes.

The following example shows you how to invoke the `createVersion` method:

```
VersionResult versionResult = authoringService.createVersion(predicate
ForVersion,comments, false);
```

We discussed some details about VersionHistory in the previous chapter, so you probably know how to get the results from `versionResult.getVersions()`.

Deleting all the versions

Performing a `deleteAllVersions` for a node means that you are removing all the versions for a specific node reference:

```
public VersionHistory deleteAllVersions(final Reference node)
throws RemoteException, AuthoringFault
```

In the following example, you can see how to invoke the `deleteAllVersions` method:

```
//Remove all the previous versions
authoringService.deleteAllVersions(checkedInNode);
```

Getting the version history

In order to get all the information about versioning for a node, you can use the `getVersionHistory` method. In this way, you can get all the version labels for a node as follows:

```
public VersionHistory getVersionHistory(final Reference node)
throws RemoteException, AuthoringFault
```

The only needed argument to invoke this method is the involved node reference. Actually, this means that you are retrieving all the previous versions of this node, so that you can get the `VersionHistory` object for a specific node reference.

You can use the following code to retrieve information about all the versions of a node:

```
VersionHistory versionHistory = authoringService.getVersionHistory(ch
eckedInNode);
Version[] versions = versionHistory.getVersions();
System.out.println("Version History of: "+checkedInNode.getPath());
for (Version version : versions) {
System.out.println("---- Version ----");
System.out.println("id: "+version.getId());
System.out.println("creator: "+version.getCreator());
System.out.println("label: "+version.getLabel());
System.out.println("created: "+version.getCreated());
System.out.println("is a major version:   " + version.isMajor());
NamedValue[] commentaries = version.getCommentaries();
System.out.println("--Properties--");
for (NamedValue namedValue : commentaries) {
System.out.println(
" Name: " + namedValue.getName() +
" | Value: " + namedValue.getValue());
```

```
}
System.out.println("--/Properties--");
System.out.println("---- /Version ----");
}
```

As you can see in the previous example, all the information is contained in the `Version` object and you can retrieve the following fields: `id`, `creator`, `label`, `creation date`, `major`, and all the other properties (named `commentaries`).

Reverting a version

In order to restore an old version of content, you can invoke the `revertVersion` method:

```
public void revertVersion(final Reference node,final String
versionLabel)
throws RemoteException, AuthoringFault
```

As you can see in the previous code, you can invoke this method providing a node and a specific version label previously retrieved from the related `VersionHistory`:

```
String versionLabel = "1.1";
authoringService.revertVersion(checkedInNode, versionLabel);
```

Managing locking explicitly

Alfresco provides you with a mechanism to manage locking in an explicit way—another sub-operation used by check-in and check-out operations.

Locking

The locking mechanism allows you to lock a node to prevent others from editing the related content. The content is locked until you unlock the node. You can lock a node using the `lock` method as follows:

```
public Reference[] lock(
final Predicate items,
final boolean lockChildren,
final LockTypeEnum lockType)
throws RemoteException, AuthoringFault
```

`lockChildren` is a boolean value used to enable locking for all the children nodes. The value of `lockType` can be read or write; both of these are `LockTypeEnum` objects that are created to let you manage the lock in two different ways. In the following example, you can see how to invoke the `lock` method to enforce a read lock without locking the related children nodes:

```
Reference[] lockedNodes =
authoringService.lock(predicateToLock, false, LockTypeEnum.read);
```

As you can see in the previous snippet, this method returns an array of node references of all the locked nodes specified in the items argument. A locked node will be shown in the Alfresco Explorer with a specific icon (a lock with a key), as shown in the following screenshot:

Unlocking

In order to unlock a node that you had previously locked, you can use the `unlock` method as follows:

```
public Reference[] unlock(
final Predicate items,
final boolean unlockChildren)
throws RemoteException, AuthoringFault
```

`Items` consists of a group of locked nodes, and the `unlockChildren` argument is a boolean value that is used to unlock all the children nodes. The following are the lines from the related example:

```
Reference[] unlockedNodes =
authoringService.unlock(predicateToUnlock, false);
```

As you can see in the previous snippet, this method returns an array of node references of all the unlocked nodes specified in the `items` argument.

Getting the lock status

If you want to check the lock status, you can use this last method dedicated to locking, named `getLockStatus`. This method allows you to retrieve information about the status of locking for nodes as follows:

```
public LockStatus[] getLockStatus(final Predicate items)
throws RemoteException, AuthoringFault
```

The following code example can help you to understand how to iterate results:

```
LockStatus[] lockStatus = authoringService.getLockStatus(predicate);
System.out.println(
"Lock Status: owner: " + lockStatus[0].getLockOwner() +
"| type: " +lockStatus[0].getLockType() +
"| node: "+lockStatus[0].getNode().getPath());
```

Notice that whenever you are iterating a `LockStatus` array, if a node is unlocked, then you could have a null value returned from these methods—`getLockOwner()` and `getLockType()`.

In the following example, you can see how to use this method during multiple operations. We will use a method named `checkLockStatus` to check and log the lock status multiple times. It can be shown as follows:

```
private static void checkLockStatus(
AuthoringServiceSoapBindingStub authoringService, Predicate predicate)
throws AuthoringFault, RemoteException{

   LockStatus[] lockStatus = authoringService.getLockStatus(predicate
);

        System.out.println(
            "Lock Status: owner: " + lockStatus[0].getLockOwner() +
            "| type: " +lockStatus[0].getLockType() +
            "| node: "+lockStatus[0].getNode().getPath());

   }
```

You can see how to use the `checkLockStatus` method in the following code example:

```
//Lock the node
Reference[] lockedNodes = authoringService.lock(predicateToCheckLock,f
alse, LockTypeEnum.write);
System.out.println("Node locked: " + lockedNodes[0].getPath());
checkLockStatus(authoringService, predicateToCheckLock);
//Unlock the node
```

```
Reference[] unlockedNodes =
authoringService.unlock(predicateToCheckLock, false);
System.out.println("Node unlocked: " + unlockedNodes[0].getPath());
checkLockStatus(authoringService, predicateToCheckLock);
```

Classification and categories

Alfresco allows you to manage contents using classifications and categories. A classification consists of a group of categories that can be structured:

- In a flat way
- With a hierarchy

Categories structured in a flat way consist of multiple categories defined in a classification at the same root level. Otherwise, you can define a classification with categories based on a hierarchy. In this way, you can classify the domain for your contents in a better way.

A category is a specific data type (d:category) for a classification and consists of a property that can be single or multiple. You can find the default classifiable aspect (cm:generalclassifiable) in the default Alfresco Content Model in the configuration root:

```
alfresco.war/WEB-INF/classes/alfresco/model/contentModel.xml
```

The default aspect cm:generalclassifiable is defined in the following way:

```
<aspect name="cm:classifiable">
<title>Classifiable</title>
</aspect>
<aspect name="cm:generalclassifiable">
<title>General Classifiable</title>
<parent>cm:classifiable</parent>
<properties>
<property name="cm:categories">
<title>Categories</title>
<type>d:category</type>
<mandatory>false</mandatory>
<multiple>true</multiple>
<index enabled="true">
<atomic>true</atomic>
<stored>true</stored>
<tokenised>false</tokenised>
</index>
</property>
</properties>
</aspect>
```

All the default categories are defined in the `categories.xml` file, which can be found at the following location:

`alfresco.war/WEB-INF/classes/alfresco/bootstrap/categories.xml.`

This is the Software Document Classification defined in the `categories.xml` file:

```
<!-- Software Document Classification -->
<cm:category view:childName="cm:generalclassifiable">
<cm:name>General</cm:name>
<cm:subcategories>
<cm:category>
<cm:name>Software Document Classification</cm:name>
<cm:subcategories>
<cm:category>
<cm:name>Software Descriptions</cm:name>
<cm:subcategories>
<cm:category>
<cm:name>Main Software Descriptions</cm:name>
<cm:subcategories>
<cm:category>
<cm:name>Short System Description</cm:name>
</cm:category>
```

All these definitions are the default categories available in the standard Alfresco installation, as you can see in the **Categories** browser on the left panel of the **Alfresco Explorer**:

But this is not the only way to manage categories; you actually have two different options for managing them:

- Create categories in a declarative way using the `categories.xml` file (bootstrap)
- Assign and remove categories programmatically using an Alfresco API

All the categories defined in the `categories.xml` file are bootstrapped by Alfresco during the startup of the repository. You can manage categories using the Web Services API using the **Classification Service**.

The Classification Service allows you to invoke the following methods:

- `getClassifications(Store store)` returns all the `classifications` defined in the store involved
- `describeClassification(String classification)` returns the classification definition
- `getCategories(Predicate items)` returns all the categories for all the nodes involved
- `setCategories(Predicate items, AppliedCategory[] categories)` sets all the applied categories for all the nodes involved
- `getChildCategories(Reference parentCategory)` returns all the children categories for the parent category

Getting classifications

You can get the classifications details by invoking the `getClassifications()` method as follows:

```
ClassificationServiceSoapBindingStub classificationService =
WebServiceFactory.getClassificationService();
Classification[] classifications = classificationService.getClassifica
tions(spacesStore);
```

For each classification, you can retrieve the `title`, `description`, `classification` (`QName`), and the `root` category:

```
for (Classification classification : classifications) {
System.out.println("Title: "+classification.getTitle());
System.out.println("Description: "+classification.getDescription());
System.out.println("Classification: "+classification.
getClassification());
System.out.println("Root category: "+classification.getRootCategory().
getTitle());
}
```

Describing a classification

In order to get information about the content model definition of a classification, you can invoke the describeClassification() method as follows:

```
String classificationQName = "{http://www.alfresco.org/model/
content/1.0}generalclassifiable";
ClassDefinition classDefinition = classificationService.describeClassi
fication(classificationQName);
```

This method invocation returns a ClassDefinition that allows you to retrieve information about the content modeling for classification. ClassDefinition is the response object to obtain all these fields for the classification: name, title, description, superclass (declared as a parent element), properties, and associations.

For instance, to get all the information from a ClassDefinition, you can take a look at the following code example:

```
System.out.println("Title: "+ classDefinition.getTitle());
System.out.println("Name: "+ classDefinition.getName());
System.out.println("Description: "+ classDefinition.getDescription());
System.out.println("SuperClass: "+ classDefinition.getSuperClass());
//Properties
PropertyDefinition[] properties = classDefinition.getProperties();
System.out.println("--Properties--");
for (PropertyDefinition propDefinition : properties) {
System.out.println("Title: " + propDefinition.getTitle());
System.out.println("Name: " + propDefinition.getName());
System.out.println("Description: "+ propDefinition.getDescription());
System.out.println("DataType: "+propDefinition.getDataType());
System.out.println("DefaultValue:"+propDefinition.getDefaultValue());
}

System.out.println("--/Properties--");
//Associations
AssociationDefinition[] associations = classDefinition.
getAssociations();
if(associations!=null){
System.out.println("--Associations--");
for (AssociationDefinition assDefinition : associations) {
System.out.println("Name: "+assDefinition.getName());
System.out.println("Title: "+assDefinition.getTitle());
System.out.println("Description: "+assDefinition .getDescription());
System.out.println("SourceRole: "+assDefinition.getSourceRole());
```

```
System.out.println("TargetRole: "+assDefinition.getTargetRole());
System.out.println("TargetClass: "+assDefinition.getTargetClass());
}
System.out.println("--/Associations--");
}
```

Getting categories

In order to retrieve categories for nodes, you have to create a `Predicate` referring to a group of nodes, and then you can invoke the `getCategories()` method as follows:

```
public CategoriesResult[] getCategories(final Predicate items)
throws RemoteException, ClassificationFault
```

This method returns an array of `CategoriesResult` that allows you to retrieve categories for each node reference as follows:

```
CategoriesResult[] categories = classificationService.
getCategories(new Predicate(new Reference[]{reference}, spacesStore,
null));
    for (CategoriesResult cats : categories) {
        for (AppliedCategory  appliedCategory : cats.getCategories()) {
            for (Reference referenceCat : appliedCategory.
getCategories()) {
                Predicate p = new Predicate(new Reference[]{referenceCat},
spacesStore, null);
                for (NamedValue property : repositoryService.get(p)[0].
getProperties()) {
                    if(property.getName().endsWith(Constants.PROP_NAME) ==
true) {
                        System.out.println(property.getValue());
                    }
                }
            }
        }
    }
```

Adding categories

If you need to add categories to nodes, you can invoke the `setCategories()` method as follows:

```
public CategoriesResult[] setCategories(
final Predicate items,
final AppliedCategory[] categories)
throws RemoteException, ClassificationFault
```

`Categories` is an array of `AppliedCategory` objects for all the categories to which you want to add the related items. This method returns an array of `CategoriesResult`, the same data type of the method, as shown in the previous section:

```
CategoriesResult[] addedCategories = classificationService.
setCategories(predicate, categories);
```

To build an array of `AppliedCategory`, you need to provide, for each node, a classification and a set of node references to apply all the categories.

Getting child categories

As you know, a classification can be based on a hierarchy of categories. So, if you need to retrieve information about the hierarchy, you can invoke the `getChildCategories()` method.

Using this method, you can retrieve all the child categories of a `parentCategory` as follows:

```
public Category[] getChildCategories(final Reference parentCategory)
throws RemoteException, ClassificationFault
```

This method returns an array of `Category` objects, and you can retrieve, for each category, all these fields: `id`, `title`, and `description`.

Authorization

When you are developing your application on top of Alfresco, you usually need to change, add, and remove permissions for content related to a single user or a group of users. The easiest way to manage authorization is to use roles associated with groups and have each group assigned directly to Alfresco spaces. A role in Alfresco is a group of permissions. A permission allows a user to perform a specific operation on the content.

Here, you can see some of the default permissions provided in Alfresco:

- `ReadProperties`
- `DeleteNode`
- `ReadContent`
- `DeleteAssociations`

In Alfresco, a permission is managed by an **Access Control Entry** (**ACE**) that allows you to associate an authority (a user, a group, or a role) to nodes. All the ACEs are stored in the **Access Control List** (**ACL**) related to the nodes in the repository.

The default roles defined in Alfresco are declared in the following configuration root file:

```
alfresco.war/WEB-INF/classes/alfresco/model/permissionDefinitions.xml
```

In order to manage permissions on contents you can use the Access Control Service as follows:

```
AccessControlServiceSoapBindingStub accessControlService =
WebServiceFactory.getAccessControlService();
```

This service allows you to invoke the methods shown in the following table:

Method	Description
getAuthorities()	Returns all the authorities (groups) for the current user
getAllAuthorities(AuthorityFilter filter)	Returns all the authorities (users or groups) available in the repository
getPermissions(Predicate predicate)	Returns all the permissions available on nodes in the predicate
getClassPermissions(String[] classNames)	Returns an array with all the permissions available for all the classNames
getACLs(Predicate predicate, ACE filter)	Returns all the ACEs related to each node in the predicate
addACEs(Predicate predicate, ACE[] aces)	Adds a set of Access Control Entries to the Access Control List of each content involved in the predicate
removeACEs(Predicate predicate, ACE[] aces)	Removes an ACE on the ACL of each content involved in the predicate
createAuthorities(String parentAuthority, NewAuthority[] newAuthorites)	Creates a group of authorities related to a parent authority (groups)
deleteAuthorities(String[] authorities)	Removes a set of authorities
getParentAuthorities(String authority, SiblingAuthorityFilter filter)	Returns a parent authority related to the filter
addChildAuthorities(String parentAuthority, String[] authorities)	Creates child authorities (users) related to a parent authority (group)
removeChildAuthorities(String parentAuthority, String[] authorities)	Removes a set of child authorities (users) from a parent authority (group)

Method	Description
`getChildAuthorities (String authority, SiblingAuthorityFilter filter)`	Returns all the child authorities related to the filter
`getOwners(Predicate predicate)`	Returns the related owner for each node involved in the predicate
`setOwners(Predicate predicate, String owner)`	Sets the owner for each node involved in the predicate
`setInheritPermission(Pred icate predicate, boolean inheritPermission)`	Sets the permissions inheritance of the nodes from their parents
`hasPermissions(Predicate predicate, java.lang.String[] permissions)`	Returns a list of node references with the related set of permissions owned by the current user

In the source code included with this chapter, you will find many examples about these methods, but we would like to describe only some of these in the book. The main methods to manage permissions are related to:

- Owners
- **Access Control Entry (ACE)**
- Authorities

Setting owners

An owner of a node can perform all the possible operations because he/she has all the permissions available for the content owned. If you need to set an owner for nodes, you should invoke the `setOwners()` method as follows:

```
public OwnerResult[] setOwners(
final Predicate predicate,
final String owner)
throws RemoteException, AccessControlFault
owner is the string value for the username of a user.
```

In the following example, you can see how to invoke this method to set the `Admin` user as the new owner for the predicate of nodes:

```
OwnerResult[] ownerResults =
accessControlService.setOwners(predicate, "admin");

for (OwnerResult ownerResult : ownerResults) {
System.out.println("Owner: "+ ownerResult.getOwner() +
"| node:" + ownerResult.getReference().getPath());
}
```

Adding permissions

In order to add specific permissions for contents, you can add or remove an ACE in the ACL of the repository. Using an ACE, you can assign a specific permission to a user or a group of users to let them execute a basic operation for a node.

The method involved for this operation is the AddACEs() method:

```
public ACL[] addACEs(final Predicate predicate, final ACE[] aces)
throws RemoteException, AccessControlFault
```

This method returns an array of ACL elements that allows you to retrieve information about permissions for the involved predicate. For instance, to add the Read permission for the content, you need to create an ACE object in this way:

```
ACE ace = new ACE();
ace.setAuthority("admin");
ace.setPermission(Constants.READ);
ace.setAccessStatus(AccessStatus.acepted);

ACL[] acl = accessControlService.addACEs(predicate, new ACE[]{ace});
for (ACL aclElement : acl) {
ACE[] aces = aclElement.getAces();
for (ACE aceElement : aces) {
System.out.println(
" | Authority: "+aceElement.getAuthority() +
" | Permission: " +aceElement.getPermission());
}
}
```

Notice that if you want to add permissions for a group or a role in Alfresco, you need to type the related prefix for the right **Authority Type.** If you need to assign permission only to users, you only need to provide their usernames. For instance, if you want to assign a permission to everyone, you need to set as authority the EVERYONE group defined in Alfresco:

```
ace.setAuthority("GROUP_EVERYONE");
```

The AccessStatus is a mandatory element and allows you to check the state for this permission, using these two different states: ACCEPTED and DECLINED. The Constants class is a utility class provided by Alfresco that helps you to use all the common permissions and roles available. In this way, you don't need to care about constants default permissions, groups, and roles:

```
/** Permission prefixes for role's and group's */
public static final String ROLE_PREFIX = "ROLE_";
public static final String GROUP_PREFIX = "GROUP_";
/** Standard authorities */
```

```
public static final String ALL_AUTHORITIES = "GROUP_EVERYONE";
public static final String OWNER_AUTHORITY = "ROLE_OWNER";
public static final String LOCK_OWNER_AUTHORITY = "ROLE_LOCK_OWNER";
public static final String ADMINISTRATOR_AUTHORITY="ROLE_
ADMINISTRATOR";

/** Common permissions */
public static final String ALL_PERMISSIONS = "All";
public static final String FULL_CONTROL = "FullControl";
public static final String READ = "Read";
public static final String WRITE = "Write";
public static final String DELETE = "Delete";
public static final String ADD_CHILDREN = "AddChildren";
public static final String READ_PROPERTIES = "ReadProperties";
public static final String READ_CHILDREN = "ReadChildren";
public static final String WRITE_PROPERTIES = "WriteProperties";
public static final String DELETE_NODE = "DeleteNode";
public static final String DELETE_CHILDREN = "DeleteChildren";
public static final String CREATE_CHILDREN = "CreateChildren";
public static final String LINK_CHILDREN = "LinkChildren";
public static final String DELETE_ASSOCIATIONS = "DeleteAssociations";
public static final String READ_ASSOCIATIONS = "ReadAssociations";
public static final String CREATE_ASSOCIATIONS = "CreateAssociations";
public static final String READ_PERMISSIONS = "ReadPermissions";
public static final String CHANGE_PERMISSIONS = "ChangePermissions";
public static final String EXECUTE = "Execute";
public static final String READ_CONTENT = "ReadContent";
public static final String WRITE_CONTENT = "WriteContent";
public static final String EXECUTE_CONTENT = "ExecuteContent";
public static final String TAKE_OWNERSHIP = "TakeOwnership";
public static final String SET_OWNER = "SetOwner";
public static final String COORDINATOR = "Coordinator";
public static final String CONTRIBUTOR = "Contributor";
public static final String EDITOR = "Editor";
public static final String GUEST = "Guest";
public static final String LOCK = "Lock";
public static final String UNLOCK = "Unlock";
public static final String CHECK_OUT = "CheckOut";
public static final String CHECK_IN = "CheckIn";
public static final String CANCEL_CHECK_OUT = "CancelCheckOut";
```

Finally, in the last part of this section, you can learn how to manage authorities in the repository. An authority, in Alfresco, can be related to:

- Groups
- Roles
- Users

Creating authorities

In order to add authorities in the repository, you need to use the createAuthorities() method as follows:

```
public String[] createAuthorities(
String parentAuthority,
NewAuthority[] newAuthorites)
throws RemoteException, AccessControlFault
```

parentAuthority is used to contain the new authorities. If this field value is null, then it means that you are referring to the root tree (only for groups and roles). To create a NewAuthority object, you need to provide an AuthorityType and a name. AuthorityType is used to define the scope of the type of authority and can be one of these constant values: ADMIN, GROUP, EVERYONE, GUEST, ROLE, OWNER, or USER. The name argument is used to define exactly the name for a specific authority.

For instance, in order to create a new group named AWSBOOK in Alfresco, you need to set a GROUP value for the authorityType and an AWSBOOK value for the name as follows:

```
NewAuthority newAuthority = new NewAuthority();
newAuthority.setAuthorityType("GROUP");
newAuthority.setName("AWSBOOK");
NewAuthority[] authorities = new NewAuthority[]{newAuthority};
accessControlService.createAuthorities(null, authorities);
```

The result of this operation allows you to manage users using a new group named AWSBOOK. After executing this example code, in the Alfresco Explorer, you will see the following **Groups** panel:

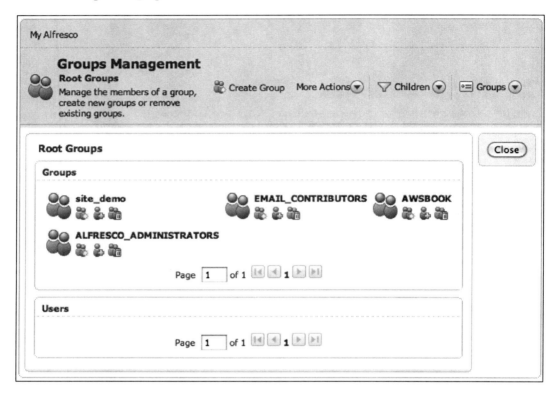

Managing actions

Alfresco allows you to execute and manage repository actions on nodes using the Action Service:

```
ActionServiceSoapBindingStub actionService = WebServiceFactory.
getActionService();
```

An action is a unit of work that can be executed on a node. For each action, it is possible to associate some conditions to set on which the nodes can be triggered. You can execute, get, attach, or remove one or more actions on a node in the repository, in a similar way to how you manage associations among nodes. But for actions, you need to use the specific ActionService to manage this type of relationship between a group of actions and a single node reference.

You can invoke all the following methods:

- `getConditionDefinitions()` — gets all the conditions to be used
- `executeActions(Predicate predicate, Action[] webServiceActions)` — executes several actions on all the nodes involved in the predicate
- `getActionDefinitions()` — gets all the action definitions
- `getActionItemDefinition(String name, ActionItemDefinitionType definitionType)` — gets the `ActionItemDefinition` for an action
- `getActions(Reference reference, ActionFilter filter)` — gets all the filtered actions available for the node reference
- `removeActions(Reference reference, Action[] webServiceActions)` — removes all the actions from the node reference
- `saveActions(Reference reference, Action[] webServiceActions)` — saves all the actions against the node reference

Getting action definitions

In order to execute actions from the Web Services API, the first step that you can follow is to query all the actions available in the repository. The method `getActionDefinitions()` helps you to achieve this goal, so you can retrieve all the actions available with all the needed parameters.

For instance, if you want to retrieve all the information about actions available in the repository, you can use the following lines of code taken from the related example:

```
ActionItemDefinition[] actionDefinitions = actionService.
getActionDefinitions();
for (ActionItemDefinition actionItemDefinition : actionDefinitions) {
System.out.println(
"-- Action: " + actionItemDefinition.getName() +
" | Title: " + actionItemDefinition.getTitle() +
" | Type: " + actionItemDefinition.getType()
);
ParameterDefinition[] parameters = actionItemDefinition.
getParameterDefinition();
if(parameters!=null) {
System.out.println("---- Parameters ----");
for (ParameterDefinition parameter : parameters) {
System.out.println(
"Name: " + parameter.getName() +
" | Type: " + parameter.getType()
```

```
    );
    }
    System.out.println("---- /Parameters ----\n");
    }
    }
```

Default actions

In a standard Alfresco installation, you can execute the following default actions:

Action	Explanation	Parameter
transform-image	Transforms and copies an image to a specific space.	Mime-type, destination-folder, association type, association name, overwrite-copy, convert-command.
mail	Sends an e-mail to specified users.	To, to_many, subject, text, from, FreeMarker template.
copy-to-web-project	Copies a node to a folder in a web project.	Destination folder.
extract-metadata	Extracts common metadata fields from content.	N/a
Counter	Increments a counter.	N/a
check-in	Checks in content.	Description.
simple-workflow	Adds a simple workflow to a node.	approve-step, approve-folder, approve-move, reject-step, reject-folder, reject-move.
script	Executes a script.	Script node reference.
transform	Transforms and copies content to a specific space.	mime-type, destination folder, association type, association name, overwrite-copy.
remove-features	Removes an aspect from a node.	destination folder, association type, association name, deep copy, overwrite-copy.
specialise-type	Specializes the type of a node.	type-name.

Action	Explanation	Parameter
import	Imports an Alfresco content package.	destination, encoding.
add-features	Adds an aspect to a node.	aspect name.
link-category	Links a node to a category.	category aspect, category value.
blog-post	Posts a blog entry.	action, result.
move	Moves a node to a specific space.	destination folder, association type, association name.
copy	Copies a node to a specific space.	destination folder, association type, association name, deep copy, overwrite-copy.
check-out	Check out node.	destination folder, association type, association name.

Getting an action definition

Now that you know more about all the default actions available in Alfresco, you can get information about a single action using the following method to retrieve a single `ActionItemDefinition` object as follows:

```
public ActionItemDefinition getActionItemDefinition(final String name,
final ActionItemDefinitionType definitionType) throws RemoteException,
ActionFault
```

The following example shows you how to get information about the `mail` action:

```
ActionItemDefinition actionItemDefinition =
actionService.getActionItemDefinition("mail",
ActionItemDefinitionType.action);
        System.out.println(
              "-- Action: " + actionItemDefinition.getName() +
              " | Title: " + actionItemDefinition.getTitle() +
              " | Type: " + actionItemDefinition.getType()
        );

ParameterDefinition[] parameters = actionItemDefinition.
getParameterDefinition();
        if(parameters!=null) {
            System.out.println("---- Parameters ----");
```

```
        for (ParameterDefinition parameter : parameters) {
            System.out.println(
                    "Name: " + parameter.getName() +
                    " | Type: " + parameter.getType()
                );
        }
        System.out.println("---- /Parameters ----\n");
    }
```

You should get the following output when the previous code is executed:

```
-- Action: mail | Title: Send an email to specified users | Type: action
---- Parameters ----
Name: to | Type: {http://www.alfresco.org/model/dictionary/1.0}text
Name: to_many | Type: {http://www.alfresco.org/model/dictionary/1.0}any
Name: subject | Type: {http://www.alfresco.org/model/dictionary/1.0}text
Name: text | Type: {http://www.alfresco.org/model/dictionary/1.0}text
Name: from | Type: {http://www.alfresco.org/model/dictionary/1.0}text
Name: template | Type: {http://www.alfresco.org/model/dictionary/
1.0}noderef
---- /Parameters ----
```

As you can see in the previous output, we can retrieve information about the description and all the input parameters that must be provided to execute this action.

Executing actions

In order to execute actions, you need to provide an array of `Action` objects. This means that you need to provide, for each action object, an `actionName` and all the related input parameters. The method used to execute actions, is named `executeActions`:

```
    public ActionExecutionResult[] executeActions(
    final Predicate predicate,
    final Action[] webServiceActions)
    throws RemoteException, ActionFault
```

You can see how to execute an action using the Action Service in the following snippet. In this example, we have created a generic content (`cm:cmobject`) and we have specialized this node to a standard content (`cm:content`), viewable from Alfresco Explorer.

As you can see, you need to set the right action name with all the related input parameters. In this example, we want to execute the `specialise-type` action, and then we need to provide the `type-name` parameter to specify the target content type for the node. You have to start creating a new `action` in this way:

```
Action action = new Action();
action.setActionName("specialise-type");
```

Then you need to provide all the input parameters for this action, in this case, the `type-name` parameter:

```
NamedValue[] actionParameters = new NamedValue[]{
new NamedValue("type-name", false, Constants.TYPE_CONTENT, null)};

action.setParameters(actionParameters);
```

Finally, you need to invoke the `executeActions()` method as follows:

```
ActionExecutionResult[] actionResults = actionService.executeActions(p
redicate, new Action[]{action});
for (ActionExecutionResult actionExecutionResult : actionResults) {
Action[] actionResult = actionExecutionResult.getActions();
Action actionPerformed = actionResult[0];
System.out.println("ActionName: " + actionPerformed.getActionName());
}
```

Saving actions

When you programmatically create your own actions or if you are using one of the default actions provided in Alfresco, you will need to save this new action instances against one or more nodes. Notice that these saved actions will never be automatically executed by the repository, you can only execute one of the stored actions manually using the `executeActions()` method described in the previous paragraph.

The method that allows you to save actions on nodes is as follows:

```
public org.alfresco.repo.webservice.action.Action[] saveActions(
final Reference reference, final Action[] webServiceActions)
throws RemoteException, ActionFault
```

In the following example, you can learn how to create an action to add the versionable aspect and how to save this action against a node:

```
//create action
Action action = new Action();
action.setActionName("add-features");

//create conditions
Condition[] conditions = new Condition[1];
Condition condition = new Condition();

//All items condition
condition.setConditionName("no-condition");
conditions[0] = condition;
action.setConditions(conditions);

//create the input parameter for this action
NamedValue parameter = new NamedValue();
parameter.setName("aspect-name");
parameter.setValue(Constants.ASPECT_VERSIONABLE);
NamedValue[] parameters = new NamedValue[1];
parameters[0] = parameter;
action.setParameters(parameters);

//save the new action against the node
Action[] actionToSave = new Action[]{action};
actionService.saveActions(reference, actionToSave);
```

Once you have executed the previous code and tried to browse the repository using **Node Browser**, you will see that all the actions are stored as new nodes. The container of these new nodes is the new child folder node in the involved node, and it is named actionFolder. Finally, the involved node will have a new aspect named actions.

Getting actions

In the previous section, you learned how to save actions against nodes in the repository; now we can see how to get these stored actions and how to use them for performing one of the operations previously described.

To get a stored action, you should use the following method:

```
public org.alfresco.repo.webservice.action.Action[] getActions(
final Reference reference, final ActionFilter filter) throws
RemoteException, ActionFault
```

Now, we can see how to get the action from the nodes:

```
Action[] savedActions = actionService.getActions(reference, new
ActionFilter());
    for (Action savedAction : savedActions) {
        System.out.println("ActionName:" +savedAction.getActionName());
        System.out.println("Description: "+savedAction.
getDescription());
        System.out.println("Id: "+savedAction.getId());
        System.out.println("Title: "+savedAction.getTitle());
        Condition[] savedActionConditions =  savedAction.
getConditions();
        for (Condition savedCondition : savedActionConditions) {
            System.out.println("-- Conditions --");
            System.out.println("Condition Name: "+savedCondition.
getConditionName());
            NamedValue[] savedConditionParameters = savedCondition.
getParameters();
            if(savedConditionParameters!=null){
                for (NamedValue savedConditionParameter :
savedConditionParameters) {
                    System.out.println("Parameter Name:
"+savedConditionParameter.getName() + " | Value:
"+savedConditionParameter.getValue());
                }
            }
            System.out.println("-- /Conditions --");
        }

        NamedValue[] savedParameters = savedAction.getParameters();
        if(savedParameters!=null){
            System.out.println("-- Parameters --");
            for (NamedValue savedParameter : savedParameters) {
                System.out.println("Parameter Name: "+savedParameter.
getName() + " | Value: "+savedParameter.getValue());
            }
            System.out.println("-- /Parameters --");
        }
    }
```

An `ActionFilter` can be used to select only some types of actions, setting all the
involved identifiers and types.

You should get the following output when the previous code is executed:

```
ActionName:add-features
Description: null
Id: 9e10d137-787c-473d-aa34-b7e9050763a9
Title: null
-- Conditions --
Condition Name: no-condition
-- /Conditions --
-- Parameters --
Parameter Name: aspect-name | Value: {http://www.alfresco.org/model/
content/1.0}versionable
-- /Parameters --
```

Removing actions

The last operation needed to manage the actions is removing actions against nodes.
The method that you need to use to remove actions is removeAction and this is
the signature:

```
public void removeActions(final Reference reference, final org.
alfresco.repo.webservice.action.Action[] webServiceActions)
throws RemoteException, ActionFault
```

The following example shows how to remove existing actions stored against nodes:

```
//create action
        Action action = new Action();
        action.setActionName("add-features");

        //create conditions
        Condition[] conditions = new Condition[1];
        Condition condition = new Condition();

        //All items condition
        condition.setConditionName("no-condition");
        conditions[0] = condition;
        action.setConditions(conditions);

        //create the input parameter for this action
        NamedValue parameter = new NamedValue();
        parameter.setName("aspect-name");
        parameter.setValue(Constants.ASPECT_VERSIONABLE);
```

```
NamedValue[] parameters = new NamedValue[1];
parameters[0] = parameter;
action.setParameters(parameters);

//remove actions against the node
Action[] actionToRemove = new Action[]{action};
actionService.removeActions(reference, actionToRemove);
```

Managing rules

When you have configured your spaces structure in Alfresco, you probably may want to create rules to manage some processes for contents in your spaces. A rule can be defined for a specific event in the repository. All the possible events are: Inbound, Outbound, and Update. Using rules, you can create actions with its conditions that can be executed automatically by the repository using the rule events. A rule event, named rule type, helps you to specify when this rule must be triggered in the repository:

- **Inbound** means that the rule will be triggered whenever a new content will be dropped in the space
- **Outbound** means that the rule will be triggered whenever content will be removed from the space
- **Update** means that the rule will be triggered whenever content will be updated

Default Conditions

To define a rule, you need to add conditions to set the scope of the involved contents in the rule. You can find some of these conditions as follows:

- All nodes
- Only nodes with a specific mime type
- Only nodes with a specific value for a property
- Only nodes with a specific aspect

All the possible condition types that you can use in an action are as follows:

Action	Explanation	Parameter
`compare-text-property`	Nodes with specific text value in property	`Property, content-property, value, operation`
`compare-property-value`	Nodes that contain a specific value in its name	`Property, content-property, value, operation`
`composite-condition`	Composite condition	`N/a`
`in-category`	Nodes with the specified category value	`Category-aspect, category-value`
`compare-mime-type`	Nodes with the specified mime type	`Property, content-property, value, operation`

In this way, you can implement procedures to transform, move, copy, or notify profiled contents, creating simple rules from the **Create Rule Wizard** in the Alfresco Explorer. Alfresco allows you to manage rules on nodes using the Action Service as follows:

```
ActionServiceSoapBindingStub actionService = WebServiceFactory.
getActionService();
```

You can invoke the following methods to manage rules:

- `getRules(Reference reference, RuleFilter ruleFilter)`: This gets all the rules filtered available for the node reference.
- `getRuleType(String name)`: This gets the rule type specified by rule name.
- `getRuleTypes()`: It gets all the available rule types (the default types are inbound, outbound, update).
- `removeRules(Reference reference, Rule[] webServiceRules`: This removes all the rules associated to the node reference.
- `saveRules(Reference reference, Rule[] webServiceRules)`: This saves all the rules associated to the node reference.

Adding rules

The `SaveRules` example is the most complete example to understand how to manage rules from the Web Services API in a good way. The following example shows you how to invoke the `saveRules()` method in order to add rules to spaces:

```
public Rule[] saveRules(
final Reference reference,
final Rule[] webServiceRules)
throws RemoteException, ActionFault
```

The involved `reference` must be a `cm:folder` content type. This means that this reference must be a space. You can assign rules only to Alfresco spaces. In this example, we want to add a new rule in a new space created using the remote API. A rule allows you to bind one or more actions to a space in the repository.

For the first step, we need to create a new action that we want to execute in the new rule. As you have seen in the previous section of the book, we need to provide an action name, all the conditions, and all the input parameters for the action.

In the following example, we are going to add the `versionable` aspect to all the items in this new space, so the action must be created as follows:

```
//create action for the rule
Action action = new Action();
action.setActionName("add-features");
//create conditions
Condition[] conditions = new Condition[1];
Condition condition = new Condition();
//All items condition
condition.setConditionName("no-condition");
conditions[0] = condition;
action.setConditions(conditions);
//create the input parameter for this action
NamedValue parameter = new NamedValue();
parameter.setName("aspect-name");
parameter.setValue(Constants.ASPECT_VERSIONABLE);
NamedValue[] parameters = new NamedValue[1];
parameters[0] = parameter;
action.setParameters(parameters);
```

In the next step, we want to create the rule with this action and with all the specified conditions:

```
//create the versionable rule
Rule[] rules = new Rule[1];
Rule rule = new Rule();
rule.setAction(action);
rule.setTitle("Add versionable aspect");
rule.setDescription("Add the versionable aspect to all the items in
the space");
rule.setExecuteAsynchronously(true);
rule.setRuleTypes(new String[]{"inbound"});
//add this rule to the new space
rules[0] = rule;
Rule[] ruleResultList = actionService.saveRules(reference, rules);
```

The `setExecuteAsynchronously()` method allows you to specify if a rule must be executed asynchronously. In this way, if you set a TRUE value for this field, each job for the rule will be executed in the background, without waiting for the response. Otherwise, each job will be executed in the foreground, waiting for each processing request. The `setRuleTypes()` method is used to set the related events (or rule types) to trigger the involved rule, as we indicated earlier, it can take the values inbound, outbound, or update.

The result of the execution of this example is that now you have a new rule saved in the new space created. So now, if you click on the new space created in the **Alfresco Explorer**, you should see the following screenshot:

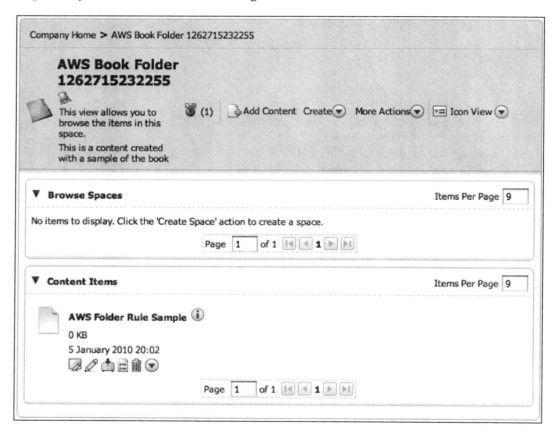

Then, if you try to create content in the new space and if you click on the **Details View** of the content, you can find all the information about versioning by expanding the **Version History** panel. If you can see the following screenshot, it means that the rule is working fine:

Finally, if we take a look at the **Details View | Manage Content Rules** of the new space, you'll see the new rule saved from the Web Services API, as shown in the following screenshot:

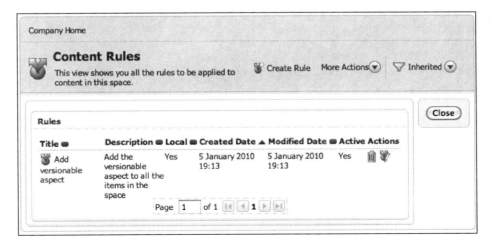

Managing users

The Administration Service allows you to manage users in Alfresco. The code snippet can be shown as follows:

```
AdministrationServiceSoapBindingStub administrationService =
WebServiceFactory.getAdministrationService();
```

You can invoke various operations to create, update, delete, and get users using the following methods:

- createUsers(NewUserDetails[] newUsers) — creates new users in the repository
- deleteUsers(String[] userNames) — removes all the users using the usernames parameter
- getUser(String userName) — returns user details from its username
- queryUsers(UserFilter filter) — returns filtered users details
- updateUsers(UserDetails[] users) — updates all the users specified in the array
- changePassword(String userName, String oldPassword, String newPassword) — changes the password for a user

The following sections explain how to add, update, delete, and search for users.

Adding users

This section shows you how to create users in the repository. The code snippet can be shown as follows:

```
public UserDetails[] createUsers(final NewUserDetails[] newUsers)
throws RemoteException, AdministrationFault
```

To invoke this method, you need to provide an array of NewUserDetails objects and you need to provide the following arguments for each object:

- A username to identify the user in the repository (String)
- A user password (String)
- A set of properties for the user (an array of NamedValue object)

In the following snippet taken from the related example, you can learn how to create users. In this case, we are creating only a single user named John Doe:

```
NewUserDetails userDetails = new NewUserDetails();
userDetails.setUserName("jdoe");
userDetails.setPassword("awsbook");

NamedValue[] properties = new NamedValue[3];
properties[0] = new NamedValue(Constants.PROP_USER_FIRSTNAME, false,
"John", null);
properties[1] = new NamedValue(Constants.PROP_USER_LASTNAME, false,
"Doe", null);
properties[2] = new NamedValue(Constants.PROP_USER_EMAIL, false,
"j.doe@example.com", null);
userDetails.setProperties(properties);
newUsers[0] = userDetails;
UserDetails[] responseUserDetails = administrationService.
createUsers(newUsers);
```

The response for this method is a UserDetails array, which you can use to check all the results as follows:

```
for (UserDetails userDetailsResponse : responseUserDetails) {
System.out.println("User created: " + userDetailsResponse.
getUserName());
NamedValue[] userProperties = userDetailsResponse.getProperties();
System.out.println("-- Properties --");
for (NamedValue namedValue : userProperties) {
System.out.println(
"Name: " + namedValue.getName() +
" | Value: " + namedValue.getValue());
}
System.out.println("-- /Properties --");
}
```

Deleting users

In order to delete users, you can use the deleteUsers() method, providing an array of strings with all the usernames involved in this operation:

```
public void deleteUsers(final String[] userNames)
throws RemoteException, AdministrationFault
```

The following script will invoke this operation without any results:

```
String[] usersToDelete = {"jdoe"};
administrationService.deleteUsers(usersToDelete);
```

usersToDelete is an array of strings that contains all the usernames involved in the deleting operation.

Updating users

In this section, you will learn how to update users using the updateUsers() method:

```
public UserDetails[] updateUsers(final UserDetails[] users)
throws RemoteException, AdministrationFault
```

In the same way as the previous method, you need to provide an array of user objects, but this time, the array is based on a different object class—UserDetails. Specifically, you can refer to the following lines:

```
//we want to update the existing user
UserDetails[] updateUserList = new UserDetails[1];
UserDetails updateUser = new UserDetails();
updateUser.setUserName("jdoe");
//update properties
NamedValue[] updateProperties = new NamedValue[3];
updateProperties[0] = new NamedValue(Constants.PROP_USER_FIRSTNAME,
false, "Johann", null);
updateProperties[1] = new NamedValue(Constants.PROP_USER_LASTNAME,
false, "Doh", null);
updateProperties[2] = new NamedValue(Constants.PROP_USER_EMAIL, false,
"j.doh@example.com", null);
updateUser.setProperties(updateProperties);
updateUserList[0] = updateUser;
//update the user
UserDetails[] updateResponse = administrationService.updateUsers(upda
teUserList);
```

This method returns an array of UserDetails objects to confirm all the changes against the repository. Finally, you can retrieve all the results in this way:

```
for (UserDetails userDetailsResponse : updateResponse) {
System.out.println("User updated: " + userDetailsResponse.
getUserName());
NamedValue[] userProperties = userDetailsResponse.getProperties();
System.out.println("-- Properties --");
for (NamedValue namedValue : userProperties) {
```

```
System.out.println(
"Name: " + namedValue.getName() +
" | " +
"Value: " + namedValue.getValue());
}
System.out.println("-- /Properties --\n");
}
```

Changing passwords

If you are using Alfresco as your authentication provider, by default, Alfresco stores all the user passwords in its own database. Then, you can let users manage their password using your application.

The method signature for this is as follows:

```
public void changePassword(final String userName, final String
oldPassword, final String newPassword) throws RemoteException,
AdministrationFault
```

The following method doesn't return any results, and you can invoke it in this way:

```
String username = "admin";
String oldPassword = "admin";
String newPassword = "secret";
administrationService.changePassword(username, oldPassword,
newPassword);
```

Getting user information

If you need to get information about a specific user, you can invoke the getUser() method as follows:

```
public UserDetails getUser(final String userName)
throws RemoteException, AdministrationFault
```

You only need to provide the username of the requested user, as you can see in the following example:

```
UserDetails userDetails = administrationService.getUser("admin");
NamedValue[] properties = userDetails.getProperties();
System.out.println("Username: "+userDetails.getUserName());
if(properties!=null){
System.out.println("---- Properties ----");
for (NamedValue namedValue : properties) {
```

```
System.out.println(
"Name: " + namedValue.getName() +
" | Value: " + namedValue.getValue());
}
System.out.println("---- Properties ----\n");
}
```

Searching users

In order to retrieve information about users, you can use the `queryUsers()` method:

```
public UserQueryResults queryUsers(final UserFilter filter)
throws RemoteException, AdministrationFault
```

`UserFilter` helps you to execute a simple search defining queries. In addition, you can use wildcards, such as "*", to perform partial matches, as shown as follows:

```
UserFilter filter = new UserFilter();
filter.setUserName("ad.*");
UserQueryResults userResults = administrationService.
queryUsers(filter);
UserDetails[] userDetailsList = userResults.getUserDetails();
for (UserDetails userDetails : userDetailsList) {
System.out.println("Username: " + userDetails.getUserName());
NamedValue[] properties = userDetails.getProperties();
if(properties!=null){
System.out.println("---- Properties ----");
for (NamedValue namedValue : properties) {
System.out.println(
"Name: " + namedValue.getName() +
" | Value: " + namedValue.getValue());
}
System.out.println("---- Properties ----\n");
}
}
```

Summary

This chapter began by introducing how to manage collaborative content editing among users. In this chapter, you learned:

- How to perform check-out and check-in operations — using versioning and locking explicitly
- How classifications allow you to manage your contents using categories
- How to change permissions and roles on contents using authorization methods
- How to perform actions in the repository and how to manage rules
- How to manage users to create, remove, update, or retrieve user information

In the next chapter, we're going to show you a complete example of using the Alfresco Web Services API.

4
A Complete Example

In this chapter, we will see an example of an application that you can build on top of Alfresco using the Web Services API. Applying all the concepts discussed in the previous chapters, now we want to focus your attention on a real case. The example proposed in this chapter is based on a bookshop application. This application allows customers to buy books and write reviews.

The chapter starts by showing you how to set up the repository to deploy the bookshop application correctly. Then it addresses an overview for each specific feature, showing the related implementation based on the Alfresco API. Specifically, you will learn how to implement the following features:

- Signing in
- Managing the home page
- Retrieving book details
- Shopping Cart
- Adding a review
- Managing reviews (only admin)
- Changing user details

Setting up the project

The implementation of this sample application is a standard J2EE web application, based on Apache Struts 1.3 as MVC framework. The project is managed using Apache Maven, and many of the resources are taken from public repositories. Instructions for downloading and installing Apache Maven can be found at the project's website at http://maven.apache.org/.

The only resource that you need to manually provide in your local Maven repository is the Alfresco Web Service client stub. To install this artifact in your local Maven repository, you need to go to the path `Alfresco SDK/lib/remote/` and run the following command:

```
mvn install:install-file -DgroupId=alfresco.community -
DartifactId=alfresco-web-service-client -Dversion=3.3 -Dpackaging=jar -
Dfile=alfresco-web-service-client-3.3.jar
```

Obviously, you have to change the `version` and `file` parameters to point to the correct Alfresco version that you want to use. Once this command is invoked, you should see a similar output:

```
[INFO] Scanning for projects...
[INFO] Searching repository for plugin with prefix: 'install'.
[INFO] --------------------------------------------------------------------
------
[INFO] Building Maven Default Project
[INFO]    task-segment: [install:install-file] (aggregator-style)
[INFO] -------------------------------------------------------------------
[INFO] [install:install-file {execution: default-cli}]
[INFO] Installing /Users/piergiorgiolucidi/Documents/Alfresco Book/
project/alfresco-community-sdk-3.3/lib/remote/alfresco-web-service-
client.jar to /Users/piergiorgiolucidi/.m2/repository/alfresco/community/
alfresco-web-service-client/3.3/alfresco-web-service-client- 3.3.jar
[INFO] -------------------------------------------------------------------
[INFO] BUILD SUCCESSFUL
[INFO] ---------------------------------------------------------------
```

Now, you have correctly installed this new artifact in your local repository, so you can build and run this example application using Maven. Notice that this example was created using Alfresco 3.3 Community. If you want to use a different version of Alfresco, you will need to install a different version of the Alfresco Web Service Client and change all the related dependency versions in the `pom.xml`.

If you are using Eclipse, you have to run the following command in order to correctly import the Maven project:

```
mvn eclipse:eclipse
```

Once you have correctly configured your local Maven repository and imported the project in your IDE, in order to test this application, you only need to run the Maven goal `jetty:run`. In this way, Maven will deploy the application in the Jetty servlet container, and you can test this application on the fly. You can configure the Alfresco endpoint address by changing the property file in this classpath of the application: `alfresco/webserviceclient.properties`.

You have to provide the following property value inside this property file, if your Alfresco instance is running in your local machine, listening at port `8080`:

```
repository.location=http://localhost:8080/alfresco/api.
```

For each feature exposed by this example application, you will find a Struts action that consists of one or more SOAP calls against the repository.

The Bookshop model

Before we start discussing features, we need to talk about the content model created for this application. The model was created to show an example of a bookshop website and you can find it in the `model` folder in the source code included with this chapter. To install the bookshop model, you should refer to the Alfresco documentation.

 For more information about how to create and deploy your custom model in Alfresco, you can find all the details in the following page: `http://wiki.alfresco.com/wiki/Data_Dictionary_Guide#Step_by_Step_Model_Definition`.

The main content type provided in this model is the `book` type that consists of these properties: `ISBN`, `authors`, `publisher`, and `reviews`. Notice that this content type extends the `cm:content` of Alfresco. This means that a `book` has all the default properties as `name`, `title`, and `description`.

A `book` is associated with one or many reviews (content type) that users can send for approval to the admin user. A `review` consists of these properties: `reviewer's name`, `reviewer's email`, `rating`, and `approved`. The last one is used to manage the approval state for all the submitted reviews.

Sign in page

The first part of the example that we are starting to discuss is the login feature. This is the first operation that a user needs to perform before entering in the bookshop application. After deploying this web application in a servlet container such as Apache Tomcat, you have to navigate at the following action to enter in the bookshop application:

```
http://localhost:8080/aws-ch4-sample
```

In this page, you will see the login form of the bookshop, as shown in the following screenshot:

Bookshop

Login

Username: jdoe

Password: ••••   (Sign in)

As you can see, all the users that can enter in this bookshop are managed in the repository. It could be useful to try to use this application using three or four users.

For this login action, we want to manage this specific web flow:

- If any user's session doesn't exist, then it will create a new user session and forward the user to the homepage
- If a previous user session exists, then it will forward to a summary page.
- If the user credentials are wrong or Alfresco returns an error, then it will forward to an error page

The unique Alfresco service needed to implement this action is the Authentication Service that you can use calling the helper class named `AuthenticationUtils`. You can see how to do this in the following code:

```
if(hasUserTicket(request)){

//if a user session exists we want to reuse it
AuthenticationDetails authenticationDetails = getUserDetails(request);

AuthenticationUtils.setAuthenticationDetails(
authenticationDetails);

   request.setAttribute(
USERNAME_ATTRIBUTE, authenticationDetails.getUserName());

        return mapping.findForward(LOGGED_IN_FORWARD);
```

```
        } else {
            //we create a new user session
            LoginFormBean loginForm = (LoginFormBean)form;
            try{

                AuthenticationUtils.startSession(
loginForm.getUsername(), loginForm.getPassword());

AuthenticationDetails userDetails =
AuthenticationUtils.getAuthenticationDetails();

            //we want to save the user session          request.
getSession().setAttribute(
USER_TICKET, userDetails);

                return mapping.findForward(HOMEPAGE_FORWARD);
            }catch(AuthenticationFault exception){
                return mapping.findForward(LOGIN_KO_FORWARD);
            }catch(RuntimeException exception){
                return mapping.findForward(LOGIN_KO_FORWARD);
            }
        }
```

In the first part of the snippet, you can see how to manage an existing user session. This means that a user is trying to re-authenticate, navigating to the login action:

```
http://localhost:8080/aws-ch4-samples/login.do
```

But this operation is not needed because there is an existing session for him/her, and then the application will show the right message that this user is logged in. This mechanism is based on using the session scope of the web application. In this way, you can set a new attribute in the web user session that you can retrieve in other actions, without invoking an authentication request each time against the repository.

The involved attribute, which is stored in the web user session, is the AuthenticationDetails object. This object is retrieved from the first authentication request of the user, and then it is stored in the web session. You will find the retrieve mechanism of the session in the base action; specifically, it is implemented inside the utility method—getUserDetails:

```
protected AuthenticationDetails getUserDetails(HttpServletRequest
request){
        return (AuthenticationDetails)request.getSession()
        getAttribute(USER_TICKET);
}
```

One of the fields included in the `AuthenticationDetails` object is the authentication ticket that you can use to bind the right credentials for each user.

In the second part of the snippet, you can see how to authenticate this user against the repository. After the request, if the authentication process returns the user details, then it means that this user can be forwarded to the homepage. Finally, the user details are stored in the web user session. Otherwise, the user will be forwarded to an error page.

Home page

Whenever a user tries to log in to the bookshop with right credentials, the sign in action will forward him to the home page. The home page is structured to have an overview of all the features, only authenticated users can start to navigate the bookshop, forwarding users to this action URL:

```
http://localhost:8080/aws-ch4-samples/homepage.do
```

At the top of this page, you will find all the available features:

Feature	Description
Home	Shows the home page
Account	Shows the account form to allow users to change their profile details.
Cart	Allows users to manage the cart, as well as adding and removing books
Sign out	Performs a logout removing the user session.
Book details	Shows all the details about the book
Manage Reviews (only admin user)	The admin user can accept or reject reviews.

The last feature is accessible only to the admin user that can manage all the reviews submitted by users.

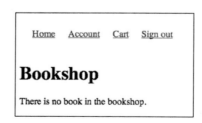

Configure the bookshop repository

As you can see, the first time that you try to use this application, there are no books in the store. This means that we need to create new books. If you have deployed the bookshop model, you can do this using the Alfresco Explorer. The first time you start this application, you need to create a **Books** space in the **Company Home**.

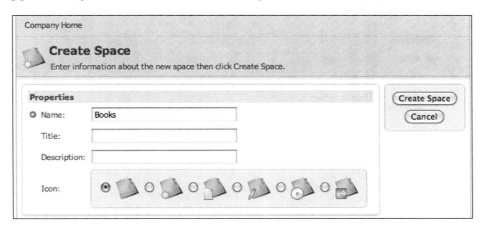

Then you need to create each book from **Company Home | Books** using the **Add Content** wizard, uploading the PDF file for the book and selecting the correct content type, as shown in the following screenshot:

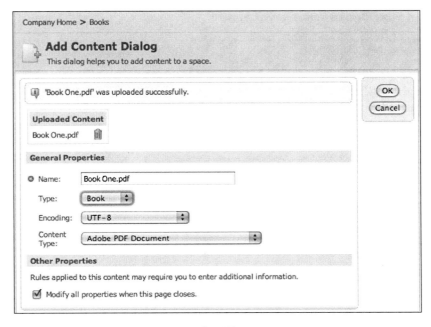

Finally, you need to set all the related properties needed by the model, as shown in the following screenshot:

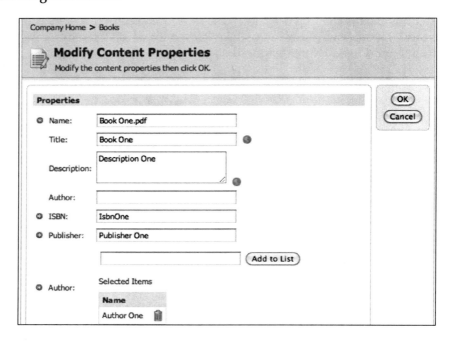

When you have created some books in your repository, you should have a similar overview of your **Books** space as follows:

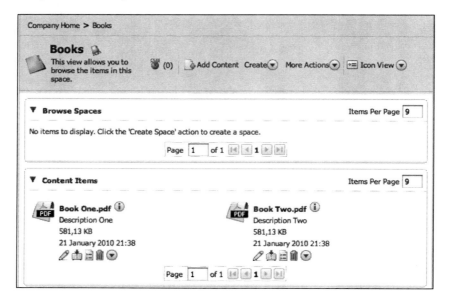

Now, if you try to refresh the bookshop home page, you should see this page updated to show all the available books provided by the store, as follows:

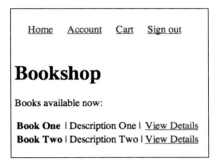

Behind the rendering of this page, the home page action executes a query to retrieve all the books in the **Company Home | Books**. Then it creates a list of books to set these to the **View** component (JSP). In order to retrieve information for a specific book, we will use specific actions using the related UUID of the involved items.

In this way, all the necessary information will be shown to the users, and you can see how to retrieve all the books in the following code of the home page action:

```
List<BookVO> booksList = new ArrayList<BookVO>();

        RepositoryServiceSoapBindingStub repositoryService =
WebServiceFactory.getRepositoryService();
        Store spacesStore = new Store(Constants.WORKSPACE_STORE,
"SpacesStore");
String luceneQuery = "PATH:\"/app:company_home/cm:Books/*\"";

Query query =
new Query(Constants.QUERY_LANG_LUCENE, luceneQuery);

        QueryResult queryResult = repositoryService.
query(spacesStore, query, false);

   ResultSet resultSet = queryResult.getResultSet();
   if(resultSet.getTotalRowCount()>0){
      ResultSetRow[] results = resultSet.getRows();
      //retrieve results from the resultSet
      if(results!=null){
         for (ResultSetRow resultRow : results) {
            ResultSetRowNode nodeResult = resultRow.getNode();
```

```
                        //create the current book bean
                        BookVO book = new BookVO();
                        book.setId(nodeResult.getId());

                        //retrieve properties from the current node
                 for (NamedValue namedValue : resultRow.getColumns()) {
                    if (Constants.PROP_TITLE.equals(namedValue.getName())) {
                            book.setTitle(namedValue.getValue());
                 } else if (Constants.PROP_DESCRIPTION.equals(namedValue.
getName())) {
                            book.setDescription(namedValue.getValue());
                 }
             }

             //add the current book to the list
             booksList.add(book);

         }
     }

}
```

Book details page

Once you have configured the bookshop repository adding books, users can click
on the **View Details** link to see all the details of a specific book. The query string
for each link is created using the UUID of the books that is used to retrieve all the
properties about a specific item in the store.

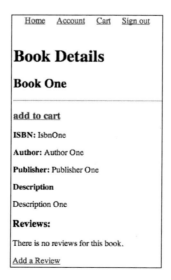

In order to render this page, the **Book Details** action performs all the following operations:

- Retrieves all the properties about the book
- Checks if this book is added in your cart
- Shows all the reviews about this book

But we also have two features:

- Add to cart
- Add a review

In the next few sections, we are going to describe all the details about these page components and features.

Getting book properties

The first service that we need to use to execute a query in the repository is the Repository Service. Using the UUID as a parameter from the query string, we can retrieve the book node and all the related properties. When you have the UUID of an item in the repository, you can invoke the `get` method to retrieve the involved nodes directly as follows:

```
String uuid = request.getParameter(BOOK_ID_PARAMETER);

RepositoryServiceSoapBindingStub repositoryService =
WebServiceFactory.getRepositoryService();

Store spacesStore =
new Store(Constants.WORKSPACE_STORE, "SpacesStore");

Reference bookReference =
new Reference(spacesStore,uuid,null);

Predicate predicateForThisBook = new Predicate(new Reference[]{bookRef
erence},spacesStore,null);

Node[] bookNode = repositoryService.get(predicateForThisBook);

NamedValue[] propertiesOfTheBook =bookNode[0].getProperties();

BookVO book = new BookVO();
        for (NamedValue bookProperty : propertiesOfTheBook) {
            if(Constants.PROP_TITLE.equals(bookProperty.getName()))
                book.setTitle(bookProperty.getValue());
```

```
            else if(Constants.PROP_DESCRIPTION.equals(bookProperty.
getName()))
            book.setDescription(bookProperty.getValue());
            else if(BookshopModel.PROP_BOOK_UUID.equals(bookProperty.
getName()))
            book.setId(bookProperty.getValue());
            else if(BookshopModel.PROP_BOOK_AUTHOR.
equals(bookProperty.getName())){

                //author is a multivalue property
                String[] authors = bookProperty.getValues();
                String authorsString = "";
                for (String author : authors) {
                   authorsString += author;
                      if(authors.length>1)
                         authorsString+=" | ";
                }

                book.setAuthor(authorsString);
            }
            else if(BookshopModel.PROP_BOOK_PUBLISHER.
equals(bookProperty.getName()))
                book.setPublisher(bookProperty.getValue());
            else if(BookshopModel.PROP_BOOK_ISBN.equals(bookProperty.
getName()))
                book.setIsbn(bookProperty.getValue());
        }
```

Notice that the book content type has an `author` field that consists of a multi-value property in the model. In the previous snippet, you can see how to get all the authors of a book. The `BookVO` is the value object used in the JSP template to correctly render the page.

Checking the cart space

In the next step, we want to verify if some books are stored in the cart of the user. For each user in Alfresco, a user home folder is defined, and in this space, the application creates the **Cart** space to manage e-commerce features. To retrieve information about the user home space, we need to use the Administration Service in order to get all the user's details by invoking the `getUser()` method:

```
String username = AuthenticationUtils.getAuthenticationDetails().
getUserName();

AdministrationServiceSoapBindingStub administrationService =
WebServiceFactory.getAdministrationService();
```

```
UserDetails userDetails = administrationService.getUser(username);

NamedValue[] userProperties = userDetails.getProperties();

String homeFolderNodeRef = null;
for (NamedValue namedValue : userProperties) {
        if(Constants.PROP_USER_HOMEFOLDER.equals(
namedValue.getName()))
              homeFolderNodeRef = namedValue.getValue();
     }
```

Then, we can use the Repository Service to execute the `queryChildren()` method to check if the cart space exists in the user home space. The **Cart** space is created by the application when a user adds a book to his/her cart for the first time. This is shown as follows:

```
Reference userHomeRef = new Reference(
spacesStore, homeFolderNodeRef.substring(24), null);

QueryResult userHomeChildren = repositoryService.queryChildren(userHo
meRef);

ResultSet resultSetHomeFolder = userHomeChildren.getResultSet();

String cartSpaceUuid = null;

if(resultSetHomeFolder.getTotalRowCount()>0
             && !ADMIN_USERNAME.equals(username)) {

ResultSetRow[] resultsUserHome = resultSetHomeFolder.getRows();

        for (ResultSetRow resultSetRow : resultsUserHome) {
           //children of the user home folder
             if(Constants.TYPE_FOLDER.equals(
resultSetRow.getNode().getType())){

NamedValue[] properties = resultSetRow.getColumns();
   for (NamedValue namedValue : properties) {    if(Constants.PROP_
NAME.equals(namedValue.getName())){

                if("Cart".equals(namedValue.getValue())){
                   cartSpaceUuid = resultSetRow.getNode().getId();
                   }
                }
             }
```

```
                    }
                }

            if(!StringUtils.isEmpty(cartSpaceUuid)){

                Reference cartReference =
                new Reference(spacesStore,cartSpaceUuid, null);

                QueryResult cartChildren =
                repositoryService.queryChildren(cartReference);

    ResultSet resultSetCart = cartChildren.getResultSet();
                (resultSetCart.getTotalRowCount()>0){
        ResultSetRow[] booksInCart = resultSetCart.getRows();

    for (ResultSetRow bookInCart : booksInCart) {
        NamedValue[] bookProperties = bookInCart.getColumns();
            for (NamedValue bookProperty : bookProperties) {    if(Constants.
    PROP_TITLE.equals(bookProperty.getName())){
            if(book.getTitle().equals(bookProperty.getValue())) {
                                    isInCart = new Boolean(true);
                        }
                    }
                }
            }
        }
    }
}
```

Getting all the associated reviews

Finally, we want to retrieve all the reviews associated with the book to show all this information in the book details page. Again, we need to use the Repository Service, invoking the `queryChildren()` method as follows:

```
List<ReviewVO> reviews = new ArrayList<ReviewVO>();

ParentReference bookReferenceParent = new ParentReference();
bookReferenceParent.setAssociationType(
BookshopModel.ASS_BOOK_REVIEWS);

bookReferenceParent.setUuid(bookReference.getUuid());
bookReferenceParent.setStore(SPACES_STORE);
```

```
QueryResult queryResultAssociated = repositoryService.queryChildren(bo
okReferenceParent);

ResultSet resultSetAss = queryResultAssociated.getResultSet();
ResultSetRow[] resultsAss = resultSetAss.getRows();
```

All the reviews are children of a specific book (the parent), this association was
defined in the bookshop model, and this is a `child-association` named `reviews`.

In the next step, we need to iterate results to retrieve details for each review. A
review is stored in the repository as a separated content. This means that if we want
to publish the content of a review to a page, we should read the related content or
provide the content URL using the Content Service as follows:

```
ContentServiceSoapBindingStub contentService = WebServiceFactory.
getContentService();

if(resultSetAss.getTotalRowCount()>0){
    for (ResultSetRow reviewAssociated : resultsAss) {
        ReviewVO review = new ReviewVO();
NamedValue[] reviewProperties = reviewAssociated.getColumns();

for (NamedValue reviewProperty : reviewProperties) {
                if(BookshopModel.PROP_REVIEW_APPROVED.equals(
reviewProperty.getName())){

    review.setApproved(new Boolean(reviewProperty.getValue()));
                } else if(BookshopModel.PROP_REVIEW_REVIEWER_NAME.
equals(
reviewProperty.getName())){
    review.setReviewerName(reviewProperty.getValue());
                } else if(BookshopModel.PROP_REVIEW_RATING.equals(
reviewProperty.getName())){
                    review.setRating(reviewProperty.getValue());

                }
            }

    Reference reviewRef = new Reference();
    reviewRef.setStore(SPACES_STORE);
    reviewRef.setUuid(reviewAssociated.getNode().getId());

    Predicate reviewPredicate = new Predicate();
    reviewPredicate.setNodes(new Reference[]{reviewRef});
    reviewPredicate.setStore(SPACES_STORE);
```

```
    Content[] reviewContent = contentService.read(reviewPredicate,
Constants.PROP_CONTENT);

String ticketURL = "?ticket="+getUserDetails(request).getTicket();

String contentUrl = URLDecoder.decode(reviewContent[0].getUrl(),
"UTF-8") + ticketURL;

            review.setContentUrl(contentUrl);
            reviews.add(review);
        }
    }
```

The created list of reviews will be set as one of the attributes in the request to render all the reviews lists in the JSP template

Adding a book to the cart

Customers can add a book to their own cart by clicking on the **Add to cart** link, as shown in the book details page. In this way, you can see how to allow users to collect items in a unique order that consists of a private space in the repository. As we have introduced in the previous section, for this application, the **Cart** space is created in the specific user's home folder, the first time a user adds a book to his cart.

The **Add to cart** action performs the following operations:

1. Check if the **Cart** space exists.
2. Only if the **Cart** space doesn't exists, then it will be created.
3. Add the book node in the **Cart** space.

Checking if the cart space exists

The first operation performed in this action is implemented using the Administration Service to get the user home folder of the current user as follows:

```
        String username = AuthenticationUtils.
getAuthenticationDetails().getUserName();

AdministrationServiceSoapBindingStub administrationService =
WebServiceFactory.getAdministrationService();

        UserDetails userDetails = administrationService.
getUser(username);
```

```
      NamedValue[] userProperties = userDetails.getProperties();
          String homeFolderNodeRef = null;
          for (NamedValue namedValue : userProperties) {
            if(Constants.PROP_USER_HOMEFOLDER.equals(
namedValue.getName()))
                homeFolderNodeRef = namedValue.getValue();
          }
```

The `homeFolderNodeRef` is the node reference of the user home that we need to use with the Repository Service to execute a Lucene query. This is used to check if the **Cart** space exists in the user home folder:

```
RepositoryServiceSoapBindingStub repositoryService =
WebServiceFactory.getRepositoryService();

String luceneQuery =
"PARENT:\""+homeFolderNodeRef+"\" AND @cm\\:name:\"Cart\"";

Query query = new Query(Constants.QUERY_LANG_LUCENE, luceneQuery);

QueryResult result = repositoryService.query(SPACES_STORE, query,
false);
```

The Lucene query used for this operation consists of a PARENT token and a metadata token. The PARENT token allows you to get all the nodes that have the specified node reference as a parent. The metadata token finds a node named `Cart` and finally, all these conditions are executed with an AND operator; this means that this query gets the node with the name property value as `Cart` and that has the user home folder as one of its own parents.

 For more information about search and how to create other types of queries, you can visit the wiki page at `http://wiki.alfresco.com/wiki/Search`

Creating the cart space

In the next step, we are going to create the **Cart** space only if it doesn't exist in the user home folder. Iterating `results` returned from the previous query, we can find the **Cart** space. If there is a result, then it means that the space exists. Otherwise, we need to create a new one in the user home folder as follows:

```
String pathCart = null;
String idCart = null;
if(result.getResultSet().getTotalRowCount()==0){
```

```
//you need to create the Cart space
ParentReference parent = new ParentReference(
    SPACES_STORE,
    homeFolderNodeRef.substring(24),
    null,
    Constants.ASSOC_CONTAINS,
    "{" + Constants.NAMESPACE_CONTENT_MODEL + "}Cart");

    //build properties
    NamedValue[] properties = new NamedValue[1];
    properties[0] = new NamedValue();
    properties[0].setName(Constants.PROP_NAME);
        properties[0].setValue("Cart");

    //create operation
    CMLCreate create = new CMLCreate();
    create.setId("1");
    create.setParent(parent);
    create.setType(Constants.TYPE_FOLDER);
    create.setProperty(properties);

    //build the CML object
    CML cml = new CML();
    cml.setCreate(new CMLCreate[]{create});

//perform a CML update to create the Cart space
UpdateResult[] resultForCart =repositoryService().update(cml);

pathCart = resultForCart[0].getDestination().getPath();

        } else {
            //the Cart space exists, we only need to add books
            ResultSet resultSet = result.getResultSet();
            ResultSetRow[] results = resultSet.getRows();
            idCart = results[0].getNode().getId();
        }
```

In the following snippet, you will see the two available ways to create a ParentReference object for the **Cart** space using the path or using the UUID:

```
//add a new book in the Cart space

    //create the Cart space
    ParentReference cartSpace = null;

    if(pathCart!=null){
```

```
                    //if you want to use the path
            cartSpace = new ParentReference(
                    SPACES_STORE,
                null,
                pathCart,
                    Constants.ASSOC_CONTAINS,
        "{" + Constants.NAMESPACE_CONTENT_MODEL + "}"+bookUuid);

    }else {

            //if you want to use the UUID
            cartSpace = new ParentReference(
                    SPACES_STORE,
                idCart,
                null,
                    Constants.ASSOC_CONTAINS,
        "{" + Constants.NAMESPACE_CONTENT_MODEL + "}"+bookUuid);
    }
```

The pathCart argument is returned from the execution of the update method invoked to create the new **Cart** space. The idCart is the UUID of the existing **Cart** space.

Adding a book in the cart

In the last step, we need to add the selected book in the **Cart**, and to do this, we need to create a CMLAddChild object. Then we need to use the Repository Service for invoking the update method as follows:

```
Reference bookToAddRef = new Reference();
bookToAddRef.setUuid(bookUuid);
bookToAddRef.setStore(SPACES_STORE);

Predicate bookToAdd = new Predicate();
bookToAdd.setNodes(new Reference[]{bookToAddRef});

CMLAddChild addBookToCart = new CMLAddChild();
addBookToCart.setWhere(bookToAdd);
addBookToCart.setTo(cartSpace);

CML cmlAddChild = new CML();
cmlAddChild.setAddChild(new CMLAddChild[]{addBookToCart});

//perform a CML update to add the node
repositoryService().update(cmlAddChild);
```

The next time a user tries to navigate to the **Cart** page, he/she will find a new book in his/her cart. In the next section, you will see how to retrieve the newly added book to the user.

Cart page

The cart page is dedicated to show all the items that users would like to buy in the bookshop. This feature is exposed by the action addressed by the **Cart** link on top of the page. In the previous section, you learned how to add a book to a user's cart, and once a user adds a book, this page consists of a list of the added books, as shown in the following screenshot:

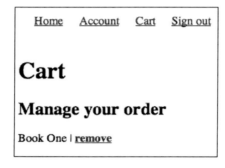

In the repository, the **Cart** space will be created in the user home folder with all the related children contents inside it. So for this feature, the page consists of the same books that exist in the repository. This means that if you try to navigate in the repository, specifically in the **Company Home | User Home | <username> | Cart**, you will see the same items, as shown in the **Cart** page as follows:

In order to render this list of books, it is necessary to use the Administration Service to get all the users details to retrieve the home folder reference for invoking the getUser() method. Then the Repository Service is used to find the **Cart** space with the related children. All the children will consist of the books added by the user in the cart.

In the first step, we need to get the user details and find the **Cart** space. But we have seen how to perform these operations in the previous section, so now we are going to see how to find all the children of the **Cart** space. We need to provide a parent reference, that is, the **Cart** space, and then we can invoke the queryChildren() method to find all the children. In this way, we can create the final list of books to show in the **Cart** page as follows:

```
Reference cartReference = new Reference(SPACES_STORE,cartSpaceUuid,
null);

QueryResult cartChildren = repositoryService.queryChildren(cartRefere
nce);

ResultSet resultSetCart = cartChildren.getResultSet();
ResultSetRow[] booksAddedToCart = resultSetCart.getRows();
```

```
if(booksAddedToCart!=null) {
   for (ResultSetRow bookAdded : booksAddedToCart) {
        BookVO book = new BookVO();
      book.setId(bookAdded.getNode().getId());
      NamedValue[] bookProperties = bookAdded.getColumns();

      //book properties
      for (NamedValue bookProperty : bookProperties) {
      if(Constants.PROP_TITLE.equals(bookProperty.getName()))
    book.setTitle(bookProperty.getValue());

else if(Constants.PROP_DESCRIPTION.equals(
      bookProperty.getName()))
      book.setDescription(bookProperty.getValue());

else if(BookshopModel.PROP_BOOK_AUTHOR.equals(
bookProperty.getName())){

         //author is a multivalue property
         String[] authors = bookProperty.getValues();
         String authorsString = "";
         for (String author : authors) {
            authorsString += " | " + author;
         }

         book.setAuthor(authorsString);
      }

else if(BookshopModel.PROP_BOOK_PUBLISHER.equals(
bookProperty.getName()))
book.setPublisher(bookProperty.getValue());

   else if(BookshopModel.PROP_BOOK_ISBN.equals(
bookProperty.getName()))
                  book.setIsbn(bookProperty.getValue());

            }
            booksAddedToCartList.add(book);
         }
      }
```

Removing a book from the cart

Once a user adds a book to his/her cart, the same user can remove this book from there. This operation is implemented with a CMLRemoveChild object to delete the association between the two involved nodes as follows:

```
ParentReference targetSpace = new ParentReference();
targetSpace.setStore(SPACES_STORE);
targetSpace.setUuid(cartSpaceUuid);
targetSpace.setAssociationType(Constants.ASSOC_CONTAINS);

Reference bookReference = new Reference(SPACES_STORE,
userPasswordForm.getBookId(), null);

Predicate nodeToRemove = new Predicate(new Reference[]{bookReference},
SPACES_STORE, null);

//remove child
CMLRemoveChild removeBook = new CMLRemoveChild();
removeBook.setFrom(targetSpace);
removeBook.setWhere(nodeToRemove);

CML cmlRemoveBook = new CML();
cmlRemoveBook.setRemoveChild(
new CMLRemoveChild[]{removeBook});
```

Adding a review

Users can add reviews to contribute to the community of the bookshop leaving a personal feedback about a book. For this feature, we have decided to implement a little workflow dedicated to publish only approved reviews. When a user would like to submit a review for approval, he/she can navigate to the details page of the interested book and he/she can click the **Add a Review** link. Then the application will render the following form to the user:

Once a user submits a review for approval, and if the admin user doesn't validate it, the review is not shown in the book details page. Only if the admin user accepts the submitted review, the involved item will be shown in the book details page. The action behind this feature is implemented to perform these operations:

1. Check if the **Reviews** space exists.
2. Only if the **Reviews** space doesn't exists, will it be created in the user home folder.
3. Create the submitted review as a child content in the private **Reviews** space.
4. Add the review as an associated node of the related book.

This feature is exposed in the book details page by clicking on the **Add a Review** link. As you saw in the previous sections, the first operation is very similar to the operation dedicated to the initialization of the **Cart** space; if the **Reviews** space doesn't exist in the user home space, we must create it. Otherwise, we must reuse the existing space:

```java
RepositoryServiceSoapBindingStub repositoryService =
WebServiceFactory.getRepositoryService();

String luceneQuery =
"PARENT:\""+homeFolderNodeRef+"\" AND @cm\\:name:\"Reviews\"";

Query query = new Query(Constants.QUERY_LANG_LUCENE, luceneQuery);

QueryResult result =
repositoryService.query(SPACES_STORE, query, false);

String pathSpaceReviews = null;
String idSpaceReviews = null;

        if(result.getResultSet().getTotalRowCount()==0){

        //you need to create the Reviews space
        ParentReference parent = new ParentReference(
        SPACES_STORE,
        homeFolderNodeRef.substring(24),
        null,
        Constants.ASSOC_CONTAINS,
        "{" + Constants.NAMESPACE_CONTENT_MODEL + "}Reviews");

            //build properties
            NamedValue[] properties = new NamedValue[1];
            properties[0] = new NamedValue();
            properties[0].setName(Constants.PROP_NAME);
```

```
        properties[0].setValue("Reviews");

    //create operation
    CMLCreate create = new CMLCreate();
    create.setId("1");
    create.setParent(parent);
    create.setType(Constants.TYPE_FOLDER);
    create.setProperty(properties);

    //build the CML object
    CML cml = new CML();
      cml.setCreate(new CMLCreate[]{create});

        //perform a CML update to create the Cart space
 UpdateResult[] resultForCart = repositoryService.update(cml);

        pathSpaceReviews = resultForCart[0].getDestination().
 getPath();

      } else {

 //the Reviews space exists, we only need to add the review
        ResultSet resultSet = result.getResultSet();
        ResultSetRow[] results = resultSet.getRows();
        idSpaceReviews = results[0].getNode().getId();
      }
```

After the execution of this operation, you should see the following screenshot from the Alfresco Explorer inside the **User Homes** space in the **Reviews** space:

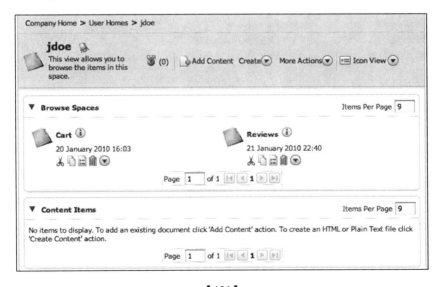

In the second step, we need to add this review in the **Users Home** space of the current user for approval. The approval state of a review is managed using the approved property defined in the **Review** content type in the bookshop model.

For a new review submitted for approval, we want to set a false default value for the approved property because an admin user will moderate the review later. If the admin user wants to publish the review, then the application will manage this, changing the approved value to true.

In order to create the node for a review, we need to create a CMLCreate object and invoke the update method from the Repository Service as follows:

```
//build properties
NamedValue[] propertiesReview = new NamedValue[5];
propertiesReview[0] = new NamedValue();
propertiesReview[0].setName(
BookshopModel.PROP_REVIEW_REVIEWER_NAME);
propertiesReview[0].setValue(reviewForm.getReviewerName());

propertiesReview[1] = new NamedValue();
propertiesReview[1].setName(
BookshopModel.PROP_REVIEW_REVIEWER_EMAIL);
propertiesReview[1].setValue(reviewForm.getReviewerEmail());

propertiesReview[2] = new NamedValue();
propertiesReview[2].setName(BookshopModel.PROP_REVIEW_RATING);
propertiesReview[2].setValue(reviewForm.getRating());

propertiesReview[3] = new NamedValue();
propertiesReview[3].setName(
BookshopModel.PROP_REVIEW_APPROVED);
propertiesReview[3].setValue("false");

propertiesReview[4] = new NamedValue();
propertiesReview[4].setName(Constants.PROP_NAME);
propertiesReview[4].setValue(bookUuid+random.nextLong());

        //create a node for the review
        CMLCreate createReview = new CMLCreate();
        createReview.setId("1");
        createReview.setParent(reviewsSpace);
        createReview.setType(BookshopModel.REVIEW_TYPE);
        createReview.setProperty(propertiesReview);
```

```
//build the CML object
CML cmlAddReview = new CML();
cmlAddReview.setCreate(new CMLCreate[]{createReview});

//perform a CML update to create the Reviews space
UpdateResult[] resultForReviews = repositoryService.
update(cmlAddReview);
```

In the next section of the code, we need to write the content for the new review using the CMLWriteContent object and invoke the update method again from the Repository Service. As you can see, we want to store a review as a text/plain mime type with UTF-8 encoding:

```
Reference reviewRef = resultForReviews[0].getDestination();
Predicate reviewPredicate = new Predicate();
reviewPredicate.setStore(SPACES_STORE);
reviewPredicate.setNodes(new Reference[]{reviewRef});

//create content for the review
ContentFormat format = new ContentFormat();
format.setMimetype("text/plain");
format.setEncoding("UTF-8");

CMLWriteContent contentReview = new CMLWriteContent();
contentReview.setFormat(format);
contentReview.setProperty(Constants.PROP_CONTENT);
contentReview.setContent(reviewForm.getContent().getBytes());
contentReview.setWhere(reviewPredicate);

CML cmlWriteReview = new CML();
cmlWriteReview.setWriteContent(new CMLWriteContent[]{contentRev
iew});

//perform a CML update to write the content the node
repositoryService.update(cmlWriteReview);
```

Finally, the review must be associated with the selected book using the reviews association, defined in the book content type. In this operation, we can assign a specific child name dedicated to the reviews association to identify each associated element as follows:

```
ParentReference bookAssociation = new ParentReference();

bookAssociation.setAssociationType(
BookshopModel.ASS_BOOK_REVIEWS);
```

```
        bookAssociation.setStore(SPACES_STORE);

    bookAssociation.setChildName(
"user_"+username+"_"+random.nextLong());

        bookAssociation.setUuid(bookUuid);

        CMLAddChild associateReview = new CMLAddChild();
        associateReview.setWhere(reviewPredicate);
        associateReview.setTo(bookAssociation);

        CML cmlAssociateReview = new CML();
        cmlAssociateReview.setAddChild(
new CMLAddChild[]{associateReview});

    //perform a CML update to associate the review to the book
        repositoryService.update(cmlAssociateReview);
```

Managing reviews page

Whenever a user submits a review for approval, this review is not shown in the book details page until it is approved by the admin user. All the reviews submitted by users are shown in the **Manage Reviews** page. This page is visible only to the admin user as one of the available features in the bookshop application:

When the admin user wants to work on approving reviews, he/she can navigate to the **Manage Reviews** link to start moderating all the items submitted by the users. The **Manage Reviews** page consists of a reviews list waiting for approval, as shown in the following screenshot:

In order to render all the information shown on this page, you can execute a Lucene query to find all the reviews with a `false` value for the `approved` property as follows:

```
String luceneQuery = "@bs\\:approved:\"false\"";

Query query =
new Query(Constants.QUERY_LANG_LUCENE, luceneQuery);

QueryResult result =
repositoryService.query(SPACES_STORE, query, false);

        ResultSet resultSet = result.getResultSet();
        ResultSetRow[] reviewsResult = resultSet.getRows();

        List<ReviewVO> reviews = new ArrayList<ReviewVO>();

        if(resultSet.getTotalRowCount()>0){
            for (ResultSetRow reviewResult : reviewsResult) {
                ReviewVO review = new ReviewVO();
                review.setId(reviewResult.getNode().getId());

    NamedValue[] reviewProperties = reviewResult.getColumns();
        for (NamedValue property : reviewProperties) {
```

```
        if(BookshopModel.PROP_REVIEW_REVIEWER_NAME.equals(property.
getName())){
                        review.setReviewerName(property.getValue());
        } else if(BookshopModel.PROP_REVIEW_REVIEWER_EMAIL.equals(
property.getName())){
                        review.setReviewerEmail(property.getValue());
        } else if(BookshopModel.PROP_REVIEW_RATING.equals(
property.getName())){
                        review.setRating(property.getValue());
                }
            }

            Reference reference = new Reference();
            reference.setStore(SPACES_STORE);
            reference.setUuid(reviewResult.getNode().getId());

            Predicate predicate = new Predicate();
            predicate.setNodes(new Reference[]{reference});
            predicate.setStore(SPACES_STORE);

Content[] content =
contentService.read(predicate, Constants.PROP_CONTENT);

String ticketURL =
"?ticket=" + getUserDetails(request).getTicket();

String contentUrl = URLDecoder.decode(content[0].getUrl(),"UTF-8") +
ticketURL;

            review.setContentUrl(contentUrl);
            reviews.add(review);
        }
    }
```

Accepting reviews

The admin user accepts a review by clicking on the **Accept Review** link. This means that he/she wants to show the approved review in the book details page. To do this, we need to change the approved property value for the selected review by setting it to true as follows:

```
String idReview = request.getParameter(REVIEW_ID_PARAMETER);

        Reference reference = new Reference();
        reference.setStore(SPACES_STORE);
        reference.setUuid(idReview);
```

```
Predicate predicate = new Predicate();
predicate.setNodes(new Reference[]{reference});
predicate.setStore(SPACES_STORE);

//review accepted
NamedValue[] reviewProperties = new NamedValue[1];
reviewProperties[0] = new NamedValue();
reviewProperties[0].setName(
BookshopModel.PROP_REVIEW_APPROVED);
reviewProperties[0].setValue("true");

CMLUpdate update = new CMLUpdate();
update.setProperty(reviewProperties);
update.setWhere(predicate);

CML cml = new CML();
cml.setUpdate(new CMLUpdate[]{update});

//perform a CML update for the review
WebServiceFactory.getRepositoryService().update(cml);
```

Whenever this action is performed, you will find a new review associated with the related book. You can check this new instance by navigating through the property sheet related to the book with the Alfresco Explorer as shown in the following screenshot:

Now in the book details page, you will find the new approved review as one of the moderated reviews, as shown in the following screenshot:

Reviews:

Add a Review

Reviewer: John Doe | Rating: 5

Read this review

> This is a great book!

This book is added in your Cart

Rejecting reviews

The admin user rejects a review by clicking on the **Reject** link. This means that he/she doesn't want to show the review in the book details page. To do this, we need to remove the review node from the reviews association of the book by performing the following operations:

- Find the book associated with the selected review
- Remove the review so that it is not a child node of the book any longer

1. In the first step of this action, we need to find the book. We start from the review node and get the parent of the node using the queryParents method of the Repository Service. The book is named with a PDF extension, so we need to find a node with the same extension:

   ```
   String idReview = request.getParameter(REVIEW_ID_PARAMETER);

   Reference reviewRef = new Reference();
   reviewRef.setStore(SPACES_STORE);
   reviewRef.setUuid(idReview);

   RepositoryServiceSoapBindingStub repositoryService =
   WebServiceFactory.getRepositoryService();
   ```

```
        QueryResult queryResult = repositoryService.
        queryParents(reviewRef);

ResultSet resultSet = queryResult.getResultSet();
Reference book = new Reference();
book.setStore(SPACES_STORE);

if(resultSet.getTotalRowCount()>0) {
    ResultSetRow[] parents = resultSet.getRows();
    for (ResultSetRow parent : parents) {
        NamedValue[] parentProperties = parent.getColumns();
        for (NamedValue parentProperty : parentProperties) {
            if(Constants.PROP_NAME.equals(parentProperty.getName())){
                if(parentProperty.getValue().endsWith(".pdf")){
                    book.setUuid(parent.getNode().getId());
                        break;
                }
            }
        }
    }
}
```

2. In the next step, we need to use the book retrieved from the previous operation to remove the review as a child of the `reviews` association. This is done as follows:

```
Predicate review = new Predicate();
review.setNodes(new Reference[]{reviewRef});
review.setStore(SPACES_STORE);

//remove child to address this review from the book
CMLRemoveChild removeReviewFromBook = new CMLRemoveChild();
removeReviewFromBook.setFrom(book);
removeReviewFromBook.setWhere(review);

CML cmlRemoveChild = new CML();
cmlRemoveChild.setRemoveChild(new CMLRemoveChild[]{removeReviewFro
mBook});

repositoryService.update(cmlRemoveChild);
```

3. In the final step, we need to remove the review node from the repository. This is done as follows:

```
CMLDelete deleteReview = new CMLDelete();
deleteReview.setWhere(review);

CML cmlDelete = new CML();
cmlDelete.setDelete(new CMLDelete[]{deleteReview});

repositoryService.update(cmlDelete);
```

Changing user details

The last feature of this chapter exposed by the bookshop application is based on an action implemented to allow users to change their account details. Each user is a user of the repository and Alfresco stores users' information and their related information as content nodes. This means that we can manage users in the same way as we manage content.

A user can change his/her account details by clicking on the **Account** link in the bookshop application, as shown in the following screenshot:

This page consists of a prefilled form with some of the existing user details. The user password is required because, in order to save user details from the Alfresco Web Services API, we need to use an admin user session on the repository to perform this operation. After the execution of this operation, we need to restore the current user session to let a user continue his/her navigation through the bookshop. The view action behind this page needs to get the Administration Service to retrieve all the user details from the repository to set values for the form as follows:

```
AdministrationServiceSoapBindingStub administrationService =
WebServiceFactory.getAdministrationService();

//get information about this current user
UserDetails userDetails = null;
try {
    userDetails = administrationService.getUser(
    authenticationDetails.getUserName());

} catch (Exception e) {
    return mapping.findForward(ERROR_FORWARD);
}

NamedValue[] properties = userDetails.getProperties();

UserProfileFormBean userProfile = new UserProfileFormBean();
    if(properties!=null){
        for (NamedValue userProperty : properties) {
            if(userProperty.getName().endsWith("firstName"))
            userProfile.setFirstName(userProperty.getValue());
            else if(userProperty.getName().endsWith("lastName"))
                userProfile.setLastName(userProperty.getValue());
            else if(userProperty.getName().endsWith("email"))
                userProfile.setEmail(userProperty.getValue());
            else if(userProperty.getName().endsWith("location"))
                userProfile.setLocation(userProperty.getValue());
            else if(userProperty.getName().endsWith("userName"))
                userProfile.setUsername(userProperty.getValue());
        }
    }
```

The userProfile object is the value object dedicated to show the user details in the page. When a user submits his/her new details, the save action needs to perform these operations:

1. Get the new user details from the form.
2. Open an admin user session.
3. Save the new user details.
4. Restore the current user session.

1. In the first step of the save action, we need to get all the form fields value and the username of the current user. This is done as follows:

```
//get input fields from the HTML form
UserProfileFormBean userProfile = (UserProfileFormBean)form;

AuthenticationDetails authenticationDetails =
getUserDetails(request);

String username = authenticationDetails.getUserName();
```

2. In the second step, we need to change the user session. We will use an admin user session because, to invoke the `updateUsers` method, Alfresco requires the use of an administrator user (a user that belongs to the `ALFRESCO_ADMINISTRATORS` group) as follows:

```
//authenticate as Admin
try {

//close the current user session
AuthenticationUtils.endSession();

//check the user credentials
AuthenticationUtils.startSession(
ADMIN_USERNAME, ADMIN_PASSWORD);

    } catch (RuntimeException e) {
       return mapping.findForward(ERROR_FORWARD);
    }
```

3. Getting properties from the form allows us to create our new user details to save in the repository. This means that we need to create a new array of `NamedValue` objects as follows:

```
//we want to update the existing user
UserDetails[] updateUserList = new UserDetails[1];
UserDetails updateUser = new UserDetails();
updateUser.setUserName(username);

//update properties
NamedValue[] updateProperties = new NamedValue[4];

updateProperties[0] = new NamedValue();
updateProperties[0].setName(Constants.PROP_USER_FIRSTNAME);
updateProperties[0].setValue(userProfile.getFirstName());
```

```
updateProperties[1] = new NamedValue();
updateProperties[1].setName(Constants.PROP_USER_LASTNAME);
updateProperties[1].setValue(userProfile.getLastName());

updateProperties[2] = new NamedValue();
updateProperties[2].setName(Constants.PROP_USER_EMAIL);
updateProperties[2].setValue(userProfile.getEmail());

updateProperties[3] = new NamedValue();
updateProperties[3].setName(PROP_LOCATION);
updateProperties[3].setValue(userProfile.getLocation());

updateUser.setProperties(updateProperties);
updateUserList[0] = updateUser;
```

4. Finally, we need to invoke the `updateUsers()` method of the Administration Service and then restore the previous user session to allow the current user to continue navigating the bookshop application. This is done as follows:

```
//restore the current user session
try {
//get Administration Service
   AdministrationServiceSoapBindingStub administrationService =
WebServiceFactory.getAdministrationService();

   //perform the user update
   administrationService.updateUsers(updateUserList);

} catch (RuntimeException e) {
   return mapping.findForward(ERROR_FORWARD);
} finally{
   AuthenticationUtils.endSession();
}

//setup user session
AuthenticationUtils.startSession(
username, userProfile.getPassword());

request.getSession().setAttribute(USER_TICKET,
 AuthenticationUtils.getAuthenticationDetails());
```

Summary

This chapter showed you a complete example of an application built on top of Alfresco using the Alfresco Web Services API. The chapter began with an overview of how to set up this project in your development environment using Apache Maven. This example application was a bookshop web application that allowed us to discuss some useful features implemented on top of Alfresco. You learned how to build a standard J2EE application on top of Alfresco and how to implement useful features using a set of operations exposed by the Web Services API.

You learned how to implement the following features for your remote application:

- The sign in process
- Changing user sessions
- Getting, changing, and removing publicly-and privately-associated content
- Managing a cart for your e-commerce application
- Changing user details

In the next chapter, you will learn how to use the Alfresco Web Services API from Microsoft .NET.

5
Using the Alfresco Web Services from .NET

This chapter shows you how to implement a Microsoft .NET application using the Alfresco Web Services API. The **.NET sample** is a standard application that performs operations against the repository.

All the data types and methods shown in this chapter are the same objects exposed by the Alfresco Web Services API, which was introduced in *Chapter 2, Creating and Modifying Content*.

For the first step, you will see how to set up the .NET project in the development environment. Then when we take a look at the sample code, we will learn how to perform the following operations from your .NET application:

- How to authenticate users
- How to search contents
- How to manipulate contents
- How to manage child associations

Setting up the project

In order to execute samples included with this chapter, you need to download and install the following software components in your Windows operating system:

- Microsoft .NET Framework 3.5
- **Web Services Enhancements (WSE)** 3.0 for Microsoft .NET
- SharpDevelop 3.2 IDE

The Microsoft .NET Framework 3.5 is the main framework used to compile the application, and you can download it using the following URL:

```
http://www.microsoft.com/downloads/details.aspx?familyid=333325fd-
ae52-4e35-b531-508d977d32a6&displaylang=en.
```

Before importing the code in the development environment, you need to download and install the Web Services Enhancements (WSE) 3.0, which you can find at this address:

```
http://www.microsoft.com/downloads/details.aspx?FamilyID=018a09fd-
3a74-43c5-8ec1-8d789091255d.
```

You can find more information about the Microsoft .NET framework on the official site at the following URL:

```
http://www.microsoft.com/net/.
```

From this page, you can access the latest news and the Developer Center where you can find the official forum and the developer community.

SharpDevelop 3.2 IDE is an open source IDE for C# and VB.NET, and you can download it using the following URL:

```
http://www.icsharpcode.net/OpenSource/SD/Download/#SharpDevelop3x.
```

Once you have installed all the mentioned software components, you can import the sample project into SharpDevelop IDE in the following way:

- Click on **File | Open | Project/Solution**
- Browse and select this file in the root folder of the samples: **AwsSamples.sln**

Now you should see a similar project tree in your development environment:

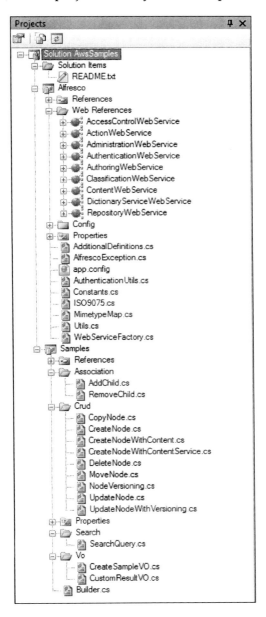

More information about SharpDevelop IDE can be found on the official site at the following address:

`http://www.icsharpcode.net/opensource/sd/.`

From this page, you can download different versions of the product; which SharpDevelop IDE version you choose depends on the .NET version which you would like to use. You can also visit the official forum to interact with the community of developers.

Also, notice that all the source code included with this chapter was implemented extending an existent open source project named **dotnet**. The dotnet project is available in the Alfresco Forge community, and it is downloadable from the following address:

`http://forge.alfresco.com/projects/dotnet/.`

Testing the .NET sample client

Once you have set up the .NET solution in SharpDevelop, as explained in the previous section, you can execute all the tests to verify that the client is working correctly. We have provided a batch file named `build.bat` to allow you to build and run all the integration tests. You can find this batch file in the root folder of the sample code.

Notice that you need to use a different version of `msbuild` for each different version of the .NET framework. If you want to compile using the .NET Framework 3.5, you need to set the following path in your environment:

`set PATH=%PATH%;%WinDir%\Microsoft.NET\Framework\v3.5`

Otherwise, you have to set .NET Framework 2.0 using the following path:

`set PATH=%PATH%;%WinDir%\Microsoft.NET\Framework\v2.0.50727`

We are going to assume that Alfresco is running correctly and it is listening on host `localhost` and on port `8080`. Once executed, the `build.bat` program should start compiling and executing all the integration tests included in this chapter. After a few seconds have elapsed, you should see the following output in the command line:

```
...

...

...

* * * * * * * * * * * * * * * *
* Running tests *
* * * * * * * * * * * * * * * *
```

```
NUnit version 2.5.5.10112

Copyright (C) 2002-2009 Charlie Poole.

Copyright (C) 2002-2004 James W. Newkirk, Michael C. Two, Alexei A.
Vorontsov.

Copyright (C) 2000-2002 Philip Craig.

All Rights Reserved.


Runtime Environment -
   OS Version: Microsoft Windows NT 5.1.2600 Service Pack 2
  CLR Version: 2.0.50727.3053 ( Net 2.0 )


ProcessModel: Default    DomainUsage: Single

Execution Runtime: net-2.0

. . . . . . . . . . . .

Tests run: 12, Errors: 0, Failures: 0, Inconclusive: 0, Time: 14.170376
seconds
  Not run: 0, Invalid: 0, Ignored: 0, Skipped: 0


********

* Done *

********
```

As you can see from the project tree, you have some of the following packages converted from the Java samples of *Chapter 2, Creating and Modifying Content*:

- Search
- Crud
- Association

The **Search** package shows you how to perform queries against the repository.

The **Crud** package contains samples related to all the CRUD operations that show you how to perform basic operations; namely, how to create/get/update/remove nodes in the repository.

The **Association** package shows you how to create and remove association instances among nodes.

Searching the repository

Once you have authenticated a user, you can start to execute queries against the repository. In the following sample code, we will see how to perform a query using the `RepositoryService` of Alfresco:

```
RepositoryService repositoryService = WebServiceFactory.
getRepositoryService();
```

Then we need to create a store where we would like to search contents:

```
Store spacesStore = new Store(StoreEnum.workspace, "SpacesStore");
```

Now we need to create a Lucene query. In this sample, we want to search the Company Home space, and this means that we have to execute the following query:

```
String luceneQuery = "PATH:\"/app:company_home\"";
```

In the next step, we need to use the `query` method available from the `RepositoryService`. In this way, we can execute the Lucene query and we can get all the results from the repository:

```
Query query =
new Query(Constants.QUERY_LANG_LUCENE, luceneQuery);

QueryResult queryResult =
repositoryService.query(spacesStore, query, false);
```

You can retrieve all the results from the `queryResult` object, iterating the `ResultSetRow` object in the following way:

```
ResultSet resultSet = queryResult.resultSet;
ResultSetRow[] results = resultSet.rows;

//your custom list
IList<CustomResultVO> customResultList =
new List<CustomResultVO>();

//retrieve results from the resultSet
foreach(ResultSetRow resultRow in results)
{
  ResultSetRowNode nodeResult = resultRow.node;

  //create your custom value object
  CustomResultVO customResultVo = new CustomResultVO();
  customResultVo.Id = nodeResult.id;
  customResultVo.Type = nodeResult.type;

  //retrieve properties from the current node
```

```
foreach(NamedValue namedValue in resultRow.columns)
  {
    if (Constants.PROP_NAME.Equals(namedValue.name))
      {
        customResultVo.Name = namedValue.value;
      } else if (Constants.PROP_DESCRIPTION.Equals(namedValue.name))
        {
    customResultVo.Description = namedValue.value;
      }
  }

    //add the current result to your custom list
    customResultList.Add(customResultVo);
}
```

In the last sample, we iterated all the results and we created a new custom list with our custom value object CustomResultVO.

 More information about how to build Lucene queries can be found at this URL:

http://wiki.alfresco.com/wiki/Search.

Performing operations

We can perform various operations on the repository. They are documented as follows:

Authentication

For each operation, you need to authenticate users before performing all the required operations on nodes. The class that provides the authentication feature is named AuthenticationUtils, and it allows you to invoke the same methods described in *Chapter 2*. This means that you will find startSession and endSession methods:

```
String username = "johndoe";
String password = "secret";
AuthenticationUtils.startSession(username, password);
try{

}
finally
{
  AuthenticationUtils.endSession();
}
```

Remember that the `startSession` method requires the user credentials: the `username` as the first argument and the `password` as the second.

Notice that the default endpoint address of the Alfresco instance is as follows:

`http://localhost:8080/alfresco`.

If you need to change the endpoint address, you can use the `WebServiceFactory` class invoking the `setEndpointAddress` method to set the new location of the Alfresco repository.

CRUD operations

Inside the `Crud` package of the sample project, you can see how to invoke basic operations to manipulate contents. In this section, we will see how to perform all the following operations on nodes:

- Create
- Update
- Copy
- Move
- Remove

Creating nodes

In order to create nodes in the repository, you need to create a `CMLCreate` object, that is, one of the CML objects described in *Chapter 2*. As you have seen, you need to use the Content Manipulation Language of Alfresco to manipulate content using the Web Services API. So, in this case, we want to create a node with some basic properties without any associated content.

The first object defined in the sample is the `Store` object. The `Store` is used to define where we want to create the new node. The `SpacesStore` is the store for all the latest versions of nodes:

```
Store spacesStore = new Store(StoreEnum.workspace, "SpacesStore");
```

Then we need to provide properties for the new node:

```
String name = "AWS Book " + DateTime.Now.Ticks;
String description =
"This is a content created with a sample of the book";

//custom value object
CreateSampleVO createSampleVo = Builder.BuildCreateSampleVO(name,
name, description);
```

The `Builder` class shows you an example of how you can create your custom object getting the new properties value (`BuildCreateSampleVO` method). Also, inside the same class, there is another method to create the `NamedValue` array required in the `CMLCreate` object. In the following snippet, you can see the `Builder` class:

```
public static class Builder
   {
      public static NamedValue[] BuildCustomProperties(CreateSampleVO
createSampleVo)
      {
        NamedValue[] properties = new NamedValue[3];
        properties[0] = Utils.createNamedValue(Constants.PROP_NAME,
        createSampleVo.Name);
        properties[1] = Utils.createNamedValue(Constants.PROP_TITLE,
        createSampleVo.Title);
        properties[2] = Utils.createNamedValue(Constants.PROP_
DESCRIPTION,
createSampleVo.Description);
        return properties;
      }

      public static CreateSampleVO BuildCreateSampleVO(String name,
      String title, String description)
      {
        CreateSampleVO createSample = new CreateSampleVO();
        createSample.Name = name;
        createSample.Title = title;
        createSample.Description = description;
        return createSample;
      }
```

In the next step, we are building the `ParentReference` object, which is the parent of the new node:

```
try
{
    ParentReference parent = new ParentReference(
      spacesStore,
      null,
      "/app:company_home",
      Constants.ASSOC_CONTAINS,
      "{" + Constants.NAMESPACE_CONTENT_MODEL + "}" + name
    );

    //build properties
    NamedValue[] properties = Builder.BuildCustomProperties(createSam
pleVo);
```

`Constants.ASSOC_CONTAINS` is the default child association `cm:contains`, which is defined in the default content model in Alfresco. This association allows you to add new nodes (children) in spaces (parents).

In order to create a new node, you need to use the `CMLCreate` object. For this object, you need to provide a parent for the new node, a content type for the node, and all the node properties:

```
//create operation
CMLCreate create = new CMLCreate();
create.id = "1";
create.parent = parent;
create.type = Constants.TYPE_CONTENT;
create.property = properties;
```

`Constants.TYPE_CONTENT` is a constant value that allows you to define new generic content in Alfresco with the following QName value: `cm:content`.

Now we have a complete `CMLCreate` object, that is, an operation for the CML language. We need to encapsulate this object in a new generic CML object to execute the operation:

```
CML cml = new CML();
cml.create = new CMLCreate[]{ create };
```

Finally, we can invoke the `update` method of the `RepositoryService` to perform the operation against the repository:

```
UpdateResult[] result = WebServiceFactory.getRepositoryService().
update(cml);
```

Creating content

In the previous paragraph, you learned how to create nodes with properties, but if you need to store a node with a related content—for example, a document—you need to upload the file to the repository.

To accomplish this task, you can follow one of two methods:

- Using the `CMLWriteContent` object
- Using the `ContentService`

Creating content using CML

If you want to encapsulate the content in a unique request for the creation of the node and its content, you have to add an instance of the CMLWriteContent object inside the previous CML request.

For the first step, you need to create an instance of the Reference object to point to the new node contained in the previous CMLCreate object:

```
//create the node reference
Reference reference = new Reference();
reference.store = spacesStore;
reference.path = "/app:company_home/cm:"+ISO9075.Encode(name);"/app:
company_home/cm:"+ISO9075.Encode(name);
```

The path field is provided encoding the space names in the ISO 9075 format because Alfresco stores node paths using XPath. Alfresco provides you with a utility class ISO9075 to allow you to encode and decode space names in the correct way.

In the following section, you need to provide a Predicate object as the group of the involved nodes. In this case, we have only a node reference:

```
//create the predicate
Predicate predicate = new Predicate();
predicate.Items = new Reference[]{ reference };
```

In this step, we are creating the ContentFormat to create all the indexes correctly for the current content:

```
//set mime type and encoding for indexing
ContentFormat format = new ContentFormat(mimeType, encoding);
```

Now that we have all the needed objects, we can build the CMLWriteContent object, and we can add this instance to the CML object.

```
//write operation
CMLWriteContent writeContent = new CMLWriteContent();
writeContent.format = format;
writeContent.where = predicate;
writeContent.property = Constants.PROP_CONTENT;
writeContent.content = new ASCIIEncoding().GetBytes("This is the
content for the new node");

//build the CML object
CML cml = new CML();
cml.create = new CMLCreate[]{ create };
cml.writeContent = new CMLWriteContent[]{ writeContent };
```

Finally, we can execute the `update` method:

```
UpdateResult[] result = WebServiceFactory.getRepositoryService().
update(cml);
```

Creating content using ContentService

Another way to create content is to use the `ContentService` as a second request after you performed the creation of the node. So, in this case, we are creating content at two occasions: during the first request we will create the node with all the properties and during the second request we will upload the content.

Let's say that we have created and performed a previous `CMLCreate` operation in the repository:

```
//perform a CML update for the CMLCreate operation
UpdateResult[] result = WebServiceFactory.getRepositoryService().
update(cml);
```

From the previous operation, we can get the new node reference:

```
//get the new node reference
Alfresco.ContentWebService.Reference referenceForContent = Alfresco.
ContentWebService.Reference.From(
result[0].destination);
```

In the next section, we create the `ContentFormat` object:

```
Alfresco.ContentWebService.ContentFormat format = new Alfresco.
ContentWebService.ContentFormat(mimeType, encoding);
```

Finally, we can get `ContentService` from `WebServiceFactory`, and then we can use it to upload the content. We have to provide the node reference, the `content` property, and the stream for the content:

```
Alfresco.ContentWebService.Content content = WebServiceFactory.
getContentService().write(
            referenceForContent,
            Constants.PROP_CONTENT,
            new ASCIIEncoding().GetBytes(
"This is the content for the new node"),
                format
            );
```

Notice that creating content using `ContentService` can cause problems with the atomicity of the operation. If you have a problem during the execution of the `write` method, the node can exist in the repository and not in the content.

Updating nodes

Once you have stored content in the repository and you need to update one of these existent nodes, you must provide an instance of the CMLUpdate object. To update a node in Alfresco, you can:

- Perform a clean update of the node and its content
- Create a new version for the involved node

Updating nodes without versioning

In the following sample code, you can see how to update existent properties values for a node previously created using the CMLUpdate object:

```
//create a predicate with the first CMLCreate result
Reference referenceForNode = result[0].destination;

Predicate sourcePredicate = new Predicate(
            new Reference[]{ referenceForNode },
            spacesStore,
            null
        );

Reference referenceForTargetSpace = result[1].destination;

//reference for the target space
ParentReference targetSpace = new ParentReference();
targetSpace.store = spacesStore;
targetSpace.path = referenceForTargetSpace.path;
targetSpace.associationType = Constants.ASSOC_CONTAINS;
targetSpace.childName = name;
```

To create a parent reference, as you can see in the previous snippet, you must provide:

- The Store object for the destination
- The path of the parent node
- The type of the association that you want to use between the space and the node
- The child name for the current instance of the association

In the following section, we are creating the new properties values for the node:

```
name = "AWS Book - Changed by CMLUpdate " + DateTime.Now.Ticks;
createSampleVo.Name = name;
createSampleVo.Title = name;
createSampleVo.Description = "Changed by CMLUpdate " + description;
```

Now, we need to create a `CMLUpdate` object to set all the new properties:

```
//update node
CMLUpdate update = new CMLUpdate();
update.property = Builder.BuildCustomProperties(createSampleVo);
update.where = sourcePredicate;
```

Finally, we can execute the `update` method to perform the CML operation:

```
CML cmlUpdate = new CML();
cmlUpdate.update = new CMLUpdate[]{ update };

//perform a CML update
WebServiceFactory.getRepositoryService().update(cmlUpdate);
```

Updating nodes with versioning

If you need to create a new version of an existing node, you can add the **versionable** aspect to the node. In this way, the repository will change the behavior for the involved node, creating a new version for each update. The repository will keep all the old versions for the node, creating a version history.

Assuming that we have an existing node previously created in the repository, we have to provide the same object seen in the previous paragraph, but by adding a new CML object named `CMLAddAspect`. This new object will add a new behavior for the node, and specifically, it will add the **versionable** aspect:

```
//create a predicate with the first CMLCreate result
Reference referenceForNode = result[0].destination;
Predicate sourcePredicate = new Predicate(new Reference[]{
referenceForNode }, spacesStore, null);

Reference referenceForTargetSpace = result[1].destination;

//reference for the target space
ParentReference targetSpace = new ParentReference();
targetSpace.store = spacesStore;
targetSpace.path = referenceForTargetSpace.path;
targetSpace.associationType = Constants.ASSOC_CONTAINS;
targetSpace.childName = name;
```

```
name = "AWS Book - Changed by CMLUpdate " + DateTime.Now.Ticks;

createSampleVo.Name = name;
createSampleVo.Title = name;
createSampleVo.Description =
"Changed by CMLUpdate " + description;
```

In the following snippet, we will create the CMLAddAspect object providing the QName of the aspect and the group of all the involved nodes (sourcePredicate). This is the object that will add the new behavior for this node:

```
CMLAddAspect aspect = new CMLAddAspect();
aspect.aspect = Constants.ASPECT_VERSIONABLE;
aspect.where = sourcePredicate;
```

Finally, we can add CMLAddAspect to the CML object, and then invoke the update method:

```
//update node
CMLUpdate update = new CMLUpdate();
update.property = Builder.BuildCustomProperties(createSampleVo);
update.where = sourcePredicate;

CML cmlUpdate = new CML();
cmlUpdate.addAspect = new CMLAddAspect[]{ aspect };
cmlUpdate.update = new CMLUpdate[]{ update };

//perform a CML update WebServiceFactory.getRepositoryService().
update(cmlUpdate);
```

Copying nodes

Creating copies for nodes is an operation that can be performed using another CML object defined for this feature, which is named CMLCopy. As in the previous samples, we are assuming that we have an existing node in the repository and we want to copy it to a different space.

We start by getting the node reference of the existing node at its new target space:

```
//create a predicate with the first CMLCreate result
Reference referenceForNode = result[0].destination;
Predicate sourcePredicate = new Predicate(new Reference[]{
referenceForNode }, spacesStore, null);

//reference for the space
Reference referenceForTargetSpace = result[1].destination;
```

```
//reference for the target space
ParentReference targetSpace = new ParentReference();
targetSpace.store = spacesStore;
targetSpace.path = referenceForTargetSpace.path;
targetSpace.associationType = Constants.ASSOC_CONTAINS;
targetSpace.childName = name;
```

Next we create the CMLCopy instance setting the where field with the group of source nodes that we want to copy from and the to field with the target space for all the copied nodes:

```
//copy content
CMLCopy copy = new CMLCopy();
copy.where = sourcePredicate;
copy.to = targetSpace;
```

Finally, we create the array of CMLCopy objects. Then we perform this operation using the update method:

```
CML cmlCopy = new CML();
cmlCopy.copy = new CMLCopy[]{copy};

//perform a CML update to move the node WebServiceFactory.
getRepositoryService().update(cmlCopy);
```

Moving nodes

The move operation is performed using the CMLMove object. In the same way, as we saw in the previous paragraph, you have to provide two mandatory objects:

- A predicate for the group of source nodes that you want to move
- A target space for the destination

In this first step, you need to create a predicate for the involved node:

```
//create a predicate with the first CMLCreate result
Reference referenceForNode = result[0].destination;
Predicate sourcePredicate = new Predicate(new Reference[]{
referenceForNode }, spacesStore, null);
```

Then we create a parent reference as the new target space for the node:

```
//create a reference for space
Reference referenceForTargetSpace = result[1].destination;

//reference for the target space
ParentReference targetSpace = new ParentReference();
```

```
targetSpace.store = spacesStore;
targetSpace.path = referenceForTargetSpace.path;
targetSpace.associationType = Constants.ASSOC_CONTAINS;
targetSpace.childName = name;
```

Next we create the CMLMove object, and we can set all the required fields:

```
//move content
CMLMove move = new CMLMove();
move.where = sourcePredicate;
move.to = targetSpace;
```

Finally, we create the CML object by setting the move operation. Then we perform the following operation using the update method:

```
CML cmlMove = new CML();
cmlMove.move = new CMLMove[]{move};

//perform a CML update to move the node WebServiceFactory.
getRepositoryService().update(cmlMove);
```

Removing nodes

CMLDelete is the CML object that can be used to remove existing nodes in the repository. In the following sample, you will see how to remove a node from the repository. The unique field required for this operation is the predicate for the involved nodes:

```
//create a predicate
Reference reference = result[0].destination;
Predicate predicate = new Predicate(new Reference[]{ reference },
spacesStore, null);
```

In next section, we create the CMLDelete object, setting the where field with the previous predicate:

```
//delete content
CMLDelete delete = new CMLDelete();
delete.where = predicate;
```

Finally, we build the CML object to use the update method:

```
CML cmlRemove = new CML();
cmlRemove.delete = new CMLDelete[]{delete};
//perform a CML update to remove the node WebServiceFactory.
getRepositoryService().update(cmlRemove);
```

Managing child associations

In this section, we will see how to manage child associations. You learned that a child association is a bidirectional association between a parent and its children.

The two CML objects used to manage child associations are:

1. CMLAddChild.
2. CMLRemoveChild.

CMLAddChild is used to add children to a parent, and CMLRemoveChild is used to remove children from a parent.

Adding child nodes

In the following sample, we want to associate two existent nodes. sourcePredicate is the predicate for the child nodes and targetSpace is the parent node:

```
Reference referenceForNode = result[0].destination;

Predicate sourcePredicate = new Predicate(new Reference[]{
referenceForNode }, spacesStore, null);

Reference referenceForTargetSpace = result[1].destination;

//reference for the target space
ParentReference targetSpace = new ParentReference();
targetSpace.store = spacesStore;
targetSpace.path = referenceForTargetSpace.path;
targetSpace.associationType = Constants.ASSOC_CONTAINS;
targetSpace.childName = name;
```

In the next section, we will create the CMLAddChild object, setting the sourcePredicate and the targetSpace as its fields:

```
//add child
CMLAddChild addChild = new CMLAddChild();
addChild.where = sourcePredicate;
addChild.to = targetSpace;

CML cmlAddChild = new CML();
cmlAddChild.addChild = new CMLAddChild[]{ addChild };

//perform a CML update to add the node WebServiceFactory.
getRepositoryService().update(cmlAddChild);
```

After the execution of the `update` method, all the involved nodes are associated by a new association instance. The child name will be the identifier for the new association instance.

Removing child nodes

Once you have associated nodes with one or more parents, you can remove children from a parent using the `CMLRemoveChild` object. You have to define:

- A predicate for all the nodes that you want to remove (`where`)
- A target space for the parent (`Item`)

In the following snippet, you can see how to get these required objects:

```
//reference for the target space
ParentReference targetSpace = new ParentReference();
targetSpace.store = spacesStore;
targetSpace.path = referenceForTargetSpace.path;
targetSpace.associationType = Constants.ASSOC_CONTAINS;
targetSpace.childName = name;

Reference refUpdate = resultAddChild[0].destination;

Predicate nodeToRemove = new Predicate(new Reference[]{ refUpdate },
spacesStore, null);
```

Now we can create the `CMLRemoveChild` instance, and we can perform the operation:

```
//remove child
CMLRemoveChild removeChild = new CMLRemoveChild();
removeChild.Item = targetSpace;
removeChild.where = nodeToRemove;

CML cmlRemoveChild = new CML();
cmlRemoveChild.removeChild = new CMLRemoveChild[]{ removeChild };

//perform a CML update to remove the node   WebServiceFactory.
getRepositoryService().update(cmlRemoveChild);
```

Summary

In this chapter, we discussed an example of a .NET application built on top of Alfresco using the Alfresco Web Services API. The chapter introduced an overview about how to set up the sample project in your development environment using the open source IDE SharpDevelop. Then it describes how to manipulate contents using .NET. Specifically, you learned the following topics:

- How to set up the sample project in your .NET environment
- How to perform queries using the Lucene query language
- How to perform basic operations to manipulate content
- How to add and remove child nodes from parents

In the following chapter, you will learn how to extend the Alfresco REST API using the Web Scripts Framework.

6
Introducing the Web Scripts Framework

In the preceding chapters, we saw how Alfresco can be integrated with disparate applications and systems by leveraging the SOAP-based Web Services APIs that it provides. In this chapter, and those that follow, you will learn about a new approach that has been available in Alfresco since version 2.1 for creating these kinds of integrations, Web Scripts.

Web Scripts allow you to develop entire web applications on Alfresco by using just a scripting language — JavaScript and a templating language — FreeMarker. They offer a lightweight framework for quickly developing even complex interfaces such as Alfresco Share and Web Studio.

Besides this, Web Scripts can be used to develop Web Services for giving external applications access to the features of the Alfresco repository. Your Web Services, implemented according to the principles of the REST architectural style, can be easily reused by disparate, heterogeneous systems.

Specifically, in this chapter, you will learn:

- What REST means and how it compares to SOAP
- What elements are needed to implement a Web Script
- How to properly design Web Scripts using the Model-View-Controller pattern
- How to configure a Web Script for things such as authentication, transactionality, and cacheability
- How clients can request a specific response format
- How to deploy Web Scripts in Alfresco

A lightweight alternative to SOAP Web Services

The term **Web Services** is generally intended to denote a large family of specifications and protocols, of which SOAP is only a small part, which are often employed to let applications provide and consume services over the **World Wide Web (WWW)**. This basically means exchanging XML messages over HTTP.

The main problem with the traditional approach to Web Services is that any implementation has to be compliant with a huge, and complicated set of specifications. This makes the application itself complex and typically hard to understand, debug, and maintain. A whole cottage industry has grown with the purpose of providing the tools necessary for letting developers abstract away this complexity. It is virtually impossible to develop any non-trivial application without these tools based on SOAP. In addition, one or more of the other Web Services standards such as **WS-Security**, **WS-Transaction**, or **WS-Coordination** are required. It is also impossible for any one person to have a reasonably in-depth knowledge of a meaningful portion of the whole Web Services stack (sometimes colloquially referred to as *WS-**).

Recently, a backlash against this heavyweight approach in providing services over the Web has begun and some people have started pushing for a different paradigm, one that did not completely ignore and disrupt the architecture of the World Wide Web. The main objection that the proponents of the REST architectural style, as this paradigm is called, raise with respect to WS-* is that the use of the term *Web* in *Web Services* is fraudulent and misleading. The World Wide Web, they claim, was designed in accordance with REST principles and this is precisely why it was able to become the largest, most scalable information architecture ever realized. WS-*, on the other hand, is nothing more than a revamped, RPC-style message exchange paradigm. It's just CORBA once again, only this time over HTTP and using XML, to put it bluntly. As it has purportedly been demonstrated, this approach will never scale to the size of the World Wide Web, as it gets in the way of important web concerns such as cacheability, the proper usage of the HTTP protocol methods, and of well-known MIME types to decouple clients from servers.

Of course, you don't have to buy totally into the REST philosophy—which will be described in the next section—in order to appreciate the elegance, simplicity, and usefulness of Alfresco Web Scripts. After all, Alfresco gives you the choice to use either Web Scripts or the traditional, SOAP-based, Web Services. But you have to keep in mind that the newer and cooler pieces of Alfresco, such as Surf, Share, Web Studio, and the CMIS service, are being developed using Web Scripts. It is, therefore, mandatory that you know how the Web Scripts work, how to develop them, and how to interact with them, if you want to be part of this brave new world of RESTful services.

REST concepts

The term **REST** had been introduced by Roy T. Fielding, one of the architects of the HTTP protocol, in his Ph.D dissertation titled *Architectural Styles and the Design of Network-based Software Architectures* (available online at `http://www.ics.uci.edu/ ~fielding/pubs/dissertation/top.htm`).

Constraints

In *Chapter 5* of his work, Dr. Fielding introduces an "architectural style for distributed hypermedia systems" called **Representational State Transfer (REST)**. It does so by starting from an architectural style that does not impose any constraints on implementations (called the Null Style) and progressively adds new constraints that together define what REST is. Those constraints are:

1. Client-Server interaction
2. Statelessness
3. Cacheability
4. Uniform Interface
5. Layered System
6. Code-On-Demand (optional)

Fielding then goes on to define the main elements of the REST architectural style. Foremost among those are resources and representations. In contrast with distributed object systems, where data is always hidden behind an interface that only exposes operations that clients may perform on said data, "REST components communicate by transferring a representation of a resource in a format matching one of an evolving set of standard data types, selected dynamically based on the capabilities or desires of the recipient and the nature of the resource."

Resources

It is important to understand what a resource is and what it isn't. A resource is some information that can be named. It can correspond to a specific entity on a data management system such as a record in a database or a document in a DMS such as Alfresco. However, it can also map to a set of entities, such as a list of search results, or a non-virtual object like a person in the physical world. In any case, a resource is **not** the underlying entity.

Resources need to be named, and in a globally distributed system such as the World Wide Web, they must be identified in a way that guarantees the universality and possibly the univocity of identifiers. On the Web, resources are identified using **Uniform Resource Identifiers (URI)**. A specific category of URIs are **Uniform Resource Locators (URL)**, which provide a way for clients to locate, that is to find, a resource anywhere on the Web, in addition to identifying it.

It is also assumed that URIs never change over the lifetime of a resource, no matter how much the internal state of the underlying entities changes over time. This allows the architecture of the Web to scale immensely, as the system does not need to rely on centralized *link servers* that maintain references separated from the content.

Representations

Representations are sequences of bytes intended to capture the current or intended state of a resource, as well as metadata (in the form of name / value pairs) about the resource or the representation itself.

The format of a representation is called its media type. Examples of media types are plain text, HTML, XML, JPEG, PDF, and so on. When servers and clients use a set of well-known, standardized media types, interoperability between systems is greatly simplified. Sometimes, it is possible for clients and servers to negotiate a specific format from a set that is supported by both.

Control data, which is exchanged between systems together with the representation, is used to determine the purpose of a message or the behavior of any intermediaries. Control data can be used by the client, for instance, to inform the server that the representation being transferred is meant to be the intended new state of the resource, or it can be used by the server to control how proxies, or the client itself, may cache representations.

The most obvious example of control data on the Web is HTTP methods and result codes. By using the `PUT` method, for example, a client usually signals to a server that it is sending an updated representation of the resource.

REST in practice

As we mentioned, REST is really just an abstract architectural style, not a specific architecture, network protocol, or software system. While no existing system exactly adheres to the full set of REST principles, the World Wide Web is probably the most well-known and successful implementation of them.

Developing Web Services that follow the REST paradigm boils down to following a handful of rules and using HTTP the way it was meant to be used. The following sections detail some of those rules.

Use URLs to identify resources

It is important that you design the URLs for your Web Service in such a way that they identify resources and do not describe the operations performed on said resources. It is a common mistake to use URLs such as:

```
/widgetService/createNewWidget
/widgetService/readWidget?id=1
/widgetService/updateWidget?id=1
/widgetService/deleteWidget?id=1
```

whenever, for instance, you want to design a web service for doing CRUD operations on widgets.

A proper, RESTful URL space for this kind of usage scenario could instead be something like the following:

`/widgets/`	To identify a collection of widgets
`/widgets/id`	To identify a single widget.

Then again, a RESTful interaction with a server that implements the previous service would be along the lines of the following (where we have indicated the HTTP verb together with the URL):

`POST /widgets/`	To create a new widget, whose representation is contained in the body of the request
`GET /widgets/`	To obtain a representation (listing) of all widgets of the collection
`GET /widgets/1`	To obtain a representation of the widget having `id=1`
`POST /widgets/1`	To update a widget by sending a new representation (the PUT verb could be used here as well)
`DELETE /widgets/1`	To delete a widget

You can see here how URLs representing resources and the appropriate usage of HTTP methods can be used to implement a correctly designed RESTful Web Service for CRUD operations on server-side objects.

Use HTTP methods properly

There are four main methods that a client can use to tell a server which kind of operation to perform. You can call them commands, if you like. These are GET, POST, PUT, and DELETE. The HTTP 1.1 specification lists some other methods, such as HEAD, TRACE, and OPTIONS, but we can ignore them as they are not frequently used.

GET

GET is meant to be used for requests that are not intended to modify the state of a resource. This does not mean that the processing by the server of a GET request must be free of side effects — it is perfectly legal, for instance, to increment a counter of page views.

GET requests, however, should be *idempotent*. The property of idempotency means that a sequence of N identical requests should have the same side effects as a single request. The methods GET, HEAD, PUT, and DELETE share this property.

Basically, by using GET, a client signals that it intends to retrieve the representation of a resource. The server can perform any operation that causes side effects as part of the execution of the method, but the client cannot be held accountable for them.

PUT

PUT is generally used to send the modified representation of a resource. It is idempotent as well — multiple, identical PUT requests have the same effect as a single request.

DELETE

DELETE can be used to request the removal of a resource. This is another idempotent method.

POST

The POST method is used to request that the server accepts the entity enclosed in the request as a new subordinate of the resource identified by the URI named in the request.

POST is a bit like the Swiss army knife of HTTP and can be used for a number of purposes, including:

- Annotation of existing resources
- Posting a message to a bulletin board, newsgroup, or mailing list

- Providing a block of data, such as the result of submitting a form, to a data-handling process
- Extending a database through an append operation

POST is not an idempotent method.

One of the main objections proponents of REST raise with respect to traditional Web Service architectures is that, with the latter, POST is used for everything. While you shouldn't feel compelled to use every possible HTTP method in your Web Service (it is perfectly RESTful to use only GET and POST), you should at least know the expectations behind them and use them accordingly.

Avoiding tight coupling

Ideally, any Web Services client should be able to talk to any server without many assumptions or the transmission of data outside the boundaries of the HTTP protocol. In general, you should eschew any practice, which tends to create unnecessary tight coupling between the client and the server.

One way to achieve this is to use standardized formats whenever possible. For instance, using Atom or RSS to represent a list of entities is generally preferable to inventing yet another markup language. Almost any client should be able to at least do *something* when served a response with a MIME type of application/atom+xml, for instance, a completely generic aggregator could act as an intermediary for clients by aggregating and caching Atom or RSS feeds, even without knowing anything about how application-specific data is encoded, for example, using foreign namespaces.

Use hyperlinks to drive the application state

One of the fundamental and mostly ignored principles of REST is that of *Hypermedia as the Engine of Application State*. This principle underlines the importance of hyperlinks as the preferred mechanism whereby clients know how to modify the state of an application hidden behind a Web Service.

In simple terms, this means that embedding links lets the clients know that, by following those links, they are acting on the server in a predetermined way.

The most egregious example of this is HTML forms. The action attribute of a form HTML element is exactly that: a link that the browser (the client) can follow by sending to its URL, using the method specified in the method attribute, a set of form data encoded using the format specified in the enctype attribute. There is no prior knowledge shared by the client and the server except what is known about the HTTP protocol itself and about the representation of form data using either the application/x-www-form-urlencoded or the multipart/form-data encodings.

By following this principle, you avoid, once again, unnecessary coupling between clients and servers—all of the information required to drive the application state is contained in the representations transmitted between them. A sure sign that you are not following REST principles is that you start writing documents about how clients should construct URLs and expect client implementers to read them. This is out-of-band transmission of information, and it should be avoided whenever possible.

Your first Web Script

That's enough with theory; in this section, we are going to show how to implement a very simple Web Script. You will see that, in order to do this, you don't have to launch your IDE, build, package, and deploy code. It is all very quick and can be done using just your browser.

You will probably have to do the write-build-package-deploy-test routine eventually, if you want to follow a repeatable, automatable development process, but not now. For now, we are going to keep things as simple as possible.

Components of a Web Script

At the very minimum, a Web Script is made up of two files:

* A descriptor
* A template

Somewhat ironically, a Web Script doesn't always need to have a script.

Creating your first Web Script

First, you are going to create the descriptor. This is an XML file, which you need to create in the **Company Home | Data Dictionary | Web Scripts Extensions** space. You can either create the descriptor locally on your computer, using your favorite programmer's editor (or even Notepad, if you like), or directly using the in-line editor of the Alfresco Explorer. Name the file `first.get.desc.xml` and type in its content as follows:

```
<webscript>
    <shortname>First</shortname>
    <description>My first Web Script</description>
    <url>/first</url>
</webscript>
```

Next, you will write the template. Create or upload a file named `first.get.html.ftl` with the following content:

```
<html>
    <body>
        <p>This is your first Web Script. Congratulations!</p>
    </body>
</html>
```

Finally, you need to register your new Web Script. It would be nice if Alfresco were able to register new Web Scripts automatically without the user's intervention. This is not the case at the moment, but luckily you only have to do this once for every new Web Script, not every time you modify it.

In order to register your new Web Script, navigate to `http://localhost:8080/alfresco/service/index` and press the **Refresh Web Scripts** button. Please note that the previous URL ends with a slash, which you must include. If you now click on the **List Web Scripts** link, you should be able to see your newly created Web Script, listed with its URL, short name, and description, exactly as you have specified them in the descriptor file.

Invoking your first Web Script

In order to execute the Web Script you just created and see its output, simply point your browser to `http://localhost:8080/alfresco/service/first` and this is what you should see:

This is your first Web Script. Congratulations!

As you can probably imagine, the URL you used to obtain this output matches what was specified in the `url` tag inside the descriptor. This underscores the fact that Web Scripts are *URL-addressable*, it means that you can design and implement your own URL space, according to whatever rules and principles you want to follow. Just remember to always add `http://localhost:8080/alfresco/service` in front of the URLs found inside the descriptor.

What happens here is that Alfresco maps all request URLs starting with `/service/` to the Web Script request dispatcher servlet. This, in turn, scans the URLs contained in all the Web Scripts' descriptors to find the one that matches most closely, and it then invokes the corresponding Web Script.

If a match is found and, as in our case, there is no controller script, the corresponding template is immediately rendered. The base logic for selecting a template is to search for a FreeMarker document having the same base name as the descriptor (`first` in this example), followed by the HTTP method used (which is always `GET` when you navigate using a browser, but is spelled in lowercase in the filename), followed by a format specification (`html` in this case, which wasn't actually specified anywhere, but is the default choice). Finally, the template must have the `.ftl` extension that indicates a FreeMarker template. The final result is exactly `first.get.html.ftl`.

The actual logic covers more complex situations, but what we outlined here is what happens in this simple case.

Adding a controller

More often than not, a Web Script will have a **controller** of some sort. While it is possible to have Web Scripts that are entirely backed by Java beans, the most often used option is to implement the controller in JavaScript, so this is what we will concentrate on initially, deferring the discussion of Java-backed Web Scripts to a later chapter.

In order to have a controller, all you need to do is create a text document called `<basename>.<method>.js` in the same folder as the descriptor and the templates. In the previous example, this would be `first.get.js`.

Let's then create a new text document called `first.get.js` in **Company Home | Data Dictionary | Web Scripts Extensions**, with the following content:

```
model.fullname = person.properties.firstName;
if (person.properties.lastName != "")
{
  model.fullname += ' ' + person.properties.lastName;
}
```

You also need to modify the template `first.get.html.ftl` to make use of the `fullname` variable that we have just added to the model:

```
<html>
    <body>
      <p>Hello ${fullname}, this is your first Web Script.</p>
    </body>
</html>
```

As we are now accessing the repository through the `person` object, we need to indicate that our Web Script must require authentication and execute it in a transaction. We do this by modifying the descriptor `first.get.desc.xml` to read:

```
<webscript>
    <shortname>First</shortname>
    <description>My first Web Script</description>
    <url>/first</url>
    <authentication>user</authentication>
    <transaction>required</transaction>
</webscript>
```

After having added a controller and modified the descriptor, you must refresh the list of Web Scripts, as explained previously. This is necessary not only when you create a new Web Script, but also every time you alter the descriptor of an existing Web Script.

Do this now and, assuming that you have logged on to Alfresco as a user named, say, Jane Doe, this is what you should see:

Hello Jane Doe, this is your first Web Script.

If you haven't logged in yet, or if you are using a different browser to test your Web Script from the one you are using to edit it, the browser will pop up a login box before it lets you run it.

What we have just shown is how it is possible for the controller to pass values to the template by means of the `model` object. Just by naming a property x of the `model` object and assigning it a value, the controller makes that value available to the template as the value of the x variable. In FreeMarker templates, you use the `${x}` syntax to evaluate the value of a variable or of an expression and output it at the position in the template that the expression occupies.

The set of objects which are available to the template includes everything that the controller adds to the model, also a number of so-called **root-scoped** objects, which are always available.

Some of these pre-defined objects, such as `args`, `headers`, and `url`, provide information about the current request.

Others, such as `status`, `cache`, and `format`, allow the script developer to manipulate the response that is being sent back to the client.

Another set of objects is only available when the user invoking the script has been authenticated. This includes `roothome`, `companyhome`, `userhome`, `people`, and `person`. These provide direct access to repository objects: `folders`, `documents`, and `users`.

Other objects, finally, are used to invoke repository services, such as `search`, `classification`, `workflows`, and `actions`.

The full list of root-scoped objects is documented at the following Wiki page: `http://wiki.alfresco.com/wiki/Web_Scripts`.

The Model-View-Controller pattern

One way of looking at the Web Scripts framework is as a platform for implementing RESTful Web Services. Although, as we have seen, your service won't actually be RESTful unless you follow the relevant guiding principles, Web Scripts technology alone does not make your services RESTful as if by magic.

Another way of looking at it is as an implementation of the **Model-View-Controller**, or **MVC** pattern. Model-View-Controller is a long-established pattern in Computer Science, often used when designing user-facing, data-oriented applications. MVC stipulates that users of the application send commands to it by invoking the controller component, which acts on some sort of **data model**, then selects an appropriate **view** for presenting the model to the users.

While the applicability of MVC to Web application has often been debated, it is still a useful framework for partitioning concerns and responsibilities and for describing the roles of the various components of the Alfresco Web Scripts framework.

In the latter, the role of controller is carried out by the scripting component. It should be stressed that, in the MVC pattern, the controller's role is purely that of governing the user interaction by selecting an appropriate model and a corresponding view for presentation, possibly determining which user actions are applicable given the present state of the application. It is not the controller's role to carry out any kind of business logic or to operate on the model directly. Rather, the controller should always delegate the execution of data manipulation operations and queries to a suitable business logic or persistence layer.

In the context of Alfresco Web Scripts, this means that your controller script should avoid doing too many things by using the repository APIs directly. It is the responsibility of the controller to:

- Validate user inputs
- Possibly convert them to data types suitable for the underlying logic layers
- Delegate operations to those layers
- Take data returned by them
- Use the data to prepare a model for the view to display
- and nothing more

All complex operations and direct manipulations of repository objects should ideally be carried out by code that resides somewhere else, like in Java Beans or JavaScript libraries, which are included by the present script.

In practice, many Web Scripts, including most of those presented in this and the following chapters, tend to be quite small and simple, so this strict separation of concerns is not always diligently applied. However, as the size and complexity of controller scripts grows, it is considered as a good practice to modularize an application's logic in order to make it easier to follow and to maintain. Some people also have a preference for the relative safety of a static language like Java, compared to JavaScript, and for the use of modern Java IDEs. Therefore, it is frequent to see Web Scripts applications that place the very minimum of logic in controller scripts that use Java Beans to carry out more complex tasks.

Coming to the view, which in Alfresco Web Scripts is implemented as FreeMarker templates, it should be noted that in a departure from the "pure" MVC pattern, the freedom accorded to the controller itself of choice between different possible views is rather limited as which view to use is determined exclusively by selecting a template for the specific output format requested by the user through the format specification in the request URL.

The model that the view can access is also only partially the responsibility of the controller. Whereas the latter can add more objects to the model available to the view, it cannot reduce the visibility of the predefined, root-scoped objects. It is therefore possible for the view to perform quite a bit of logic without even having a controller to do it. This is why Web Scripts without a controller are acceptable. Whether this is a good practice or not is open to debate.

The following diagram illustrates the steps that are involved when a Web Script is executed:

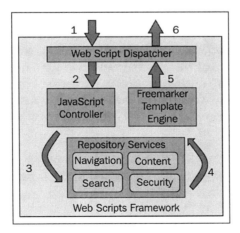

The diagram can be explained as follows:

1. An HTTP request, specifying a method and a URI is received.
2. The dispatcher uses the HTTP method and the URI to select a Web Script to execute and executes the controller script.
3. The controller script accesses the repository services by means of the Alfresco JavaScript API.
4. The model is populated and passed to the FreeMarker template engine for rendering.
5. FreeMarker renders a response using the appropriate template.
6. The response is returned to the client.

URL matching

We've already seen how the dispatcher selects a particular Web Script by matching the URL of the HTTP request against the value of the `url` element in the descriptors of the registered Web Scripts. There is actually a bit more to this process than simple, exact matching, as we are going to see.

First, let's have a look at the structure of a Web Script's request URL:

```
http[s]://<host>:<port>/[<contextPath>/]/<servicePath>[/
<scriptPath>][?<scriptArgs>]
```

The meaning of `host` and `port` should be obvious. `contextPath` is the name of the web application context, that is, where your application is deployed in your application server or Servlet container. It will often be `alfresco`, but could be `share`, as the Share application is able to host Web Scripts. It could be missing, if the application is deployed in the root context, or it could really be anything you want.

The value of `servicePath` will usually be either `service` or `wcservice`. Using the former, if the Web Script requires authentication, this is performed using the HTTP Basic method. This means that the browser will pop up a username/password dialog box. When the latter is used, authentication is performed by the Alfresco Explorer (also known as Web Client). This means that no further authentication is required if you are already logged into the Explorer, otherwise you will be redirected to the Explorer login page.

`scriptPath` is the part of the URL that is matched against what is specified in the descriptor. Arguments can optionally be passed to the script by specifying them after the question mark, as with any URL.

With this in mind, let's look at the value of the `<url>`element in the descriptor. This must be a valid **URI template**, according to the JSR-311 specification. Basically, a URI template is a (possibly relative) URI, parts of which are tokens enclosed between curly braces, such as:

1. `/one/two/three`
2. `/api/login/ticket/{ticket}`
3. `/api/login?u={username}&pw={password?}`

Tokens stand for variable portions of the URI and match any value for a path element or a parameter. So, the first template in the previous list only matches `/one/two/three` exactly, or more precisely:

```
http[s]://<host>:<port>/[<contextPath>/]/<servicePath>/one/two/three
```

The second template here matches any URI that begins with `/api/login/ticket/`, whereas the third matches the `/api/login` URI when there is a `u` parameter present and possibly a `pw` parameter as well. The `?` symbol at the end of a token indicates that the parameter or path element in question is not mandatory. Actually, the mandatory character of a parameter is not enforced by Alfresco, but using the question mark is still valuable for documentation purposes to describe what the Web Script expects to receive.

We can now precisely describe the operation of the dispatcher as follows: When the dispatcher needs to select a Web Script to execute, it will select the one matching the specific HTTP method used by the request and whose URI template more specifically matches the script path and arguments contained in the request URL.

A Web Script descriptor can also have more than one URI template specified in its descriptor, simply by having more than one `<url>`element. All of them are consulted for matching.

The actual values of the path elements specified as tokens are available to the script as entries in the `url.templateArgs` map variable. For instance, when the `/x/foo` URL is matched by the `/x/{token}` template, the value of the expression `url.templateArgs["token"]` will be equal to `foo`.

Values of request arguments are accessible from the script or template as properties of the `args` object, such as `args.u` and `args.pw` for the third example here.

The format requested, which can be specified in the URL by means of the filename extension or of a `format` argument, need not be specified in the URI template.

Authentication

In the last version of our Web Script, we specified a value of `user` for the `<authentication>` element. When you use this value, users are required to authenticate when they invoke the Web Script's URL, but they can use any valid credentials.

When a value of `none` is present, the Web Script will not require any authentication and will effectively run anonymously. This tends to not be very useful, as all operations using repository objects will require authentication anyway. If you require no authentication, but try to access the repository anyway, the script will throw an exception.

A value of `guest` requires authentication as the guest user. This can be used for scripts accessed from the Explorer, where users are automatically logged in as **guest**, unless they log in with a different profile.

A value of `admin` requires authentication as a user with the administrator role, typically **admin**.

Run as

Scripts can be run as if they were invoked by a user, other than the one who actually provided the authentication credentials. In order to do this, you need to add a `runAs` attribute to the `<authentication>` element:

```
<authentication runAs="admin">user</authentication>
```

This can be used, as in the previous example, to perform operations which require administrator privileges without actually logging in as an admin.

As this can be a security risk, only scripts loaded from the Java `classpath`, and not those loaded from the Data Dictionary, can use this feature.

The Login service

Web Scripts that render as HTML and are therefore intended to be used by humans directly can either use HTTP Basic authentication or Alfresco Explorer authentication, as it is assumed that some person will fill in a login dialog with his username and password.

When a script is meant to implement some form of Web Service that is intended for consumption by another application, HTTP Basic or form-based authentication is not always convenient. For this reason, Alfresco provides the login service, which can be invoked using the following URL:

```
http[s]://<host>:<port>/[<contextPath>/]/service/api/login?u={username
}&pw={password?}
```

If authentication is successful, the script returns an XML document with the following type of content:

```
<ticket>TICKET_024d0fd815fe5a2762e40350596a5041ec73742a</ticket>
```

Applications can use the value of the `ticket` element in subsequent requests in order to avoid having to provide user credentials with each request, simply by adding an `alf_ticket=TICKET_024d0fd815fe5a2762e40350596a5041ec73742a` argument to the URL.

As the username and the password are included, unencrypted, in the request URL, it is recommended that any invocations of the login service be carried out over HTTPS.

Transactions

Possible values of the `transaction` element are:

1. `none`
2. `required`
3. `requiresnew`

When `none` is used, scripts are executed without any transactional support. Since most repository operations require a transaction to be active, using `none` will result in an error whenever the script tries to call repository APIs.

`required` causes the execution of the script to be wrapped in a transaction, which is the normal thing to do. If a transaction is already active when the script is invoked, no new transaction is started. `requiresnew`, on the other hand, always initiates a new transaction, even if one is already active.

Requesting a specific format

The `format` element in the Web Script descriptor indicates how clients are expected to specify which rendering format they require. This is what the element looks like:

```
<format [default="default format"]>extension|argument</format>
```

A value of `extension` indicates that clients should specify the format as a filename extension appended to the Web Script's path. For example:

```
http://localhost:8080/alfresco/service/myscript.html
http://localhost:8080/alfresco/service/myscript.xml
```

A value of `argument` indicates that the format specification is to be sent as the value of the `format` URL parameter:

```
http://localhost:8080/alfresco/service/myscript?format=html
http://localhost:8080/alfresco/service/myscript?format=xml
```

When the client fails to specify a particular format, the value of the `default` attribute is taken as the format to use.

Once a format has been determined, the corresponding template is selected for rendering the model, after the script finishes its execution, on the basis of the template's filename, which must be of the form:

```
<basename>.<method>.<format>.ftl
```

Status

Sometimes it can be necessary for the Web Script to respond to a request with an HTTP status code other than the usual **200 OK** status, which indicates that the request has been processed successfully. There might also be a requirement that the response body be different depending on the status code, like, for instance, when you want to display a specific message to indicate that some resource could not be found, together with a status code of **404 Not Found**.

You can easily do this by manipulating the `status` object:

```
if (document != null)
{
    status.code = 404
    status.message = "No such file found."
    status.redirect = true
}
```

You need to set the value of `status.redirect` to `true` in order for Alfresco to use an alternative error handling template.

When you do this, the Web Scripts framework goes looking for a template with a file name of `<basename>.<method>.<format>.<code>.ftl`, like, for instance, `myscript.get.html.404.ftl` and uses it, if found, instead of the usual `myscript.get.html.ftl`.

In this template, you can access the following properties of the `status` variable to customize your output:

Property name	Meaning
status.code	Numeric value of the HTTP status code (for example, 404)
status.codeName	String value of the status code (for example, Not Found)
status.message	Possibly set by the script
status.exception	The exception that caused this status

If your script sets a status code between 300 and 399, which usually means a redirection, you can set the value of `status.location` to control the value of the `location` HTTP header:

```
status.code = 301; // Moved permanently
status.location = 'http://some.where/else'
```

Configuring Web Scripts

In order to make Web Scripts configurable, it is recommended to avoid hard-wiring parameters in controller scripts or to read them from a database. The Web Scripts Framework provides a simple way to store parameters in an XML file that can be bundled with the rest of the files making up the Web Script. Following the usual naming conventions, the name of the file should be `<basename>.<method>.config.xml`. The format of the file can be any valid XML, but for storing a list of simple parameter values, the following would probably work best:

```
<config>
    <par1>value 1</par1>
    <par2>value 2</par2>
</config>
```

In order to read the configuration parameters, the **ECMAScript for XML** library (also known as **E4X**), which is included in JavaScript, is used:

```
var conf = new XML(config.script)
var par1 = conf.par1 // "value 1"
var par2 = conf.par2 // "value 2"
```

Cache control

Web Scripts can control whether clients or intermediaries, like caching proxies, should cache their output or not. You can control how caching is performed by placing a `cache` element in the Web Script's descriptor. The `cache` element can have the following three child elements, whose value can be either true or false:

1. `never`: When `true`, it signals intermediaries that they should never cache the output of this Web Script because it might be different upon the next request. This is the default.

2. `public`: This applies to authenticated responses. When `true`, it signals intermediaries that they are allowed to store responses in public caches even if they have been obtained from a URL that requires authentication. As authenticated responses typically contain sensitive data, they should not normally be made publicly available, so the default value for this element is `false`.

3. `mustrevalidate`: If `true`, it signals intermediaries that they should always check that the cached version of the response is up to date.

The default values of these configuration elements are set up for maximum safety and minimal cacheability of the content. Basically, they signal intermediaries that responses are never cacheable, which is the default, safe thing to do, unless you, as the developer of a Web Script, can guarantee the cacheability of a particular response.

If you are sure that a specific Web Script's response will never change, you can let intermediaries cache it for as long as they like by using the following configuration:

```
<cache>
<never>false</never>
<public>false</public>
<mustrevalidate>false</mustrevalidate>
</cache>
```

This rarely happens in practice. However, a more usual scenario is that your Web Script might be able to tell intermediaries to cache responses for a limited amount of time. If this is the case, you can let them know by manipulating the maxAge property of the cache object available in the scripting environment, like this:

```
cache.maxAge = 3600; // in seconds
```

The value of maxAge is interpreted as seconds since the request. This example tells intermediaries that the response should not change before one hour has passed, so they can safely cache it for up to one hour.

More realistic scenarios involve some kind of revalidation. This uses the cache validation protocol for HTTP described in RFC 2616 (http://www.w3.org/Protocols/rfc2616/rfc2616-sec14.html) and can be controlled again by manipulating the ETag and lastModified properties of the cache object. The former is some kind of opaque string that can be computed by the server and compared against a previously generated value that has been stored in a cache. The latter represents the last modification date of the resource whose representation the Web Script is supposed to generate (remember we are talking in REST terms here, so we have resources whose representations are transferred via HTTP).

For example, let's assume that your Web Script is meant to return an RSS feed of the ten documents most recently added to or modified in a particular space. Intermediaries are allowed to cache the feed as long as no new document is added to the space and no document belonging to the space has been modified.

Therefore, in order to control caching, our script needs to find which document is the newest and set the cache control headers accordingly:

```
var lastModifiedNode = … // determine which node is newest
cache.ETag = lastModifiedNode.id
cache.lastModified =
    lastModifiedNode.properties["cm:modified"]
```

These instructions will make the following headers appear in the response:

```
ETag: "16340341-2452-408f-9eee-589ce80ca7c2"
Last-Modified: Mon Dec  7 16:15:59 CET 2009
```

 Note that the value of the ETag header is enclosed in double quotes.

The RSS reader, which sent that request, could store those two values together with a cached copy of the RSS feed received. When the time comes to fetch the feed again, the client will send back those values using the If-None-Match and If-Modified-Since headers:

```
If-None-Match: "16340341-2452-408f-9eee-589ce80ca7c2"
If-Modified-Since: Mon Dec  7 16:15:59 CET 2009
```

It is now the responsibility of the Web Script to read those headers, which are accessible as members of the headers array and determine whether it should tell the client that its cached copy is still valid or not. It can do so, for instance, by comparing the GUID of the most recent node with the value of the If-None-Match header: if they are different, the RSS feed must be generated again. If they are equal, the value of the If-Modified-Since header must be compared with the date of the last modification of the most recently modified document. This is necessary because the document that was most recent when the previous request occurred might have been modified before the current request.

If the date of the last modification is not after the value of If-Modified-Since, then we can tell the client that its copy of the response is still valid by emitting a response with a 304 Not Modified status and an empty body, saving the work necessary for the rendering and transmission of a new RSS feed.

Here is a complete script that implements the logic described here. Save it as recent.get.js.

```
var results =
    search.luceneSearch(
        'PATH:"/app:company_home/app:guest_home/*"',
        "@cm:modified",
        false)
if (results.length > 0) {
    var top = results[0]
    cache.ETag = top.id
    cache.lastModified = top.properties["cm:modified"]

    // Check if feed needs regenerating
    var etag = headers["If-None-Match"]

    // We must strip off extra quotes
    if (etag != undefined && etag.replace(/\"/g,"")
== top.id) {
        if (headers["If-Modified-Since"] != undefined) {

            // Truncate time values to the second
            var ims = Math.floor(Date.parse(
```

```
headers["If-Modified-Since"]) / 1000)
            var lastmodified = Math.floor(
                top.properties["cm:modified"].getTime() /
                1000)
            if (lastmodified <= ims) {
                status.code = 304; // Not Modified
                status.redirect = true;
            }
        }
    }
}
model.results = results
```

For this to work properly, you should use the following caching configuration:

```
<cache>
    <never>false</never>
    <public>false</public>
    <mustrevalidate>true</mustrevalidate>
</cache>
```

A simplified template for producing an RSS feed listing the recent documents as selected by the controller script could look like the following:

```
<?xml version="1.0"?>
<rss version="2.0">
<channel>
<title>Recent Documents</title>
<link>http://localhost:8080/alfresco/service/recent</link>
<description>Recently created or modified documents in the Guest Home
space.</description>
<generator>Alfresco ${server.edition?xml} ${server.version?xml}</
generator>
  <#list results as item>
    <item>
      <title>${item.properties["cm:name"]?xml}</title>
      <link>${absurl(url.context + item.url)?xml}</link>
       <#if item.properties["cm:description"]??>
         <description>${item.properties["cm:description"]?xml}
         </description>
      </#if>
      <pubDate>${item.properties["cm:modified"]?datetime}</pubDate>
      <guid>${item.id?xml}</guid>
    </item>
  </#list>
</rss>
```

Save the template as a document called `recent.get.rss.ftl`. You must also provide an empty template to use when the `304` status is selected (just create an empty file called `recent.get.rss.304.ftl`).

The complete descriptor is listed as follows. Copy these lines to a file called `recent.get.desc.xml`. Note that we are using a value of `guest` for the `authentication` element; when you invoke the script by requesting the `http://localhost:8080/alfresco/service/recent` URL, you need to specify **guest** as both the username and the password.

We are also using a value of `required` for the transaction element. This is necessary because we are now accessing the repository via the `search` object.

```
<webscript>
    <shortname>Recent Documents</shortname>
    <description>Lists the 10 most recently created or modified
    documents in the Guest Home space</description>
    <url>/recent</url>
    <authentication>guest</authentication>
    <transaction>required</transaction>
    <format default="rss">any</format>
    <cache>
    <never>false</never>
    <public>false</public>
    <mustrevalidate>true</mustrevalidate>
    </cache>
</webscript>
```

It must be noted that enabling caching with the previous configuration does not cause Alfresco itself to cache anything. Caching is entirely the responsibility of the client or of the intermediary. What was demonstrated in this section will only cause the Web Scripts framework to emit the correct headers that tell clients what and when to cache.

Deployment

Web Scripts can be deployed to a running Alfresco instance in one of two places: either in the repository itself, under the **Company Home | Data Dictionary | Web Scripts Extensions** or the **Company Home | Data Dictionary | Web Scripts** spaces or in the Java `classpath`, inside the `alfresco/extension/templates/webscripts` or the `alfresco/templates/webscripts` folders.

These locations are consulted by Alfresco in the specific order listed here, when looking for a Web Script; Web Scripts located in the **Web Scripts Extensions** space are used in preference to Web Scripts with the same name located in the **Web Scripts** space. Those, in turn have precedence over Web Scripts loaded from the Java `classpath`. Web Scripts found under `alfresco/extension/templates/webscripts` in the `classpath` have higher precedence than those found in `alfresco/templates/webscripts`. In the latter, you will be able to find all the Web Scripts that are distributed as part of a typical Alfresco installation.

What this means is that it is possible for you to override existing Web Scripts just by placing your alternative implementation higher on the chain of locations searched by the dispatcher.

It is even possible to override only parts of an existing Web Script. For example, if you want to customize the output of a built-in Web Script, found in `alfresco/templates/webscripts`, the easiest way to do this is to upload only a modified template, either in `alfresco/extension/templates/webscripts` or in the Data Dictionary, using the same package and filename, without having to provide copies of the descriptor or of the controller script.

Summary

This chapter introduced the Web Scripts framework that has been an important part of Alfresco since version 2.1 and whose relevance is continually growing.

In this chapter, you learned:

1. The basic principles of the REST architectural style and how it compares to the traditional Web Services stack of specifications based on SOAP.
2. How the adoption of these principles impacts aspects like URL design and the choice of representation formats.
3. How to build and deploy a very simple Web Script and saw how this can be done very quickly and with very simple tools.
4. The components that make up a Web Script and various configuration options available.

In the following chapters, you will learn how to develop rich templates using the FreeMarker language and how to implement complex functionalities using JavaScript and Java.

 More information about Web Scripts can be found on the Alfresco wiki at `http://wiki.alfresco.com/wiki/Web_Scripts`.

7
Templating with FreeMarker

In this chapter, we introduce the FreeMarker templating engine that is used by Alfresco Web Scripts to provide a mechanism for generating a response at the end of the execution of a Web Script.

You will learn the basics of the FreeMarker language and a number of features that will be useful when developing templates for Alfresco. These are as follows:

- Variables and how to interpolate values in the output
- Operators and built-ins that can be used to build more complex expressions from simple variables
- Directives and their effect on the flow of execution of the template
- How to define macros for reusing blocks of code

FreeMarker has many uses, in addition to its use in Alfresco, so covering all the uses is outside the scope of this chapter. The FreeMarker documentation, which is available online at `http://freemarker.org`, is very good and complete, and you should refer to it whenever you have doubts about the syntax and the semantics of the language.

FreeMarker concepts

FreeMarker is an open source template engine for the Java Virtual Machine that was created a few years ago by Benjamin Geer and Mike Bayer and has subsequently gone through various iterations. The version included in Alfresco, as of release 3.3 Community, is FreeMarker 2.3.13.

A template is a text document that, when applied to some kind of input model, produces an output document having a structure that resembles the structure of the template.

Templating languages have long been used by Web application frameworks to produce dynamic HTML pages. PHP, for instance, is often used as a templating language—a PHP page has the structure of an HTML page, with PHP instructions interspersed throughout the document. The PHP interpreter executes those instructions and replaces them in the output document with the result of the execution. JSP pages play a similar role in many Java Web applications.

With PHP and JSP, you can build whole applications as a collection of pages, embedding the complete logic of the application inside the templates. This is not normally regarded as a good practice, for reasons of readability and maintainability of the resulting code, as was explained in the *The Model-View-Controller pattern* section in the previous chapter.

FreeMarker is more of a pure templating language, compared to PHP and JSP, in that it does not permit you to implement complex business procedures inside its templates. FreeMarker instructions (called directives) provide only very basic programming constructs, not much more than iterating over lists and the if...then...else construct.

Moreover, FreeMarker templates do not have access to the full complement of Java classes available to the underlying JVM environment like JSP pages do. They can see only a restricted model, made up of whatever objects the code invoking the template decides to make available. In the case of Alfresco Web Scripts, this includes the full set of root-scoped objects listed in the previous chapter, in addition to whatever the controller script adds as properties of the model variable.

This fact arguably makes it easier for application writers to avoid putting too much business logic in the templates themselves.

If you are familiar with **Apache Velocity**, another popular templating language for the Java platform, you will find it easy to pick up FreeMarker programming, as the basic concepts are pretty similar.

Variable interpolation

As we saw in the previous chapter, FreeMarker templates can contain expressions inside the ${...} symbols. When the FreeMarker engine finds those sequences inside a template, it evaluates the expression inside the curly braces and substitutes its value for the whole sequence. Have a look at the following template, which is used as part of a Web Script:

```
<html>
<body>
<p>The name of the user's home space is
```

```
        "${userhome.name}"</p>
    </body>
    </html>
```

This will produce the following output document (depending on the authenticated user's identity and the name of his/her home space):

```
<html>
<body>
<p>The name of the user's home space is
    "Alice's Home"</p>
</body>
</html>
```

FreeMarker expressions

An expression in FreeMarker is a sequence of variable names and operators that, when evaluated, produces a **value**.

Variables and expressions always have a value and a **type**. Some languages treat every value as a string, but this is not the case with FreeMarker, which is a typed language.

FreeMarker types can either be scalars or containers; the former contains a single value, which can be a string, a number, a boolean, or a date. The latter contains multiple values and includes hashes, sequences, or collections.

FreeMarker actually has some less frequently used types, such as methods, functions, and nodes, but we will not be dealing with them. You can find a detailed explanation of the FreeMarker type system in its online documentation at http://freemarker.org.

Scalars

FreeMarker supports only four scalar types: string, boolean, number, and date.

Strings

Strings are very common to all programming languages and therefore need no specific explanation. The only thing that you have to remember is that string constants are enclosed in double quotes ("), but like JavaScript, single quotes (') are also allowed. If the string contains the quoting character used to delimit the string itself, you can escape it by preceding it with the backslash (\) character.

Other escape sequences are similar to the Java ones, with the addition of the following, which can be useful for producing well-formed XML or HTML documents:

\l	Less-than sign: <
\g	Greater-than sign: >
\a	Ampersand: &

Booleans

Boolean values can be either true or false and can be used in `if` directives. You don't need to put quotes around `true` or `false`.

Numbers

There is only one numeric type in FreeMarker, which makes no distinction between integer and floating point numbers, or between single- and double-precision values.

It is not recommended to carry out anything but the simplest computations in FreeMarker.

Numeric constants are written without quotes, can have a sign (+ or -) in front, and use the decimal point (.) as a separator between the whole part and the decimals. You cannot use scientific notation, such as `1E3`, and you cannot omit the zero before the decimal point.

Dates

A date variable in FreeMarker can be used to store either just a date (year, month, and day of the month), time of day (hour, minute, second, and milliseconds), and date-time.

In most circumstances, FreeMarker can keep track of which of these three variants a given variable actually is, but sometimes, especially when using dates passed from the controller or obtained by the Alfresco repository, it can't. This is due to the fact that the standard Java libraries use a single type (`java.util.Date`) for all cases.

This can happen, for instance, while trying to output the last modification time of an Alfresco node. The following expression will cause the template execution to be stopped and an error message to be displayed:

```
${companyhome.properties["cm:modified"]}
```

In this case, you need to tell FreeMarker which part of the `date` objects to display, using one of the three **built-ins**: `date`, `time`, or `datetime`. Built-ins are a kind of operator that can, among other things, modify the way a value is displayed; you use a built-in by appending a question mark (?) to an expression, followed by the name of the built-in.

For example, to correct the previous expression and display the full modification date, including the timestamp, use:

```
${companyhome.properties["cm:modified"]?datetime}
```

This will effectively display the full timestamp, using the default Java format for dates, which depends on the current locale. More often than not, you will want to control the format used. You can do this by using the `string` built-in:

```
${companyhome.properties["cm:modified"]?string("MM/dd/yyyy HH:mm:ss")}
```

Containers

Containers are variables and constants that can contain zero or more values. Therefore, we need a way to refer to the single values in addition to the whole container.

Hashes

Hashes are sometimes called associative arrays. The closest thing to a hash in the Java language is a `java.util.Map`.

FreeMarker hashes are collections of values, called **members** that are indexed using a string, called the **key**, not any kind of object like Java maps. You access members of the hash using the square-brackets notation:

```
hashname["key"]
```

The `key` can be any string and doesn't have to be a valid identifier. When it is a valid identifier, though, FreeMarker permits the use of a short-hand notation:

```
hashname.key
```

The data model of FreeMarker templates itself is actually one big hash, indexed by the name of objects stored in it. The only difference with user-defined hashes is that you don't need to prefix keys with the name of the hash, `model`.

Hashes are not ordered. Therefore, you cannot access the first, last, or n-th value and FreeMarker does not guarantee that the order of entries will be preserved after insertions or deletions. You can, however, iterate over the keys to retrieve all of the values, as shown in the following template:

```
<#assign beatles = {
"John":"Lennon",
"Paul":"McCartney",
"George":"Harrison",
"Ringo":"Starr" }>
<#list beatles?keys as b>
    ${b} ${beatles[b]}
</#list>
```

Which generates the following output:

```
John Lennon

Paul McCartney

George Harrison

Ringo Starr
```

Members of a hash can be of any scalar value or containers and they can be of different types. Hashes can be members of hashes, of course, so you can use hashes to build complex data structures of any depth.

Sequences

Sequences are ordered collections of values that are indexed by number. Index values are integers and start with 0.

Sequences are similar to arrays in traditional programming languages, but with the important distinction that the values can be of different types.

Collections

Collections are restricted sequences. They hold an ordered collection of values, but the values cannot be accessed by index. They are typically only used in a list directive.

Operators

You can combine FreeMarker variables into expressions, and those expressions into more complex expressions yet, using a set of operators that are designed to resemble the ones of the Java language. If you know the latter, you will have no problems reading a FreeMarker expression, in most cases.

String operators

The following operators act on strings:

Concatenation and interpolation

You concatenate string values in FreeMarker using the '+' operator:

```
<#assign x="Hello" + " World">
${x} <#-- Outputs "Hello World" -->
```

It is actually more common to use interpolation for concatenating strings:

```
<#assign x="Hello">
<#assign y="World">
<#assign z="${x} ${y}">
```

This example also underscores the fact that you can use interpolations inside string literals, in addition to textual content.

Getting a single character

You can obtain the seventh character in a string by using the following syntax (positions inside a string are numbered, starting with 0):

```
<#assign x="Hello World">
${x[6]}  <#-- Outputs 'W' -->
```

The result of this operator is a string of length 1, as FreeMarker does not have a character type like the type found in Java.

Sequence operators

The following operators act on sequences and collections:

Concatenation

To concatenate sequences, you use the '+' operator:

```
<#assign beatles=["John", "Paul"] + ["George", "Ringo"]>
```

Slicing

You can get a portion of a sequence (called a "slice") by using the [startindex..endindex] operator. For instance, beatles[1..3] equals ["Paul", "George", "Ringo"].

You can omit the end index of the slice, as in beatles[1..], in which case, the slice will comprise all the elements of the sequence from the start index until the end of it.

Hash operators

Hashes support only the concatenation operator '+'. It is not possible to access hash entries using a numerical index.

Arithmetical operators

FreeMarker supports the four basic arithmetical operations ('+', '-', '*', '/') plus the modulus (or remainder) operation ('%').

Comparison operators

You can test two values for equality in FreeMarker using either the '=' or the '==' operator. As there is no chance for ambiguity between comparison and assignment in FreeMarker, you can use a single equals sign, or two, depending on your taste.

Inequality is tested with '!=', and the usual symbols '<', '<=', '>=', and '>' are used with numeric expressions to test whether the left-hand side of the comparison is less than, less than or equal to, greater than or equal to, or greater than the right-hand side, respectively:

```
<#if x < 0>
<div class="error">Negative values are not allowed</div>
</#if>
```

FreeMarker templates are not XML files, so you do not normally need to escape the '<' and '>' symbols. However, notice how the comparison in the following example is enclosed in parentheses:

```
<#if (x > 100)>
<div class="error">Value is too large</div>
</#if>
```

This is necessary whenever an expression used inside a directive's tag contains the '>' symbol, otherwise FreeMarker would think that it signals the closing of the tag. Instead of using parentheses, we could have written the greater-than sign as gt, \gt, or even >.

Logical operators

FreeMarker has the usual **or** ('||'), **and** ('&&'), and **not** ('!') operators. These work only on boolean values.

Missing values

FreeMarker is quite picky when you try to use variables that do not have values. For instance, assuming the x variable has not been assigned a value using the **assign** directive and is not part of the data model, the following interpolation:

```
${x}
```

will cause the rendering process to stop with an error, instead of outputting an empty string or "null".

The same is true for properties of objects that are undefined, or Java methods that return **null**.

Fortunately, FreeMarker offers a couple of ways to avoid this kind of error. One way is by using default values and the other is by testing whether a value is defined or not.

Specifying default values

You can specify a default value to be output, when the actual value of an expression is missing, by appending an exclamation mark to the expression, followed by the default value:

```
${x!"Hello"}
${y!42}
```

You can also omit the default value, in which case, an empty string or sequence, depending on the context, will be assumed:

```
${x!}
```

Testing for missing values

The ?? characters, when appended to an expression, will cause the whole expression to evaluate to true or false, depending on whether the original expression has a value or not:

```
${foo??} => outputs "false"
<#assign foo "bar">
${foo??} => outputs "true"
```

This kind of test is typically used in conditionals:

```
<#if foo??>
  ${foo}
<#else>
'foo' has no value.
</#if>
```

Built-ins

FreeMarker built-ins are like method calls and they are available for the native FreeMarker types. You apply a built-in to an expression by appending a question mark at the end of the expression, followed by the built-in's name, possibly followed by a list of arguments in parentheses.

In the following sections, we are going to show a handful of FreeMarker built-ins that are mostly useful when generating machine-parsable data, like when developing Web Services, where you typically need to ensure that your output is well-formed XML, where dates are displayed using standard formats or white space is treated correctly.

There are many more built-ins in FreeMarker than the ones described here. You can find a full reference in the online documentation.

Built-ins for strings

The following built-ins expect a string value on their left-hand side:

html, xhtml, xml

They turn the string into a version which is "safe" to use as text content for HTML, XHTML, and XML documents, respectively. This basically means replacing all the occurrences of reserved characters, such as '<', '>', and '&', with the corresponding entities (`&lt;`, `&gt;`, `&amp;`, and so on).

js_string

This escapes special characters, like single and double quotes, so that the result is safe to use inside a JavaScript string literal.

url

This encodes all characters that have a special meaning in a URL, such as colon, slash, question mark, space, and so on into their equivalent hexadecimal codes.

trim

This removes all leading and trailing whitespace from the string.

Built-ins for dates

The following built-ins expect a date value on their left-hand side:

string

Converts a date into its string representation. This built-in can take an argument, representing the desired format with the same rules used by the `java.text.DateFormat` class. For example, if `somedate` represents 7:55PM, December 18th, 2009, then the following expression:

```
${somedate?string("MM/dd/yyyy HH:mm:ss")}
```

will output the following:

```
12/18/2009 19:55:00
```

date, time, datetime

As we mentioned before, due to the ambiguity of the `java.util.Date` type, sometimes FreeMarker cannot easily determine whether an instance of the `Date` class should be taken to represent the date, the timestamp part of a time value, or both. In those cases, the ambiguity can be resolved by using one of the `date`, `time`, or `datetime` built-ins.

Once again, if `somedate` represents 7:55PM, December 18th, 2009, then the following expressions:

```
${somedate?date}
${somedate?time}
${somedate?datetime}
```

will output the following strings, respectively:

```
Dec 18, 2009
7:55:00 PM
Dec 18, 2009 7:55:00 PM
```

 As we didn't specify a format, the actual values that are output will depend on the current locale.

Directives

In FreeMarker, directives are used to control the "flow" of execution in a template and provide features like conditionals and loops that are typical of traditional programming languages.

Directives are recognizable by the `<#directive-name parameters>` syntax. If a directive includes some content, the end of the directive is marked by the `</#directive-name>` syntax.

Remember that a FreeMarker template is not a well-formed XML document: the # character would not be allowed as the first character of an XML element name. Also, directives that don't have nested content need not be closed with the / character like in XML.

Assign

The `assign` directive can be used to store a value in a variable, to create a new variable, or to update an existing one. The simplest form of the assign directive is as follows:

```
<#assign name1=value1 name2=value2 ... nameN=valueN>
```

For convenience, you can set the value of multiple variables at once, if you like:

```
<#assign foo=bar n=4+2>
```

If

The `if` directive can be used to render a portion of a template or not, depending on the value of a boolean expression:

```
<#if (results?size > 0)>
  <p>Number of results: ${results?size}</p>
</#if>
```

Alternative choices can be evaluated using the `<#else>` and `<#elseif>` tags inside the `if` directive:

```
<#if (results?size > 1)>
  <p>The search returned ${results?size} documents.</p>
<#elseif (results?size > 0)>
  <p>The search returned one document.</p>
<#else>
  <p>No documents match the specified criteria.</p>
</#if>
```

List

The `list` directive is used to iterate over members of a sequence or of a collection:

```
<ul>
  <#list results as r>
  <li>${r.properties.name}</li>
  </#list>
</ul>
```

The general form of a `list` directive is as follows:

```
<#list sequence as loop-variable>
  ...
</#list>
```

The directive's nested content is output once for every element of the sequence. Inside the nested content, you can use the `loop-variable` to refer to the current element in the iteration.

Between the directive's start and end tags, you also have access to a couple of special variables:

- `loop-variable_index`: a numerical index, starting at 0, that counts the iterations of the loop

- `loop-variable_has_next`: a boolean variable that is true only when the current element is not the last one in the sequence

You could use these variables, for instance, to print out a numbered list of items, each one of them followed by a semicolon, except for the last one, which is followed by a full stop.

```
<#assign beatles = [ "John", "Paul", "George", "Ringo" ]>
<#list beatles as b>
  ${b_index + 1}. ${b}
<#if b_has_next>;<#else>.</#if><br/>
</#list>
```

The output from this template would be:

1. John;
2. Paul;
3. George;
4. Ringo.

You can use the `<#break>` tag to exit prematurely from iteration:

```
<ul>
<#list results as r>
  <#if r_index == 10>
    <#break>
  </#if>
  <li>${r.properties.name}</li>
</#list>
</ul>
```

You can also use the `list` directive to count numbers, using a **numerical range sequence expression**:

```
<#list 1..100 as counter>
  ${counter}
</#list>
```

Include

The general form of an `include` directive is:

```
<#include path [options]>
```

Where `path` is a string expression that evaluates to the path of the file to be included and `options` is an optional set of `name=value` pairs.

Since `path` can be an expression, it need not be a constant, thus the following is perfectly legal:

```
<#include ${companyhome.path} + "/Data Dictionary/Templates/template.
ftl">
```

The allowed options are the following:

- `encoding`: A string denoting the character set of the included file. If no encoding option is present, it is assumed that the included file has the same encoding as the including one.

- `parse`: A boolean value. When `parse=true`, any FreeMarker constructs inside the included file are processed as if they were present in the including file. When `parse=false`, the file is included verbatim and no constructs are processed. When the `parse` option is absent, a value of `true` is assumed.

The `include` directive is typically used to include common elements, such as headers and footers of HTML pages, inside a template, or to import libraries of macro definitions. This is a convenient method for avoiding code duplication.

Here is an example of an `include` directive with a full set of options:

```
<#include "commons/header.html" parse=false encoding=UTF-8>
```

Macro

The `macro` directive introduces a **user-defined directive**. This snippet defines a directive called `foo`:

```
<#macro foo>
bar
</#macro>
```

You can recall the directive anywhere in the template where it is defined or in a template that includes the file where the macro is defined. You use the syntax `<@ macro-name/>` to invoke a macro. The following snippet:

```
<p>The value is <@foo/>.</p>
```

will output the following text:

The value is bar.

Nested content

Notice that we wrote the macro invocation as `<@foo/>`, with a trailing slash. Whereas this is not necessary for built-in directives, as the FreeMarker engine knows which directives can have content between the opening and the closing tag. But this becomes mandatory for user-defined macros, as FreeMarker has no way of knowing whether to expect a closing tag or not.

If you want to define a macro that makes use of the content included between the start and end tags, you can do so and access the content from within the macro definition by using the `nested` directive. The following macro:

```
<#macro generator>
<generator><#nested> ${server.edition?xml}
    ${server.version?xml}</generator>
</#macro>
```

When invoked as:

```
<@generator>Alfresco</@generator>
```

will produce the following output (depending on the version of Alfresco in which it is executed):

<generator>Alfresco Community 3.2.0 (r2 2440)</generator>

Macros with parameters

User-defined macros can take parameters too. You must declare those parameters in the macro definition using the following syntax:

```
<#macro name [parname [=defaultvalue]] * >
macro body
</#macro>
```

This is an example of a macro that takes two mandatory parameters and an optional one with a default value:

```
<#macro mymacro par1 par2 par3=defval>
par1 = ${par1}<br />
par2 = ${par2}<br />
par3 = ${par3}<br />
</#macro>
```

You must invoke the macro by passing as many parameters as are declared in the macro definition, save for those that have a default value, so you can either call the macro as:

```
<@mymacro par1="foo" par2="bar" />
```

or as:

```
<@mymacro par1="foo" par2="bar" par3="baz"/>
```

You cannot pass any parameter that was not declared in the macro definition; doing so will result in an error and processing will immediately be stopped.

Comments

Everything that is included between the `<#--` and `-->` sequences in FreeMarker is considered a comment and is not included in the output.

Using FreeMarker in Web Scripts

As mentioned in the previous chapter, the model that is available to a template, which is used to render the output of a Web Script, includes a number of objects that give the template direct access to a significant subset of Repository Services. Keep in mind that in order to use most of the objects that are described in this section, the Web Script must be configured to use authentication and must require transactions.

The model that is made available to templates cannot be used to perform modifications to the repository. It is essentially a read-only model.

The TemplateNode API

Some objects that make up the default model are listed in the following table:

roothome	The root node of the repository
companyhome	The Company Home space
userhome	The user's home folder
person	The currently logged-in user

These objects are of a common type, called **TemplateNode**, that represents a node in the Alfresco repository. As they are of the same type, they share a common set of properties and methods. A full reference of the TemplateNode API is available on the Alfresco Wiki at `http://wiki.alfresco.com/wiki/Template_Guide#TemplateNode_Model_API`. Here we present a short description of the most commonly used properties and methods:

properties	A hash of node properties, for example, `companyhome.properties["cm:name"]`
children	A sequence containing the children of this node
assocs	A hash, keyed by association name of this node; each value in the hash is an array of associated targets
aspects	A sequence of the aspects of this node
hasAspect(aspectName)	Returns true if this node has the aspect named `aspectName`
isContainer	Returns true if the node is a container (folder)
isDocument	Returns true if the node is a document
content	The content of the node, as a string

url	The URL pointing to this node's content stream
id	The UUID of this node
parent	The parent node of this node
permissions	The list of this node's permissions, represented as strings
hasPermission(permiss ion)	Returns true if the node has the named permission

Searching

The TemplateNode API includes a handful of methods that let templates execute searches on the contents of the repository and present their results. Together with the properties and methods listed in the previous two tables, these methods allow developers to create a Web Script that navigates the repository without using a controller script.

childrenByXPath

The `childrenByXPath` property of a TemplateNode is a hash-valued property whose value is a sequence of nodes matching the **XPath** expression used as the look-up key. For example, the following expression will return all the descendants of the **Company Home** space that are named `foo.txt`:

```
companyhome.childrenByXPath[".//*[@cm:name='foo.txt']"]
```

For more information about XPath, see `http://www.w3.org/TR/xpath/`.

childByNamePath

The `childByNamePath` property is a hash having the node as its only entry whose pathname, relative to this node, is equal to the hash key:

```
companyhome.childByNamePath["Data Dictionary/Web Script Extensions/
readme.html"];
```

childrenByLuceneSearch

`childrenByLuceneSearch` is a hash-valued property whose value is the sequence of nodes returned by executing the Lucene query used as the key:

```
companyhome.childrenByLuceneSearch["@cm\:name:foo.txt"]
```

The query is performed against the whole repository, regardless of the node that you use to access the `childrenByLuceneSearch` property.

childrenBySavedSearch

This is once again a hash-valued property that returns the results of a saved search. Saved searches are stored as nodes in the repository. Therefore, you need to specify the NodeRef of the saved search as the hash key:

```
companyhome.childrenBySavedSearch["workspace://SpacesStore/92005879-
996a-11da-bfbc-f7140598adfe"]
```

A simple example

In this section, we are going to revisit the template for generating an RSS feed of Alfresco nodes, which were presented in the previous chapter to make it more readable with the use of macros.

Here is the original version again:

```
<?xml version="1.0"?>
<rss version="2.0">
  <channel>
    <title>Recent Documents</title>
    <link>http://localhost:8080/alfresco/service/recent</link>
    <description>Recently created or modified documents in the Guest
Home space.</description>
    <generator>Alfresco ${server.edition?xml} ${server.version?xml}</
generator>
    <#list results as item>
    <item>
      <title>${item.properties["cm:name"]?xml}</title>
      <link>${absurl(url.context + item.url)?xml}</link>
      <#if item.properties["cm:description"]??>
      <description>${item.properties["cm:description"]?xml}</
description>
      </#if>
      <pubDate>${item.properties["cm:modified"]?datetime}</pubDate>
      <guid>${item.id?xml}</guid>
    </item>
    </#list>
  </channel>
</rss>
```

First of all, we are going to define a macro for producing the `<generator>` element that gives information about the version of Alfresco used. This macro does not take any parameters, but generates the element's value by appending the server's edition and version to whatever the nested content of the macro invocation is. The server object is also part of the default model.

```
<#macro generator>
<generator><#nested> ${server.edition?xml} ${server.version?xml}</
generator>
</#macro>
```

Next, we will define a macro for producing an RSS element if an expression is not null:

```
<#macro optelem elemname value>
<#if value??>
<${elemname}>${value?xml}</${elemname}>
</#if>
</#macro>
```

With these changes, the full code of the template is as follows:

```
<?xml version="1.0"?>
<#macro generator>
<generator><#nested> ${server.edition?xml} ${server.version?xml}</
generator>
</#macro>

<#macro optelem elemname value>
<#if value??>
<${elemname}>${value?xml}</${elemname}>
</#if>
</#macro>

<?xml version="1.0"?>
<rss version="2.0">
  <channel>
    <title>Recent Documents</title>
    <link>http://localhost:8080/alfresco/service/recent</link>
    <description>Recently created or modified documents in the Guest
Home space.</description>
    <@generator>Alfresco</@generator>
    <#list results as item>
     <item>
```

```
      <@optelem "title" item.properties["cm:title"]/>
      <link>${absurl(url.context + item.url)?xml}</link>
      <@optelem "description" item.properties["cm:description"]/>
      <pubDate>${item.properties["cm:modified"]?datetime}</pubDate>
      <guid>${item.id?xml}</guid>
    </item>
  </#list>
 </channel>
</rss>
```

Generating an Atom Categories Document

In the following example, you will use the knowledge that you have acquired in this chapter and the preceding one to develop a simple Web Script that produces an Atom Categories Document, listing a set of categories defined as part of the Alfresco classification hierarchy.

Atom

In the remainder of the book, a number of examples of RESTful Web Services will be shown. These examples will generate representations of collections and lists, such as documents in a space, search results, and categories. In the previous example, we used RSS as an XML-based format for representing lists. In the upcoming examples, we will use the **Atom Syndication Format** instead.

As a format for representing lists, Atom is slightly more powerful and better specified than RSS, but the real reason for using it here is that Atom as a syndication format is also the basis for the definition of the **Atom Publishing Protocol**, an HTTP-based protocol for managing collections of resources following REST principles.

AtomPub is also important because one of the protocol bindings of the **CMIS** standard, which will be introduced in *Chapter 10, Overview of CMIS,* is an extension of AtomPub.

Chapter 9, Putting it All Together will provide a much more thorough introduction to Atom and AtomPub. In this chapter, we are using only one of the possible Atom document types, the **Categories Document**.

The Alfresco Bookshop

In *Chapter 4, A Complete Example*, we also introduced the fictitious Alfresco Bookshop, an Internet bookshop that provides a number of Web Services to other applications. Using these services, remote clients will be able to search for books, retrieve descriptions, create and update resources about books, tag and review them, and so on.

In this chapter, we are reusing the same domain model used for the Web Services-based Alfresco Bookshop application, but implement a REST version of one of the services using a Web Script.

The service we are going to implement will provide a list of the top-level categories that are used to classify books. In the bookshop, books are classified as belonging to one or more categories. We will be storing books as Alfresco documents and will use the Alfresco classification system to categorize them.

Categories in Atom

The Atom Publishing Protocol specifies a format for enumerating which categories are supported by a server. This is useful for letting clients know that some collections are expected to contain resources belonging to a limited set of categories, and for listing the categories a given resource belongs to. The basis for this is the **Categories** document, an example of which is shown here, as copied verbatim from the RFC 5023 specification:

```
<app:categories
xmlns:app="http://www.w3.org/2007/app"
xmlns:atom="http://www.w3.org/2005/Atom"
fixed="yes" scheme="http://example.com/cats/big3">
  <atom:category term="animal" />
  <atom:category term="vegetable" />
  <atom:category term="mineral" />
</app:categories>
```

The scheme attribute is used as a namespace to disambiguate between categories having the same name (term) but belonging to different classification schemes.

When describing an Atom entry or feed, you would use the following syntax to refer to a category listed in a category document:

```
<atom:category scheme="http://example.com/cats/big3" term="mineral"/>
```

Categories in Alfresco

For our example, we need to define a set of categories for the purpose of classifying books. These categories might look like **Fiction**, **Science**, **Mystery**, and **Computers & Internet**. Look at the list of categories on the **Books** section of the www.amazon.com website for a useful set of categories.

For our Web Script to work, you need to define a suitable set of categories using the Alfresco Category Management application. Log in as admin onto Alfresco, browse to the **Administration** console and, from there, create the **Books** top-level category and then add as many child categories as you like. In the end, your category should look like the following:

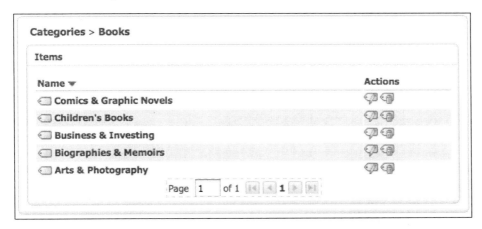

Don't bother creating nested categories. Whereas Alfresco supports these, Atom does not.

Creating the Web Script

Our Web Script consists of a descriptor, a controller script, and one template.

The descriptor

In order to have a descriptor for your Web Script, create a file named categories. get.desc.xml in a suitable location, either in the Java classpath or under **Data Dictionary | Web Script Extensions**, with the following content:

```
<webscript>
  <shortname>Top Level Categories</shortname>
  <description>Lists all the top level categories</description>
```

```
<url>/bookshop/categories</url>
<authentication>user</authentication>
<transaction>required</transaction>
<format default="atom">any</format>
</webscript>
```

The controller

The controller script is very simple. All it does is finding the children of the **Books** top-level category. Create a file named `categories.get.js` in the same folder as the descriptor with the following content:

```javascript
var topcats = classification.getRootCategories("cm:
generalclassifiable")
for (var i in topcats) {
    if (topcats[i].name == "Books") {
        model.categories = topcats[i].subCategories
        break;
    }
}
```

The script uses the `classification` root object to access the Alfresco categories. Unfortunately, there is no method to obtain a category by name, so we have to iterate over all top-level categories to find the one named "Books". Once we have it, we store its children and descendants in the `categories` property of the data model for access by the template.

 As explained in the previous chapter, it would have been possible, but not really recommended, to do the same directly in the template and avoid the need for the controller script. It's better to keep every bit of domain-specific logic in the controller and use the template for presentation only.

The template

Save the following template in a file named `categories.get.atom.ftl`:

```
<?xml version="1.0" ?>
<app:categories
    xmlns:app="http://www.w3.org/2007/app"
    xmlns:atom="http://www.w3.org/2005/Atom"
    fixed="yes" scheme="http://www.packtpub.com/a3ws/bookshop/
categories">
<#list categories as cat>
<atom:category term="${cat.name?xml}"/>
</#list>
</app:categories>
```

Notice that we used the `xml` built-in to escape any special characters that could be present in the name of a category like **Arts & Photography**.

Using the Web Script

Refresh the list of Web Scripts using the console at `http://localhost:8080/alfresco/service/` and invoke your Web Script via its URL:

```
http://localhost:8080/alfresco/service/bookshop/categories
```

If you do this with a browser, it will probably offer to save the response as a file, since browsers normally do not know what to do with an Atom Categories document. You might find it easier to examine the output using the `curl` command-line utility as follows:

```
curl -u admin:admin http://localhost:8080/alfresco/service/bookshop/categories
```

In any case, this is the kind of output you should expect:

```
<?xml version="1.0" ?>
<app:categories
    xmlns:app="http://www.w3.org/2007/app"
    xmlns:atom="http://www.w3.org/2005/Atom"
    fixed="yes" scheme="http://www.packtpub.com/a3ws/bookshop/categories">
  <atom:category term="Arts &amp; Photography"/>
  <atom:category term="Biographies &amp; Memoirs"/>
  <atom:category term="Business &amp; Investing"/>
  <atom:category term="Children&apos;s Books"/>
  <atom:category term="Comics &amp; Graphic Novels"/>
</app:categories>
```

Categories as JSON

A data format that has recently grown in popularity is **JSON**. JSON (`http://www.json.org`) is an acronym which stands for **JavaScript Object Notation** and a JSON document is basically a serialized representation of a JavaScript data structure.

The advantage of JSON is apparent if your client understands JavaScript. In this case, you can simply reconstruct the original data structure from JSON by using the `eval` function.

This is why using JSON is comparatively easier than XML if your client is an in-browser, JavaScript application that uses AJAX to talk to the server: you don't have to deal with the DOM and its quirks.

Creating JSON output is also made very easy in Alfresco Web Scripts, thanks to the `jsonUtils` root object.

Here is a template that generates a JSON array of categories. Save it as `categories.get.json.ftl`

```
[
<#list categories as cat>
  "${jsonUtils.encodeJSONString(cat.name)}"<#if cat_has_next>,</#if>
</#list>
]
```

and invoke it as

`http://localhost:8080/alfresco/service/bookshop/categories.json`.

The output should look something like this:

```
[
    "Arts & Photography",
    "Biographies & Memoirs",
    "Business & Investing",
    "Children's Books",
    "Comics & Graphic Novels"
]
```

Summary

This chapter covered the following topics:

- The FreeMaker language—its syntax and semantics
- How the FreeMarker default model is extended in Alfresco Web Scripts in order to let templates access the repository

You also had a brief introduction to the Atom Publishing Protocol that will be used extensively in the upcoming chapters.

In the next chapter, you are going to learn about programming with JavaScript in Alfresco Web Scripts and the most important objects of the Alfresco JavaScript APIs. Having learned about FreeMarker templates and JavaScript controllers, you should be well equipped to start developing even the most complex Web Script-based applications.

8
Writing a Web Script Controller in JavaScript and Java

After the descriptor and the templates, the third typical element of a Web Script is the controller which is often mostly implemented as a JavaScript program.

Alfresco provides a JavaScript execution environment that is composed of an interpreter and a number of *root* objects that, taken together, make up the Alfresco JavaScript APIs. These APIs let scripts access and manipulate repository objects and present a useful encapsulation of most services provided by the Alfresco repository.

In this chapter, a brief overview of the main concepts of the Alfresco JavaScript APIs will be presented, including:

- Which root objects are available to the scripts for performing operations
- General scripting techniques, such as including libraries, logging, and debugging
- Searching the repository using Lucene
- Manipulating nodes and their content
- Augmenting a Web Script controller with Java code

Armed with this knowledge, we will then perform a step-by-step implementation of a simple Web Service.

Providing a Web Script with a JavaScript controller

As we saw in *Chapter 6, Introducing the Web Scripts Framework*, a Web Script may have a controller in the form of a JavaScript program that must be contained in a file called `basename.method.js`.

When the Web Script is invoked, the controller script is executed, and values can be passed by the controller to the template through the `model` variable.

The Alfresco JavaScript implementation is provided by the Mozilla Rhino interpreter. You can find more information about Mozilla Rhino at its website: `http://www.mozilla.org/rhino`. The version of JavaScript that Mozilla Rhino understands is 1.6.

You are expected to understand a bit of JavaScript syntax in order to be able to follow the code samples that follow. If you are familiar with Java syntax, it shouldn't be a problem, but if you want to become really proficient in JavaScript, there are a number of tutorials available online and books that you can peruse.

Root objects

Every controller script in an Alfresco Web Script has access to a number of so-called root-scoped objects that it can use to access the underlying Alfresco Foundation Services.

The root-scoped objects are JavaScript objects that wrap the Foundation Services, which are Java objects whose public methods are not always suitable for calling directly from JavaScript code. This is why Alfresco created the JavaScript APIs to provide JavaScript code with usable interfaces and, sometimes, to implement higher-level functionalities on top of lower-level ones.

The set of root-scoped objects that implement the Alfresco JavaScript API is similar to the one available to templates and introduced in *Chapter 6, Introducing the Web Scripts Framework*, with the important difference that the JavaScript API allows the manipulation of repository nodes; that is, creating, updating, and deleting them, not just reading them.

At the time of writing this chapter, the most up-to-date reference of the Alfresco JavaScript API is available online on the Alfresco wiki at `http://wiki.alfresco.com/wiki/3.3_JavaScript_API`.

General scripting techniques

In this section, we introduce a number of techniques that are useful for making your scripts more modular and easier to diagnose and debug.

Importing scripts

One of the foremost principles of good programming practice is avoiding the duplication of code. Following this principle leads to the need for defining reusable portions of code and making them available to other code.

In the Alfresco scripting environment, you can put the reusable code in separate files, either on the Java `classpath` or in the repository, and import them where needed by using the `import` tag:

```
<import resource="location">
```

The value of location can be either a name-based path as:

```
<import resource="/Company Home/Data Dictionary/Scripts/mylibrary.js">
```

A node reference:

```
<import resource="workspace://SpacesStore/a26150a1-e9a1-4463-be2c-04d65c35d8f8">
```

or a location on the `classpath`:

```
<import resource="classpath:alfresco/extension/scripts/mylibrary.js">.
```

In any case, all of the `import` tags must be at the very beginning of the importing file.

A typical use of the `import` feature is for including libraries of functions. Functions in JavaScript are defined using the `function` keyword:

```
function fib(n){
    return n<2?n:fib(n-1)+fib(n-2);
}
```

Save the previous function definition in a document called `fib.js` inside **Company Home | Data Dictionary | Scripts**, and then create a new Web Script with the following script as the controller:

```
<import resource="/Company Home/Data Dictionary/Scripts/fib.js">

model.fib = [ fib(1), fib(2) , fib(3), fib(4), fib(5), fib(6), fib(7),
fib(8), fib(9), fib(10) ]
```

Use the following code as the template:

```html
<html>
  <body>
    <ul>
      <#list fib as f>
      <li>${f}</li>
      </#list>
    </ul>
  </body>
</html>
```

The following is the output you should get when you execute the Web Script:

```
1
1
2
3
5
8
13
21
34
55
```

Logging

The `logger` object can be used to output messages to the `alfresco.log` file. In order for log messages from scripts to be visible, you need to set the logging level of the JavaScript interpreter to DEBUG, either by editing the `log4j.properties` file (which you can find in `tomcat/webapps/alfresco/WEB-INF/classes` if you are using the Tomcat bundle) or via JMX. If you modify the `log4j.properties` file, it is necessary to restart Tomcat in order for the changes to be applied. In either case, set:

```
log4j.logger.org.alfresco.repo.jscript.ScriptLogger=DEBUG
```

and look for log messages in the `alfresco.log` file.

The logger object exposes only two methods:

```
boolean isLoggingEnabled()
```

It returns true if logging has been configured, as shown before.

```
void log(string)
```

It logs a string message to the log file.

You should always test whether logging is enabled with the former method before wasting unnecessary CPU cycles formatting log messages that nobody will see.

To test that logging works as expected, configure `log4j`, as explained, and add the following lines to the script shown in the preceding section:

```
if (logger.isLoggingEnabled()) {
    logger.log("fib = " + model.fib)
}
```

If you did everything correctly, you should see a message similar to the following, appear in `alfresco.log` when you invoke the script again:

```
17:37:43,593 DEBUG [org.alfresco.repo.jscript.ScriptLogger] fib =
1,1,2,3,5,8,13,21,34,55
```

Debugging

The Mozilla Rhino JavaScript engine includes a handy, interactive debugger. To activate the debugger, navigate to the URL:

`http://localhost:8080/alfresco/service/api/javascript/debugger.`

Now click on the **Enable** button. A window, similar to the one shown in the following screenshot, should pop up:

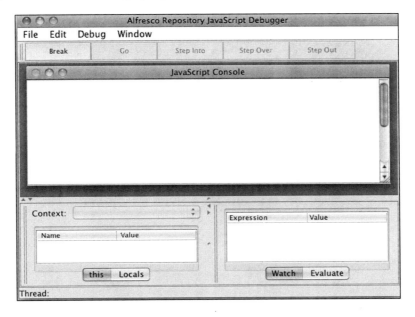

Now, whenever you invoke a Web Script, or any other server-side script, its execution will be suspended at the first JavaScript statement encountered and the debugger window will show the code of the current script, as shown in the following image.

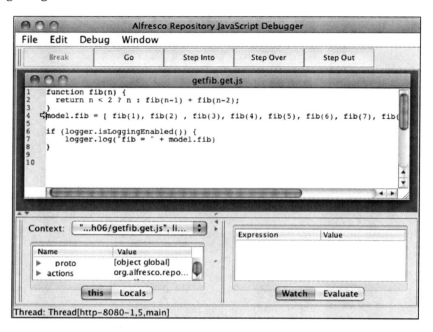

The debugger is now waiting for your input, and you can tell it to continue the execution or to step over code, using the buttons in the toolbar. You can also set breakpoints, examine variables, and evaluate expressions.

 Sometimes, the debugger does not pause at the first statement automatically. We found that you can make it work as expected, in this case, by refreshing the list of existing Web Scripts.

Notice that the JavaScript debugger executes as part of the Alfresco server application. This means that if you are using a remote server, the debugger window will pop up on the server's desktop, not your workstation's desktop. The only way to use the debugger effectively is to run Alfresco on `localhost`.

Searching the repository

One of the most frequently used root objects of the scripting environment is `search`. This object lets you search for nodes across the whole Alfresco repository using a variety of techniques.

The `search` object allows one to do searches using the Lucene search engine, which is embedded in Alfresco and is used for indexing metadata fields and textual content of documents.

It also gives the option of performing searches using the XPath syntax and of accessing and recalling saved searches. In the following sections, we are concerning ourselves only with Lucene searches. If you are interested in XPath queries, you can use the Wiki as a further source of information.

Performing a simple Lucene search

To perform a search using the Lucene syntax, use the `luceneSearch` method of the `search` object. The following snippet will search the repository for all documents containing the phrase "alfresco".

```
var results = search.luceneSearch("TEXT:alfresco")
```

If you wish, you can search only a specific store with the following variant:

```
var results = search.luceneSearch("workspace://SpacesStore", "TEXT:
alfresco")
```

The return value of the method call is an array of nodes that match the specified search criteria. Notice that the list of results is already filtered according to the permissions of the user executing the script. In other words, only nodes that the current user can read are returned; you do not need to filter them yourself or expect permission errors when the user tries to actually access the content or the properties of the nodes.

A primer on Lucene query syntax

The Lucene search engine that is embedded in Alfresco understands a rich and powerful query language that you can use to quickly and easily find documents in Alfresco. The full syntax of the language is described in detail on the Lucene website, `http://lucene.apache.org`.

In order to understand the basics of Lucene, it is important to know that a Lucene search index is a collection of **documents**. Each document is a set of **fields**, that is, name-value pairs.

When you build a Lucene query string, you string together a number of **terms**, possibly using AND rather than OR conjunctions. Each term is written as a field name, followed by a semicolon, and then by a search **phrase**. The following is a term used for searching for occurrences of the phrase "Web Scripts" in the text of Alfresco documents:

```
TEXT:"Web Scripts"
```

Take care to include the search phrase in double quotes. You don't need to do that if the phrase is a single word.

You can combine different terms using AND, OR, and NOT operators:

```
TEXT:"Web Scripts" AND NOT TYPE:"bs:book"
```

You can use wildcards, such as '*' and '?', to perform partial matches. Even though Lucene does not allow you to put a wildcard at the beginning of a phrase, Alfresco has extended Lucene to let you do just that:

```
TEXT:"*lfresco"
```

If your search term does not include a field name, Lucene will use the so-called *default* field. In Alfresco, the default field is TEXT. Therefore, the search term "alfresco" is interpreted as "TEXT:alfresco".

Fields in the Alfresco index

When Alfresco indexes a node, it stores it in the Lucene index as a set of fields that include TEXT, TYPE, PATH, and a number of other fields that are documented on the Alfresco wiki.

In addition, it stores a field for every metadata property for which the domain model specifies that the field needs to be indexed:

```
<property name="cm:title">
<index enabled="true">
```

The name of the field is the property's name, prefixed by '@' and the namespace prefix. Take care that, when writing queries using metadata fields, the semicolon used to separate the prefix from the local name of the property is not interpreted by Lucene as the separator between the field name and the search phrase. In order to avoid this, you need to escape the first semicolon:

```
@cm\:title:"the catcher in the rye"
```

Sorting results

Search results can be sorted based on the value of a property, by using the following method:

```
Array luceneSearch(string store, string query, string sortColumn,
boolean asc)
```

Or one of its variants, which assume default values for the missing arguments:

```
Array luceneSearch(string query)
Array luceneSearch(string store, string query)
Array luceneSearch(string query, string sortColumn, boolean asc)
```

The `asc` argument can be used to specify that the results have to be returned in ascending order if `true` is passed as the actual value, or descending if `false` is passed. The following call, copied from the example in *Chapter 6*, will return all nodes under **Company Home | Guest Home**, from the most recently to the least recently modified one.

```
var results =
    search.luceneSearch(
        'PATH:"/app:company_home/app:guest_home/*"',
        "@cm:modified",
        false)
```

The ScriptNode API

Many of the JavaScript root-scoped objects, such as `companyhome`, `userhome`, `person`, and a number of other objects returned from method calls performed on root objects, such as search results, are of a type meant to represent a node in the repository. This type is called **ScriptNode**.

All ScriptNodes support the same set of properties and methods. In the upcoming sections, we give a brief list of the most relevant properties used for obtaining information about nodes and of the methods typically used for manipulating nodes.

The ScriptNode API is similar to the TemplateNode API that was described in *Chapter 7, Templating with FreeMarker*. So you can expect that most of the properties and methods listed there will work on ScriptNodes too. What the ScriptNode API gives you, in addition, is the possibility of actually modifying the contents of the repository, and not just reading them.

Properties of nodes

You can read and modify properties of nodes by accessing the `properties` associative array of every ScriptNode. This array contains all the metadata for a given node, indexed by the property name.

In Alfresco, properties defined as part of a type definition have a name that is composed of a namespace URI and of a local part. Therefore, the most precise and unambiguous way to access a given property's value would be the following:

```
node.properties["{http://www.alfresco.org/model/content/1.0}modified"]
```

As this can be a bit unwieldy, using the namespace prefix is allowed:

```
node.properties["cm:modified"]
```

For properties that are defined in the default Alfresco content model, which have names belonging to the `http://www.alfresco.org/model/content/1.0` namespace, you can leave out the prefix:

```
node.properties["modified"]
```

This can be simplified further, if the property name is a valid JavaScript identifier, as follows:

```
node.properties.modified
```

Writing properties

Properties of nodes can be added or modified by setting the corresponding value in the `properties` array:

```
node.properties.title = "Gravity's Rainbow"
```

Notice that when this line of code is executed, Alfresco does not immediately write the new property value to the node. This only happens when you call:

```
node.save()
```

It is easy to forget to add this call and then wonder why the actual node's properties are not set.

Navigating the repository

You can navigate up and down the tree of folders and documents by accessing the `children` and `parent` properties of a ScriptNode. For instance, to list all children of a node, you can use the following code:

```
for each (child in node.children) {
    logger.log(child.name)
}
```

Instead of accessing the immediate children of a node, you can also find nodes deeper in the hierarchy by using the `childByNamePath` method:

```
var templatesFolder = companyhome.childByNamePath("Data Dictionary/
Templates")
```

The `childrenByXPath` method works exactly as in the TemplateNode API.

You can also use the `assocs` property to follow associations from one node to another.

Performing operations on nodes

Besides modifying a node's properties, as explained before, there are many other things that you can do to nodes, including creating and deleting them.

Creating new nodes

New folders and documents are created by calling the `createFolder` and `createFile` methods of the ScriptNode interface, respectively. You just need to specify the name of the new folder or file. These methods return a ScriptNode representing the newly created node:

```
var letters = userhome.createFolder("Correspondence")
var newFile = letters.createFile("A New Letter")
```

If you need to create a node of a type which is neither `cm:folder` nor `cm:content`, you can do so by invoking the `createNode` method:

```
var newnode = userhome.createNode("foo.txt", "my:nodeType")
```

Other variants of the `createNode` method let you specify an initial set of properties for the new node or a specific type of association to be used for linking the parent to the new child, instead of the default `cm:contains`.

A full reference of all methods that can be used to modify and create content can be found online at http://wiki.alfresco.com/wiki/3.3_JavaScript_API#Modifying_and_Creating_API.

Deleting nodes

You can remove a node from the repository by calling its `remove` method. You can also remove a node from the list of its parent's children by calling:

```
parent.removeNode(child)
```

This will not cause the child to be deleted, unless the parent happens to be the *primary* one.

> Child nodes in Alfresco can have more than one parent. Only one of them, the one under which the node was first created, is considered its *primary* parent.

Copying and moving nodes

You create a copy of a node in another folder by invoking the `copy` method. This copies `node` to your user's home folder:

```
var copy = node.copy(userhome, true)
```

The second argument to the method call is used to specify whether this is a **deep copy** operation or not: if `true` is passed, children of the node are copied too.

Nodes can be moved to another folder by using the `move(ScriptNode destination)` method.

Manipulating content

Using the ScriptNode APIs, you can manipulate the content of Alfresco documents (nodes of type `cm:content`) or of any custom type that has a property of type `cm:content`. You do so by accessing, either for reading or for writing, the `content` property of a ScriptNode.

```
node.content = "some text"
var txt = node.content
```

The `content` property is of string type, so it is suitable for embedding directly in templates, when the type of a document is text-based (plain text, HTML, XML, and so on).

You can also manipulate textual content using string operators, as shown here:

```
// Append some text to the end of a document
document.content += "\r\nAppended text.\r\n"
```

Care should be taken when manipulating content as if it were a string that the document actually contains text and not binary data. You should check the value of the mimetype property of the node:

```
if (document.mimetype == "text/plain") {
  // … do something with content
}
```

You should also check the character set used to encode the textual content, especially if you want to embed it in a web page that is served using a different encoding, as this is likely to cause troubles with international characters. You can do so by reading the value of the encoding property of the node.

When the content is not of a textual nature, you should not manipulate it as if it were a string, nor try to embed it in a web page. In this case, you will probably want to provide a download link by embedding in the page the value of the url property:

```
<a href="${document.url}">Download</a>
```

About the only other thing you can do to binary content using the JavaScript APIs is copying a node's content to another node. This operation is performed using the write method:

```
thisNode.write(otherNode.content)
```

More complex operations on binary content, such as transformations or conversions, should probably be carried out in Java code, as JavaScript is not suitable for the manipulation of huge quantities of binary data. You can also build Alfresco extension components, such as custom transformers and metadata extractors, to achieve this.

A step-by-step example—posting reviews

This section introduces a complete, working implementation of a simple use case for our Alfresco Bookshop application that was introduced in the preceding chapters.

Requirements

We are tasked with developing a Web Service that lets client applications post reviews of the books present in the bookshop.

Reviews need to have a reviewer's name and e-mail address, some text, and a rating expressed as a number between 1 and 5.

It should not be possible for someone to write more than one review for a single book.

We are going to satisfy these requirements in stages, starting with a simpler version that does not bother to check that someone is trying to review a book twice. We will add this feature in a second version.

For the sake of simplicity, we are also not going to check the validity of the request submitted by the client. In the real world, you should always check your inputs thoroughly to defend against malicious, or simply mistaken, clients.

The protocol

Clients are expected to create a new review by posting a request to a URI that represents the collection of reviews for a given book. We are going to use the ISBN number to identify a book, so we will use the following URI template in our descriptor:

```
/books/{isbn}/reviews/
```

When a client posts a request and the server successfully creates a new review, the server will reply with an HTTP status code of **201 Created**. The response will contain a `Location` header that links to a suitable representation of the newly created review:

```
HTTP/1.1 201 Created
```

```
Location: http://localhost:8080/alfresco/service/books/978-1-849511-52-0/
reviews/1262534379466.json
```

Representations

We want our Web Service to support two different representation formats for reviews, namely, JSON and Atom entries. JSON is particularly suitable for clients written in JavaScript and is arguably simpler than Atom, so we will stick to JSON only in our first version.

The Alfresco Web Scripts runtime provides some helper objects for dealing easily with JSON and Atom requests, so you will not have to write a parser yourself or re-use a third-party one.

Implementing the first version

For our first version, we need a custom domain model that defines suitable content types for books and reviews, then we'll create a Web Script that satisfies the initial requirements.

If you are not familiar with the way Alfresco custom domain models are defined, it would be a good time now to read a good tutorial on the subject, for example, `http://wiki.alfresco.com/wiki/Data_Dictionary_Guide` or the excellent article by *Jeff Potts*, *Working with Custom Content Types*, which is available online at `http://ecmarchitect.com/archives/2007/06/09/756`.

Extending the content model

In *Chapter 4*, we introduced a custom domain model for representing books and reviews, by extending the built-in Alfresco content model. In order to save you the hassle of having to go back and forth between chapters to consult the model, we are reprinting it here in its entirety:

```xml
<?xml version="1.0" encoding="UTF-8"?>

<!-- Bookshop Model -->

<model name="bs:bookshopModel" xmlns="http://www.alfresco.org/model/
dictionary/1.0">

    <description>Bookshop Model for the A3WS Samples</description>
    <author>Ugo Cei, Piergiorgio Lucidi</author>
    <version>1.0</version>

    <imports>
        <import uri="http://www.alfresco.org/model/dictionary/1.0"
prefix="d"/>
        <import uri="http://www.alfresco.org/model/content/1.0"
prefix="cm"/>
    </imports>

    <namespaces>
        <namespace uri="http://www.packtpub.com/a3ws/samples/bookshop"
prefix="bs"/>
    </namespaces>

    <types>
```

```xml
<type name="bs:book">
   <title>Book</title>
   <parent>cm:content</parent>
   <properties>
      <property name="bs:isbn">
         <title>ISBN</title>
         <type>d:text</type>
         <mandatory>true</mandatory>
         <index enabled="true">
            <atomic>true</atomic>
            <stored>false</stored>
            <tokenised>false</tokenised>
         </index>
      </property>
      <property name="bs:publisher">
         <title>Publisher</title>
         <type>d:text</type>
         <mandatory>true</mandatory>
      </property>
      <property name="bs:author">
         <title>Author</title>
         <type>d:text</type>
         <mandatory>true</mandatory>
         <multiple>true</multiple>
      </property>
      <property name="bs:price">
         <title>Price</title>
         <type>d:float</type>
         <mandatory>false</mandatory>
      </property>
   </properties>
   <associations>
      <child-association name="bs:reviews">
         <source>
            <mandatory>false</mandatory>
            <many>true</many>
         </source>
         <target>
            <class>bs:review</class>
            <mandatory>false</mandatory>
            <many>true</many>
         </target>
      </child-association>
   </associations>
</type>
```

```
<type name="bs:review">
    <title>Review</title>
    <parent>cm:content</parent>
    <properties>
        <property name="bs:reviewer_name">
            <title>Reviewer's name</title>
            <type>d:text</type>
            <mandatory>true</mandatory>
        </property>
        <property name="bs:reviewer_email">
            <title>Reviewer's email</title>
            <type>d:text</type>
            <mandatory>true</mandatory>
        </property>
        <property name="bs:review_rating">
            <title>Rating</title>
            <type>d:int</type>
            <mandatory>true</mandatory>
        </property>
        <property name="bs:approved">
            <title>Approved</title>
            <type>d:boolean</type>
            <mandatory enforced="true">true</mandatory>
            <default>false</default>
        </property>
    </properties>
</type>

</types>

</model>
```

Configuring the Alfresco Explorer

We also need a bit of Alfresco Explorer customization in order to be able to create documents of the type "Book" and display their properties:

```
<alfresco-config>

    <config evaluator="string-compare" condition="Content Wizards">
        <content-types>
            <type name="bs:book" />
        </content-types>
    </config>
```

```
<config evaluator="node-type" condition="bs:book">
   <property-sheet>
      <show-property name="bs:isbn" />
      <show-property name="bs:publisher" />
      <show-property name="bs:author" />
      <show-property name="bs:price" />
      <show-child-association name="bs:reviews" />
   </property-sheet>
</config>

<config evaluator="node-type" condition="bs:review">
   <property-sheet>
      <show-property name="bs:reviewer_name" />
      <show-property name="bs:reviewer_email" />
      <show-property name="bs:review_rating" />
      <show-property name="bs:approved" />
   </property-sheet>
</config>

</alfresco-config>
```

You should be able to deploy a custom model and an extended Explorer configuration. If you need to refresh your memory on how to do it, refer to the Alfresco documentation online or to the *Alfresco Developer Guide* book by *Jeff Potts* from Packt Publishing.

It is now possible to create a new book using the Explorer. Be sure to select the **Book** content type when uploading a document:

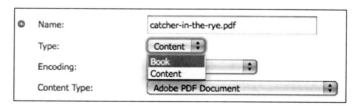

Creating the Web Script descriptor

Our descriptor is very similar to the ones that you have already seen. Save it in a file called `review.post.desc.xml`, as we specified that the client uses the POST method to create reviews:

```
<webscript>
  <shortname>Post Book Review</shortname>
  <description>Post a Review to a Book</description>
  <url>/books/{isbn}/reviews</url>
  <authentication>user</authentication>
  <transaction>required</transaction>
  <format default="json">any</format>
</webscript>
```

Creating the controller

Normally, you would name the controller script file `review.post.js`, but here we are going to do something different. Our controller will be named `review.post.json.js`.

If you do so, and if the request body is a JSON document, the set of root objects accessible from the controller will include one more (called `json`) that provides a convenient way to read the properties of the JSON object (or array of objects) represented in the request.

Finding the book

Remember that the URI template we specified for our Web Script is `/books/{isbn}/reviews`. We can use the `templateArgs` variable to retrieve the values of the various variable parts of the actual URI such as `isbn`:

```
var isbn = url.templateArgs.isbn
```

Once we have the ISBN, we use it to search for the corresponding book (we assume that the ISBN is unique among all books):

```
var results = search.luceneSearch("@bs\\:isbn:" + isbn)
```

We need to check that there actually is a book with the given ISBN. If there isn't, we return a suitable error response to the client:

```
if (results.length <= 0) {
    status.code = 404 // Not Found
    status.message = "No book with ISBN " + isbn + " found."
    status.redirect = true
}
```

Creating the review

Here is the code for creating a new node of type bs:review, as a child of the book we just found. We use the current time, in milliseconds, to create an identifier for the review:

```
var book = results[0]
var id = new Date().getTime()
var review = book.createNode(id, "bs:review", [], "bs:reviews")
review.mimetype = "text/plain"
review.content = json.get("content")
```

The fourth argument passed to the createNode method is the name of the association created between the book and the review, bs:reviews, as specified by our custom content model.

We store the text of the review as the document's content, that's why we specify a MIME type of text/plain. The text itself is read from the content property of the JSON object.

Setting the review's properties

We could have passed all the properties of the review in the initial createNode call, but we chose to do it later only because we find it more readable this way:

```
review.properties["cm:title"] = json.get("title")
review.properties["bs:reviewer_name"] = json.get("author").get("name")
review.properties["bs:reviewer_email"] = json.get("author").
get("email")
review.properties["bs:rating"] = json.get("rating")
review.save()
```

Just remember to call the save method at the end to persist all changes to the properties.

Returning the response

As per the protocol we described earlier, we return a 201 Created response in case of success.

```
status.code = 201 // Created
status.location = url.server + url.serviceContext + "/books/" + isbn +
"/reviews/" + id + ".json";
status.redirect = true
```

The value of the `Location` header will look as shown in the following code:

```
http://localhost:8080/alfresco/service/books/978-0316769488/
reviews/1262539260503.json
```

While this is not part of the example, there should be a Web Script that responds to that request URI and returns a JSON representation of the review.

This concludes our controller, which is listed here in its entirety:

```
var isbn = url.templateArgs.isbn
var results = search.luceneSearch("@bs\\:isbn:" + isbn)
if (results.length <= 0) {
    status.code = 404 // Not Found
    status.message = "No book with ISBN " + isbn + " found."
    status.redirect = true
} else {
    if (json != undefined) {
        var book = results[0]
        var id = new Date().getTime()
        var review = book.createNode(id, "bs:review", [], "bs:
reviews")
        review.mimetype = "text/plain"
        review.content = json.get("content")
        review.properties["cm:title"] = json.get("title")
        review.properties["bs:reviewer_name"] = json.get("author").
get("name")
        review.properties["bs:reviewer_email"] = json.get("author").
get("email")
        review.properties["bs:rating"] = json.get("rating")
        review.save()
        status.code = 201 // Created
        status.location = url.server + url.serviceContext + "/books/"
+ isbn + "/reviews/" + id + ".json";
        status.redirect = true
    } else {
        status.code = 400 // Bad Request
        status.message = "Format of request not recognized"
        status.redirect = true
    }
}
```

Creating the template

When the client succeeds in posting a new review, the server redirects it to the location of the review by means of the `Location` HTTP header. It does not need to read the server's response, so the server might as well not provide any. The best way to do so is to create an empty file and name it `review.post.json.201.ftl`.

 This style of interaction, whereby the server sends back an empty response with a `Location` header in response to a `POST`, is sometimes called the **post-redirect-get** pattern. The server does not send back a representation of the newly created entity in the response because the client might be tempted to resubmit the request in case it could not read the response. However, this would cause another entity to be created, which is not what we want. The client must issue a `GET` request to the redirect URL. The `GET` request is idempotent and can therefore be issued as many times as needed.

For all other result codes, Alfresco will use a default fallback template. You might want to provide a custom one, if you wish to serve a specific response in case of an error.

Testing the Web Script

The easiest way to test our Web Script is probably to use the `curl` command-line utility. Just create a JSON file (call it `review.json`) with some review data:

```
{
   author: {
      name: "John Doe",
      email: "johndoe@example.com"
   },
   title: "A timeless masterpiece",
   content: "The quick brown fox jumps over the lazy dog.",
   rating: 5
}
```

Then post it with `curl`:

```
curl -v -u admin:admin -d @review.json -H 'Content-Type:application/json'
http://localhost:8080/alfresco/service/books/978-0316769488/reviews
```

This is the kind of output you should see:

```
* About to connect() to localhost port 8080 (#0)
*   Trying ::1... connected
* Connected to localhost (::1) port 8080 (#0)
* Server auth using Basic with user 'admin'
> POST /alfresco/service/books/978-0316769488/reviews HTTP/1.1
> Authorization: Basic YWRtaW46YWRtaW4=
> User-Agent: curl/7.19.4 (universal-apple-darwin10.0) libcurl/7.19.4
OpenSSL/0.9.8k zlib/1.2.3
> Host: localhost:8080
> Accept: */*
> Content-Type:application/json
> Content-Length: 177
>
< HTTP/1.1 201 Created
< Server: Apache-Coyote/1.1
< Cache-Control: no-cache
< Pragma: no-cache
< Location: http://localhost:8080/alfresco/service/books/978-0316769488/
reviews/1262541153459.json
< Content-Type: application/json;charset=UTF-8
< Content-Length: 0
< Date: Sun, 03 Jan 2010 17:52:33 GMT
<
* Connection #0 to host localhost left intact
* Closing connection #0
```

The review you just created is not directly visible in the Alfresco Explorer, as it is not contained in any folder. You could make it a child of some folder, if you want, but using the Explorer to navigate reviews is not required for this application, so we did not consider this.

You can always use the Node Browser to find the node representing the book and, from there, navigate to its child reviews and check that their properties and their content are as expected.

Using Atom

Even though JSON is arguably much simpler, we want to demonstrate what it would take to implement the same use case, but allowing the client to send the review as an Atom entry instead.

We have already briefly introduced Atom and the Atom Publishing Protocol in the previous chapter, when we talked about the Categories document. In this chapter, we will use another bit of Atom, namely, an **Entry** document, deferring a complete presentation of Atom and AtomPub to the next chapter.

Anatomy of an Atom entry

The following example shows how we could represent a review as an Atom entry:

```
<?xml version="1.0"?>
<entry xmlns="http://www.w3.org/2005/Atom"
       xmlns:bs="http://www.packtpub.com/a3ws/samples/bookshop">
  <title>A timeless masterpiece</title>
  <id>urn:uuid:1225c695-cfb8-4ebb-aaaa-80da344efa6a</id>
  <updated>2003-12-13T18:30:02Z</updated>
  <author>
    <name>John Doe</name>
    <email>johndoe@example.com</email>
  </author>
  <content type="text">The quick brown fox jumps over the lazy dog.</
content>
  <bs:rating>5</bs:rating>
</entry>
```

We mapped most of the properties of a review, such as title, author, and text, to basic Atom entry elements, namely, `title`, `author`, and `content`. We had to use an extension element, `bs:rating`, to represent the reviewer's given rating, which does not map clearly to an existing entry element.

The Atom syndication format mandates that all entries must have an `id` element and an `updated` element. A server implementing the Atom Publishing Protocol is free to ignore those, and this is what we will do in this case. However, the client still has to include them, so we just used random values.

Save this example to a file named `review.atom.xml`, since you are going to use it in a while to test your new service.

A controller that accepts Atom entries

The new controller is a modified version of the one shown before, which accepted JSON documents. Add this one to your Web Script as `review.post.atom.js` and refresh the list of Web Scripts:

```
var isbn = url.templateArgs.isbn
var results = search.luceneSearch("@bs\\:isbn:" + isbn)
if (results.length <= 0) {
    status.code = 404 // Not Found
    status.message = "No book with ISBN " + isbn + " found."
    status.redirect = true
} else {
    if (entry != null) {
        var book = results[0]
        var id = new Date().getTime()
        var review = book.createNode(id, "bs:review", [], "bs:
reviews")
        review.mimetype = "text/plain"
        review.content = entry.content
        review.properties["cm:title"] = entry.title
        review.properties["bs:reviewer_name"] = entry.author.name
        review.properties["bs:reviewer_email"] = entry.author.email
        var ratingQName = new Packages.javax.xml.namespace.
QName("http://www.packtpub.com/a3ws/samples/bookshop", "rating", "bs")
        var rating = entry.getExtension(ratingQName);
        if (rating != null) {
            review.properties["bs:rating"] = rating.text
        }
        review.save()
        status.code = 201 // Created
        status.location = url.server + url.serviceContext + "/books/"
+ isbn + "/reviews/" + id + ".atom";
        status.redirect = true
    } else {
        status.code = 400 // Bad Request
        status.message = "Format of request not recognized"
        status.redirect = true
    }
}
```

Notice that when the Alfresco Web Scripts framework detects that the request contains an Atom entry document, it will automatically add to the script context an object named `entry`. This is actually an instance of `org.apache.abdera.model. Entry`, a class included in the Apache Abdera library, which is distributed as part of Alfresco.

The correct `MIME` type for an Atom entry is `application/atom+xml;type=entry`, so this is what we need to specify when we want to post a new review as an Atom entry:

```
curl -v -u admin:admin -d @review.atom.xml -H 'Content-Type:application/
atom+xml;type=entry' http://localhost:8080/alfresco/service/books/978-
0316769488/reviews.xml
```

This concludes the implementation of the first version of our Web Service.

Checking for duplicate reviews

We now need to modify our Web Script so that it doesn't allow people to review the same book twice. For this, we will use the reviewer's e-mail address as a user identifier.

Of course, this is very unsecure, as it allows anyone to post any number of reviews and artificially inflate (or deflate) the ratings of a book, simply by using a huge number of fake e-mail addresses. As previously mentioned, we are not interested in security at this stage, and we basically trust the client, which has to authenticate anyway.

Finding duplicates

Finding out whether a given user has already created a review for a given book is easy using Lucene. Here is a function that does just that:

```
function checkDuplicateReview(book, email) {
    var query = '@bs\\:reviewer_email:"' + email +
        '" AND PARENT:"' + book.nodeRef + '"'
    var results = search.luceneSearch(query)
    return results.length > 0
}
```

Basically, we search for nodes having the `bs:reviewer_email` property equal to the value of the `email` parameter and which are children of the `book` node. Remember that in our domain model, reviews are associated to books by means of a parent-child association.

Store this function in a file called `reviewLib.js`, because you are going to need it in a while.

The revised controller

We rewrote the controller to include the previous function and we also refactored it a bit in order to avoid having too many nested `if-else` blocks. The Atom version is as follows:

```
<import resource="classpath:alfresco/extension/templates/webscripts/
com/packtpub/aws3/samples/ch07/bookshop/reviewLib.js">

function postReview() {
    var isbn = url.templateArgs.isbn
    var results = search.luceneSearch("@bs\\:isbn:" + isbn)
    if (results.length <= 0) {
        status.code = 404 // Not Found
        status.message = "No book with ISBN " + isbn + " found."
        status.redirect = true
        return
    }
    if (entry != null) {
        var email = entry.author.email
        var book = results[0]
        if (checkDuplicateReview(book, email)) {
            status.code = 400 // Bad Request
            status.message = "Attempt to post a duplicate review
detected"
            status.redirect = true
            return
        }
        var id = new Date().getTime()
        var review = book.createNode(id, "bs:review", [], "bs:
reviews")
        review.mimetype = "text/plain"
        review.content = entry.content
        review.properties["cm:title"] = entry.title
        review.properties["bs:reviewer_name"] = entry.author.name
        review.properties["bs:reviewer_email"] = email
        var ratingQName = new Packages.javax.xml.namespace.
QName("http://www.packtpub.com/a3ws/samples/bookshop", "rating", "bs")
        var rating = entry.getExtension(ratingQName);
        if (rating != null) {
            review.properties["bs:rating"] = rating.text
        }
        review.save()
        status.code = 201 // Created
        status.location = url.server + url.serviceContext + "/books/"
+ isbn + "/reviews/" + id + ".atom";
        status.redirect = true
```

```
        } else {
            status.code = 400 // Bad Request
            status.message = "Format of request not recognized"
            status.redirect = true
        }
    }

    postReview()
```

Now, when you try to post a review twice, this is the response that you will get:

```
< Server: Apache-Coyote/1.1
< Cache-Control: no-cache
< Pragma: no-cache
< Content-Type: text/xml;charset=UTF-8
< Content-Length: 446
< Date: Wed, 06 Jan 2010 17:02:33 GMT
< Connection: close
<
<?xml version="1.0" encoding="UTF-8"?>
<response>
  <status>
    <code>400</code>
    <name>Bad Request</name>
    <description>Request sent by the client was syntactically
incorrect.</description>
  </status>
  <message>Attempt to post a duplicate review detected</message>
  <exception></exception>
</response>
```

Writing Web Scripts in Java

Most of the examples presented in this chapter as well as the following ones make use of the JavaScript language for the implementation of the Web Script controller.

While JavaScript is a powerful and expressive language, there can be some advantages in using a more traditional, compiled programming language, such as Java, to write application logic. You can use your favorite IDE (such as Eclipse, Idea, Netbeans, or others) to write code. You can use unit testing tools, such as JUnit, to test that your code does what it is expected to do. You can directly access the Alfresco Foundation APIs and not only the subset of it that is made available through the JavaScript APIs. In addition to this, you can reuse any one of the myriad of Java libraries that perform every kind of task and are freely available for download and use.

What is more important is that application developers are typically more familiar with Java and the Java APIs than with JavaScript, a language that has traditionally been the domain of Web developers writing scripts to make Web pages more dynamic by manipulating the HTML in the browser.

Another situation where you might want to use Java instead of JavaScript is when you need to stream large quantities of binary data such as videos. The JavaScript language is not particularly well suited for these kinds of tasks.

For all these reasons, it might make sense to implement some of the controller's logic in Java instead of JavaScript. Fortunately, Alfresco makes it easy to do so, and it also allows you to mix Java and JavaScript parts in the same Web Script.

Types of Java-backed Web Scripts

Alfresco provides two ways to implement Web Scripts using Java, depending on which base class you choose to extend: **Abstract** Web Scripts and **Declarative** Web Scripts.

While the former allow maximum flexibility, letting you govern every aspect of the response generation process, the latter trade some flexibility for ease of development and configuration. In the remainder of this section, we will concentrate exclusively on Declarative Web Scripts.

Declarative Web Scripts

A Java-backed Web Script can partially be implemented by a Java class that implements the `org.alfresco.web.scripts.WebScript` interface; directly doing so means having to implement every single aspect of the Web Script in your class. Fortunately, the Alfresco libraries include a base class, called `org.alfresco.web. scripts.DeclarativeWebScript`, that provides some base functionalities and that you can extend instead.

When you want to create a Java-backed, declarative Web Script, you do all the steps described in this chapter and the previous ones: you create a descriptor, a template, and possibly a controller script. In addition, you must compile a Java class that extends the `org.alfresco.web.scripts.DeclarativeWebScript` base class. In your class, you override the `executeImpl` method. The `executeImpl` receives three arguments from the Web Scripts runtime:

- *WebScriptRequest* req: contains information about the request, such as URI, arguments, content, and URI template matching information
- *Status* status: contains information about the status JavaScript variable; this can be used to control the output of the Web Script
- *Cache* cache: used for controlling the HTTP response headers relevant to caching

An example of such a class is displayed here:

```
package com.packtpub.a3ws.samples.ch07;

import java.util.HashMap;
import java.util.Map;

import org.alfresco.web.scripts.Cache;
import org.alfresco.web.scripts.DeclarativeWebScript;
import org.alfresco.web.scripts.Status;
import org.alfresco.web.scripts.WebScriptRequest;

public class HelloWorldJavaWebScript extends DeclarativeWebScript {

    @Override
    protected Map<String, Object> executeImpl(WebScriptRequest req,
    Status status, Cache cache) {
        Map<String, Object> model = new HashMap<String, Object>();
        model.put("message", "Hello, world");
        return model;
    }
}
```

When the Web Script is invoked, the Alfresco dispatcher first invokes the `executeImpl` method of your class, and then executes the JavaScript controller, if present, and finally renders the template.

Your class can add any values to the template's data model, in addition to any values that will be set by the JavaScript controller, by saving them in a Java Map and returning it from the `executeImpl` method just like the previous example.

Wiring the class to the Web Script

When Alfresco looks up the components of a Web Script, controller, and templates, it does so based on a naming convention that is based on the Web Script's identifier, the HTTP method, and the output format. But how does it look up a corresponding Java class, which cannot be named according to this convention?

The answer is that the Alfresco dispatcher does not look for a Java class with a specific name. Instead, it looks for a Spring bean with a name such as `webscript.<package>.<webscript-id>.<method>`, where `package` is the Web Script's own package (derived from the path of the directory where it is found), not the Java class's package.

For instance, if you have a Web Script named `jhello` stored in the `com/packtpub/a3ws/samples/ch07` directory, you need to define a bean in the Spring application context that looks like the following:

```
<bean
  id="webscript.com.packtpub.a3ws.samples.ch07.jhello.get"
  class=
  "com.packtpub.a3ws.samples.ch07.HelloWorldJavaWebScript"
  parent="webscript" />
```

 Remember to include the `parent="webscript"` attribute in the definition.

Of course, as with all Spring beans, you can add to the bean definition any number of references that your Java controller will need, as long as you implement the corresponding setters in the class. An example of such a declaration is shown in the following code:

```
<bean
  id="webscript.com.packtpub.a3ws.samples.ch07.foo.get"
  class=
  "com.packtpub.a3ws.samples.ch07.FooJavaWebScript"
  parent="webscript" />
  <property name="nodeService" ref="NodeService" />
  <property name="contentService" ref="ContentService" />
</bean>
```

Here is the corresponding class:

```
package com.packtpub.a3ws.samples.ch07;

import org.alfresco.web.scripts.DeclarativeWebScript;

public class FooJavaWebScript extends
    DeclarativeWebScript {

    private NodeService nodeService;
    private ContentService contentService;

    public void setNodeService(NodeService ns) {
        nodeService = ns;
    }

    public void setContentService(ContentService cs) {
        contentService = cs;
    }

    protected Map<String, Object> executeImpl
        (WebScriptRequest req,
            Status status, Cache cache) {
    }
}
```

Posting reviews: The Java version

To conclude the topic of writing Web Scripts in Java, we present the Java version of the controller used to accept reviews posted as JSON documents whose JavaScript version was introduced earlier. The following code is of the executeImpl method of the PostReviewJavaWebScript class. The full source code for this example, together with the configuration files, is available for download from the book's website.

```
protected Map<String, Object> executeImpl(
        WebScriptRequest req,
        Status status,
        Cache cache) {

    Map<String, Object> model = new HashMap<String, Object>();

    // Search for the book given the ISBN contained
    // in the request URI
    String isbn =
```

```
        req.getServiceMatch().getTemplateVars().get("isbn");
String query = "@bs\\:isbn:" + isbn;
ResultSet results = searchService.query(store,
    SearchService.LANGUAGE_LUCENE, query);
if (results.length() <= 0) {
    status.setCode(HttpServletResponse.SC_NOT_FOUND);
    status.setRedirect(true);
    return model;
}


// Check that the request body is a JSON document
Object content = req.parseContent();
if (!(content instanceof JSONObject)) {
    status.setCode(HttpServletResponse.SC_BAD_REQUEST);
    status.setRedirect(true);
    return model;
}
JSONObject json = (JSONObject) content;
try {

    // Set a name for the association based on the review's
    // title
    String title = json.getString("title");
    NodeRef book = results.getNodeRef(0);

    // Read the review's properties from the JSON input
    Map<QName, Serializable> properties =
        new HashMap<QName, Serializable>();
    String id = String.valueOf(System.currentTimeMillis());
    QName assocQName = QName.createQName(BOOKSHOP_NS_URI, id);
    properties.put(ContentModel.PROP_NAME, id);
    properties.put(ContentModel.PROP_TITLE, title);
    properties.put(PROP_REVIEWER_NAME,
        json.getJSONObject("author").getString("name"));
    properties.put(PROP_REVIEWER_EMAIL,
        json.getJSONObject("author").getString("email"));
    properties.put(PROP_RATING, json.getInt("rating"));

    // Create the review as a child of the book
    ChildAssociationRef caref = nodeService.createNode(book,
        ASSOC_REVIEWS, assocQName, TYPE_REVIEW, properties);
    NodeRef child = caref.getChildRef();
```

```
        // Write the review's content
        ContentWriter writer = contentService.getWriter(child,
            ContentModel.PROP_CONTENT, true);
        writer.setEncoding("UTF-8");
        writer.setMimetype("text/plain");
        writer.putContent(json.getString("content"));

        // Redirect to the review's URI
        status.setCode(HttpServletResponse.SC_CREATED);
        status.setLocation(req.getServerPath() +
            req.getServiceContextPath() + "/books/" + isbn +
            "/reviews/" + id + ".json");
        status.setRedirect(true);
        return model;
        } catch (JSONException e) {
        status.setCode(HttpServletResponse.SC_BAD_REQUEST);
        status.setRedirect(true);
        status.setException(e);
        return model;
        }
    }
}
```

Summary

This chapter introduced the Alfresco JavaScript APIs, a set of objects and methods that let Web Scripts access and manipulate the Alfresco repository, its content, and the services that it provides.

In this chapter, you saw:

- What we can achieve using the JavaScript scripting. Many more features, of which you can find a detailed reference online, are available to scripts than the ones that are described here.

- A step-by-step implementation of a Web Service that lets client review books present in our imaginary Alfresco Bookshop. With just a handful of lines of JavaScript, we were able to build a service that accepts posted reviews in JSON or in the Atom format, all while adhering to a clean design based on REST principles.

- How it is possible to implement the Web Script controller as a Java class instead of, or in addition to, a JavaScript program.

In the next chapter, we will look at the complete implementation of a RESTful Web Service for manipulating books, composed of a set of Web Scripts.

9
Putting it All Together

In this chapter, you will use the knowledge of the Alfresco Web Scripts framework that you have acquired from the preceding three chapters to implement a RESTful Web Service that lets clients manipulate books in our bookshop using a *CRUD* (Create, Read, Update, Delete) interface.

We will demonstrate an actual, albeit simplified, implementation of the following operations:

- Retrieving a list of books belonging to a category
- Creating a new book
- Uploading a book's content
- Updating a book's metadata and content
- Deleting a book

You will also be able to test that the service is working according to the specifications, using a command-line tool and writing Java client code as well.

The Atom Publishing Protocol

The Atom Publishing Protocol is a RESTful protocol for publishing resources, such as blog entries, news articles, multi-media files, and documents over the Internet. We decided to reuse this protocol for implementing our Bookshop service, instead of inventing one specifically for this application.

A bit of history

In July 2005, the **Internet Engineering Task Force (IETF)**, which is the organization tasked with developing and promoting new Internet standards, published a **Request For Comments (RFC)** document titled *The Atom Syndication Format*.

This document, which is identified as RFC 4287, specifies "Atom is an XML-based Web content and metadata syndication format".

As the introduction explains, Atom is an XML format for representing collections of Web resources to give an example such as blog entries and news headlines. It plays a role in syndication applications, very similar to the one played by the **RSS** format, which pre-dated Atom. However, it does so in a way that is much more rigorously specified and, therefore, avoids a lot of the ambiguities inherent in RSS.

Atom has been a successful format since its inception, and is nowadays supported by many websites and by virtually all existing syndication applications.

Enter AtomPub

In October 2007, the IETF published the second of the two Atom specifications. This one, dubbed RFC 5023 and titled *The Atom Publishing Protocol*, builds on top of the former with the aim of turning the world of syndication from being essentially read-only to being a read-write medium.

Using only the Atom Syndication format, applications are limited to reading feeds and, possibly, transforming and aggregating them. On the contrary, using the Atom Publishing Protocol (**AtomPub**, for short), applications can now create new Web resources by posting their representations to collections or updating and deleting existing resources.

AtomPub does all of this by adhering, as closely as possible, to the principles of the REST architectural style that was described in *Chapter 6, Introducing the Web Scripts Framework*.

AtomPub-enabled applications interact by transferring representations of resources identified by proper URIs. They use the four basic HTTP verbs—GET, POST, PUT, and DELETE, as intended. They exchange metadata and control information using HTTP headers and follow explicit links to manipulate an application's state.

AtomPub concepts

The Atom Publishing Protocol specification deals with the concepts such as resources and entries, collection of resources, and feeds.

Resources and entries

An Atom-enabled server exposes a number of objects, known as **resources**, to the external world. In the context of a Content Management System, such as Alfresco, these resources could be anything, from documents to folders, persons, saved searches, categories, and more.

Every resource must be identified by a URI (technically, the Atom specification talks about **IRIs**, that is, **Internationalized Resource Identifiers**, but we can ignore that distinction for the moment).

 Note that using the Alfresco `NodeRef` as a URI would not be permitted, as a `NodeRef` is not a valid URI, though it might resemble one. The reason is that the store protocol (for example, `workspace` or `avm`) that begins a `NodeRef` is not a URI scheme registered with the **Internet Assigned Numbers Authority (IANA)**.

In Atom, resources are represented as entries. An Atom entry is an XML element that looks like the following:

```
<entry xmlns="http://www.w3.org/2005/Atom">
<title>Atom-Powered Robots Run Amok</title>
<link href="http://example.org/2003/12/13/atom03"/>
<id>urn:uuid:1225c695-cfb8-4ebb-aaaa-80da344efa6a</id>
<updated>2003-12-13T18:30:02Z</updated>
<summary>Some text.</summary>
<author>
    <name>John Doe</name>
</author>
</entry>
```

Every valid Atom entry *must* have the `id`, `updated`, and `author` elements. Valid Atom entries must also have either of a `content` element or a `link` element with a relation type (as specified by the `rel` attribute) of `alternate`. The value `alternate` for the relation type of links is the default one, assumed in case the attribute is missing, as in the previous example.

An example of an entry having a content element that points to the URL of the binary stream representing the actual contents of the resource, a PDF document in this case, could be written as follows:

```
<entry xmlns="http://www.w3.org/2005/Atom">
<author>
    <name>John Doe</name>
</author>
    <content type="application/pdf"
        src="http://localhost:8080/…/content.pdf"/>
<id>urn:uuid:a68530a3-bdd4-4d5f-865a-45e154e80f92</id>
<title>document.pdf</title>
<summary>A random PDF document</summary>
<updated>2010-02-20T15:38:24.028+01:00</updated>
</entry>
```

When thinking of Alfresco nodes as resources, it is natural to represent them as Atom entries containing all, or a subset, of their metadata. A document node, when represented as an Atom entry, will have a content element pointing to the document's content stream.

Extensions

In the previous examples shown, we were able to represent some of the typical properties of Alfresco nodes, such as title, description, author, modified, as Atom entry elements, namely, title, summary, author, and updated. The set of possible elements of an Atom entry, however, is limited, and we can't think of mapping every imaginable Alfresco node property, including custom ones, to Atom elements.

The solution to this problem resides in using extension elements belonging to foreign namespaces, different from the http://www.w3.org/2005/Atom namespace to which the Atom-defined elements belong.

Let's imagine that you wanted to include in your entries a link to the icon representing the node's type. As there is no standard Atom element for icons, what you can do is define your own namespace, such as http://www.alfresco.org, and add an icon element belonging to that namespace to your entries:

```
<entry xmlns="http://www.w3.org/2005/Atom"
        xmlns:alf="http://www.alfresco.org">
<author>
    <name>John Doe</name>
</author>
<content type="application/pdf"
    src="http://localhost:8080/…/content.pdf"/>
```

```
<id>urn:uuid:a68530a3-bdd4-4d5f-865a-45e154e80f92</id>
<title>document.pdf</title>
<summary>A random PDF document</summary>
<updated>2010-02-20T15:38:24.028+01:00</updated>
    <alf:icon>
    http://localhost:8080/alfresco/images/filetypes/pdf.gif
    </alf:icon>
</entry>
```

This is more than a hypothetical example: Entries produced by the Alfresco CMIS service typically include the `alf:icon` element, as previously shown.

CMIS itself, as we will see, defines a number of Atom extension elements using the following two namespace declarations:

```
xmlns:cmis="http://docs.oasis-open.org/ns/cmis/core/200908/"
```

and:

```
xmlns:cmisra=
    "http://docs.oasis-open.org/ns/cmis/restatom/200908/"
```

Collections and feeds

A collection is a concept that can have many practical applications in a content management system. All the children of a space in Alfresco naturally form a collection. You can have a collection of search results, users, categories, types, and possibly others.

Using Atom, collections are represented as feeds. An Atom **feed** is an XML document whose root element is called `feed` and whose children can be metadata elements describing the feed itself, such as `title`, `id`, `updated`, `generator`, in addition to zero or more `entry` elements like the ones we saw in the preceding section.

In other words, a feed represents a collection of resources as a list of entries, with some additional metadata about the collection itself. Here's an example of an Atom feed containing a single entry, taken verbatim from the text of RFC 4287:

```
<feed xmlns="http://www.w3.org/2005/Atom">
<title type="text">dive into mark</title>
<subtitle type="html">
A &lt;em&gt;lot&lt;/em&gt; of effort went into making
  this effortless
</subtitle>
<updated>2005-07-31T12:29:29Z</updated>
<id>tag:example.org,2003:3</id>
```

```
<link rel="alternate" type="text/html" hreflang="en"
href="http://example.org/"/>
<link rel="self" type="application/atom+xml"
 href="http://example.org/feed.atom"/>
<rights>Copyright (c) 2003, Mark Pilgrim</rights>
<generator uri="http://www.example.com/"
  version="1.0">Example Toolkit</generator>
<entry>
<title>Atom draft-07 snapshot</title>
<link rel="alternate" type="text/html"
href="http://example.org/2005/04/02/atom"/>
        <link rel="enclosure" type="audio/mpeg" length="1337"
        href="http://example.org/audio/ph34r_my_podcast.mp3"/>
        <id>tag:example.org,2003:3.2397</id>
        <updated>2005-07-31T12:29:29Z</updated>
        <published>2003-12-13T08:29:29-04:00</published>
        <author>
            <name>Mark Pilgrim</name>
            <uri>http://example.org/</uri>
            <email>f8dy@example.com</email>
        </author>
        <contributor>
            <name>Sam Ruby</name>
        </contributor>
        <contributor>
            <name>Joe Gregorio</name>
        </contributor>
        <content type="xhtml" xml:lang="en"
        xml:base="http://diveintomark.org/">
            <div xmlns="http://www.w3.org/1999/xhtml">
                <p><i>[Update: The Atom draft is
                finished.]</i></p>
            </div>
        </content>
    </entry>
</feed>
```

Notice that, in this example, the feed has two link elements: One with a relationship type of `self` and another one with a relationship type of `alternate`. The former always points to the URL from which a client can retrieve the most recent version of the feed itself, while the latter points to an alternate representation of the collection underlying the feed.

In a blog application, which is the first use case the designers of Atom had in mind, a feed can be used to represent the collection of the most recently posted entries. The `alternate` link would, in this case, point to the home page of the blog itself.

In a document management system, a feed can be used, as mentioned before, to represent the collection of children of a folder. In this case, the Atom feed will have one entry for each child, and the `alternate` link might point to a web page listing the contents of the folder, such as the Alfresco space browse page, for instance.

You could also have more than one `alternate` link, as long as each one has a different `type` attribute. You could have a link pointing to a web page, in which case, you would use a type of `text/html`. You could also have a link pointing to a JSON representation of the collection, in which case, you would use a type of `text/json`. Clients would be able to choose the representation that best suits their needs and capabilities.

It goes without saying that clients will retrieve a feed by issuing a GET request to the feed's URL.

Paging

While a feed is usually the representation of a collection of resources belonging to some web server, it is by no means necessary that all feeds always include a complete listing of all resources. In some situations, collections might be very large and it could be impractical or too time-consuming to generate, transmit, and parse a complete feed.

In these cases, a feed could represent a window over the collection, including only a limited number of entries, and provide links for clients to follow, in order to move the window forwards and backwards.

A useful metaphor for this behavior is that of scrolling through pages in a book. The feed contains only the lines of a single page, and clients can require the previous and the next page from the server. It would also be useful for a client to be able to turn to the first or the last page of the book.

The way Atom feeds do this is by means of links with relationship types of `next`, `previous`, `first`, and `last`, as shown in the following example:

```
<feed xmlns="http://www.w3.org/2005/Atom">
    <link rel="first" href="http://example.org/entries" />
    <link rel="previous" href="http://example.org/entries?p=3" />
    <link rel="next" href="http://example.org/entries?p=5" />
    <link rel="last" href="http://example.org/entries?p=10" />

</feed>
```

The Service Document

The feed and entry document types are already part of the Atom syndication format (RFC 4287), and AtomPub doesn't add much to them. An entirely new type of document, however, is defined by AtomPub (RFC 5023), the **Service Document**.

The Service Document is an XML document whose root element is service in the namespace http://www.w3.org/2007/app. It is served with a MIME type of application/atomsvc+xml.

A given server's Service Document, basically, describes all the collections that the server exposes via the Atom Protocol. When interacting with a server, a client only needs to know the URL of the Service Document. Every other URL can be determined by looking at it, and by following links contained in the documents received subsequently.

In a Service Document, collections are grouped in **workspaces**. The standard, however, does not assign any specific meaning to workspaces. They are simply descriptive and a server is not required to support more than one workspace.

Here is a simplified version of the CMIS Service Document served by Alfresco 3.2 (we have removed all elements that are CMIS-specific and kept only the pure AtomPub ones):

```
<service xmlns="http://www.w3.org/2007/app"
    xmlns:atom="http://www.w3.org/2005/Atom">
    <workspace>
        <atom:title>Main Repository</atom:title>
        <collection
            href="http://localhost:8080/alfresco/…/children">
          <atom:title>root collection</atom:title>
        </collection>
        <collection
            href="http://localhost:8080/alfresco/…/types">
            <atom:title>type collection</atom:title>
        </collection>
        <collection
            href="http://localhost:8080/alfresco/…/checkedout">
            <atom:title>checkedout collection</atom:title>
            <accept>application/atom+xml;type=entry</accept>
        </collection>
        <collection
            href="http://localhost:8080/alfresco/…/unfiled">
            <atom:title>unfiled collection</atom:title>
            <accept>application/atom+xml;type=entry</accept>
```

```
        </collection>
        <collection
            href="http://localhost:8080/alfresco/.../queries">
            <atom:title>query collection</atom:title>
            <accept>application/cmisquery+xml</accept>
        </collection>
    </workspace>
</service>
```

This document describes a service as having a single workspace, titled `Main Repository`. This workspace contains five collections.

Collections must have a URI, pointed to by the `href` attribute, and a title. They can also have zero or more `accept` child elements, listing the types of entries or files that clients can submit (using `POST`) to the collection.

Creating resources

A client can create a new resource by sending an `HTTP POST` request to a collection's URI, the one that appears in the Service Document. The body of the request will usually be an Atom entry, with a MIME type of `application/atom+xml;type=entry`, but see the next section for more options.

If the server accepts the posted entry, it should reply with an HTTP status code of **201 Created** and include a (possibly modified) copy of the entry in the response body. This is useful, since the server can alter the original entry in many ways, for instance, by assigning it a new identifier.

The response must also include a `Location` header, whose value is the URI of the newly created resource. This is called a **Member URI** and can be used by the client to retrieve the entry again, for instance, to edit it.

The following is an example of a request-response dialog between a client posting a new entry and the server accepting it. First, the client's request:

```
POST /edit/ HTTP/1.1
Host: example.org
Content-Type: application/atom+xml;type=entry
Content-Length: 100

<?xml version="1.0"?>
<entry xmlns="http://www.w3.org/2005/Atom">
    <title>Atom-Powered Robots Run Amok</title>
    <id>urn:uuid:1225c695-cfb8-4ebb-aaaa-80da344efa6a</id>
```

```
    <updated>2003-12-13T18:30:02Z</updated>
    <author><name>John Doe</name></author>
    <content>Some text.</content>
</entry>
```

Then, the server's response:

```
HTTP/1.1 201 Created
Date: Fri, 7 Oct 2005 17:17:11 GMT
Content-Length: 130
Content-Type: application/atom+xml;type=entry;charset="utf-8"
Location: http://example.org/edit/first-post.atom
ETag: "c180de84f991g8"

<?xml version="1.0"?>
<entry xmlns="http://www.w3.org/2005/Atom">
    <title>Atom-Powered Robots Run Amok</title>
    <id>urn:uuid:1225c695-cfb8-4ebb-aaaa-80da344efa6a</id>
    <updated>2003-12-13T18:30:02Z</updated>
    <author><name>John Doe</name></author>
    <content>Some text.</content>
    <link rel="edit"href="http://example.org/edit/first-post.atom"/>
</entry>
```

Entry and media resources

In the previous example, the client posted an Atom entry to a server collection. Depending on the type of content that our application is managing, this is all that might be necessary. A news server, for instance, might deal exclusively with content that is textual, either plain text or HTML. Textual content can easily be embedded in the entry itself as a child of the `content` element. This is called an **Entry Resource**.

When dealing with binary data, this approach tends to not work very well, as binary streams and XML do not mix together well. For small files, it might still be feasible to encode the binary stream as Base64, but for files measuring megabytes, or more, this is horribly inefficient, both in terms of bandwidth usage and memory / CPU consumption.

Our news service, to stay with the previous scenario, might accept images and videos, and we want to transfer those to the server as efficiently as possible.

To satisfy this requirement, AtomPub introduces the concept of Media Resources.

Typically, the server will advertize which resource types it accepts in the
Service Document:

```
<collection    href="http://example.org/images">
    <atom:title>Images Collection</atom:title>
    <accept>image/png</accept>
    <accept>image/jpeg</accept>
    <accept>image/gif</accept>
</collection>
```

When the client posts an image file to such a collection, the server will create two
new resources: one corresponding to the file sent with the request, called the **Media
Resource**, and associated Atom entry, called the **Media Link Entry**, as a member
of the collection. The Media Link Entry, which appears in the collection's feed,
will contain a description of the Media Resource and a link to its URI.

Clients can use the link to the Media Resource contained in the Media Link Entry
to retrieve the original file. The Media Link Entry should also contain a link, with a
relationship type of edit-media, which clients can use to submit an updated version
of the file.

As an example, consider the following case, where the client sends a POST request,
containing a PNG image:

```
POST /edit/ HTTP/1.1
Host: media.example.org
Content-Type: image/png
Content-Length: nnn
```

…binary data…

The server responds, as usual, with a **201 Created** status code and a representation of
the Media Link Entry:

```
HTTP/1.1 201 Created
Date: Fri, 7 Oct 2005 17:17:11 GMT
Content-Length: 245
Content-Type: application/atom+xml;type=entry;charset="utf-8"
Location: http://example.org/media/edit/the_beach.atom

<?xml version="1.0"?>
<entry xmlns="http://www.w3.org/2005/Atom">
    <title>The Beach</title>
    <id>urn:uuid:1225c695-cfb8-4ebb-aaaa-80da344efa6a</id>
    <updated>2005-10-07T17:17:08Z</updated>
```

```
    <author><name>Daffy</name></author>
    <content type="image/png"
        src="http://media.example.org/the_beach.png"/>
    <link rel="edit-media"
        href="http://media.example.org/edit/the_beach.png" />
</entry>
```

There are two links in the previous entry. The first one is the value of the `src` attribute of the content element. This points to the Media Resource URI: `http://media.example.org/the_beach.png`. The second one is the `href` of the `edit-media` link: `http://media.example.org/edit/the_beach.png`.

Updating resources

Updating an existing entry generally entails retrieving its current representation by issuing a `GET` request against the entry's Member URI. The entry thus retrieved should contain a link with a relationship of `edit`. The client must issue a `PUT` request to the edit URI. The body of the request must be the modified version of the entry. The server will respond with a **200 OK** result code if it is able to perform the update.

Servers can guard against lost updates due to concurrent modifications by different clients by using the conditional HTTP update mechanism. When employing this technique, the server includes an `ETag` header in the response to `GET` requests that identify the current version of the resource.

When the client submits the update, it must include an `If-Match` header with the same `ETag` value that it received previously. If the server detects that the `ETag` is not valid anymore, possibly because some other client performed an update in the meantime, it should reply with a **412 Precondition Failed** status code.

Deleting resources

To delete a resource, a client must send a `DELETE` request to the entry's Member URI.

Listing books by category

This service is meant to let client applications retrieve a list of books belonging to a given category.

Service URI

The service will respond to the `/books/category/{category}` URI, where `{category}` must match an existing category's name, that is, a child of the **Books** top-level category. You should create a number of categories using the Alfresco Category Management tool before proceeding, as shown in the following screenshot:

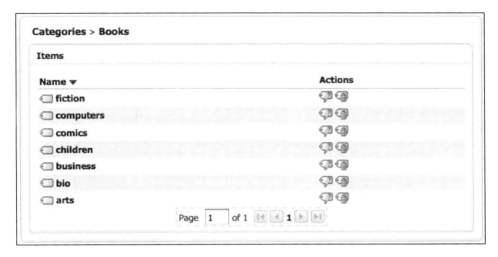

Notice that we used simple identifiers for the category names shown above. You are, of course, free to use more descriptive phrases, for example Children's Books instead of **children**, but remember to properly escape characters, such as the space or the ampersand, which are not allowed nor have a special meaning in URIs.

After having created one or more categories, upload some books using the custom domain model that was introduced in the preceding chapters, and assign them to one or more of the categories that were just created. You can use the **Category** section of the document details page in the Alfresco Explorer to do so.

Response format

Naturally, the format of the response is going to be an Atom feed where each entry describes a particular book. Here is an example:

```
<?xml version="1.0" ?>

<feed
    xmlns="http://www.w3.org/2005/Atom"
    xmlns:app="http://www.w3.org/2007/app"
    xmlns:bs="http://www.packtpub.com/a3ws/samples/bookshop">
```

```
<title>Literature &amp; Fiction</title>
<link href="http://localhost:8080/alfresco/service/books/category/
fiction"/>
<updated>2010-01-16T16:03:50+0100</updated>
<id>http://localhost:8080/alfresco/service/books/category/fiction</id>
<generator version="3.2.0 (r2 2440)">Alfresco (Community)</generator>
<entry
    xmlns="http://www.w3.org/2005/Atom"
    xmlns:app="http://www.w3.org/2007/app"
    xmlns:bs="http://www.packtpub.com/a3ws/samples/bookshop">
<id>1ecdf8fd-3939-492a-9670-eeb381568a1a</id>
<link rel="self"
    href="http://localhost:8080/alfresco/service/books/978-
0684833392"/>
<link rel="alternate" type="application/pdf" href="http://
localhost:8080/alfresco/d/d/workspace/SpacesStore/1ecdf8fd-3939-492a-
9670-eeb381568a1a/catch22.pdf"/>
<updated>2010-01-14T14:20:24+0100</updated>
<title>Catch-22</title>
    <author><name>Joseph Heller</name></author>
    <category term="fiction" scheme="http://www.packtpub.com/a3ws/
bookshop/categories" />
    <bs:isbn>978-0684833392</bs:isbn>
    <bs:publisher>Simon &amp; Schuster</bs:publisher>
</entry>
<entry
    xmlns="http://www.w3.org/2005/Atom"
    xmlns:app="http://www.w3.org/2007/app"
    xmlns:bs="http://www.packtpub.com/a3ws/samples/bookshop">
<id>4f9c6be7-6512-4e0c-86c1-fd477e99d208</id>
<link rel="self"
    href="http://localhost:8080/alfresco/service/books/978-
0316769174"/>
<link rel="alternate" type="application/pdf" href="http://
localhost:8080/alfresco/d/d/workspace/SpacesStore/4f9c6be7-6512-4e0c-
86c1-fd477e99d208/catcher.pdf"/>
<updated>2010-01-14T14:21:04+0100</updated>
<title>The Catcher in the Rye</title>
    <author><name>Jerome D. Salinger</name></author>
    <category term="fiction" scheme="http://www.packtpub.com/a3ws/
bookshop/categories" />
    <bs:isbn>978-0316769174</bs:isbn>
    <bs:publisher>Back Bay Books</bs:publisher>
</entry>
</feed>
```

We used existing Atom elements, such as title and author, where appropriate. For properties that are not easily mapped to an Atom element, such as an ISBN or a publisher's name, we used extension elements in the `http://www.packtpub.com/a3ws/samples/bookshop` namespace.

Implementing the service

The following sections present the various pieces of the implementation of the Web Script: the descriptor, the controller, and the template.

The descriptor

The Web Script's descriptor is simple. Here it is in its entirety:

```
<webscript>
    <shortname>Category Listing</shortname>
    <description>Lists all the books belonging to
    category</description>
    <url>/books/category/{category}</url>
    <authentication>user</authentication>
    <transaction>required</transaction>
    <format default="atom">any</format>
</webscript>
```

Save this as `category.get.desc.xml`.

The controller

The controller is also simple. The only part that needs some explanation is the loop that tries to find the category specified in the request URI. Unfortunately, the Alfresco Classification JavaScript API, embodied by the `classification` object, does not provide a convenient method to get a single category based on its name; we have to loop through all the top-level categories to find the one named **Books** and then loop through its children to find the one we want.

We must also make sure that every member of the array that is passed to the template is actually a book. This is why we check each result's type before adding it to `model.books`:

```
var category = url.templateArgs.category
var bookType = "{http://www.packtpub.com/a3ws/samples/bookshop}book"
model.books = []
model.categoryDesc = "Unknown category"
model.updated = new Date()
var topcats = classification.getRootCategories("cm:
generalclassifiable")
```

```
    for (var i in topcats) {
        if (topcats[i].name == "Books") {
            var cats = topcats[i].subCategories
            for (var j in cats) {
                if (cats[j].name == category) {
                    model.categoryDesc =
                        cats[j].properties.description
                    for (var k in cats[j].categoryMembers) {
                        var b = cats[j].categoryMembers[k]
                        if (b.type == bookType) {
                            model.books.push(b)
                        }
                    }
                }
            }
            break;
        }
    }
```

Save this as `category.get.js`.

The template

The FreeMarker template is kept readable and simple by the fact that we moved a couple of user-defined macros to the `atomlib.ftl` file and included the latter in the template. These macros are also going to be useful in other templates that we will develop later.

Here is the template, contained in the `category.get.atom.ftl` file:

```
<#include "atomlib.ftl">
<?xml version="1.0" ?>

<feed
    xmlns="http://www.w3.org/2005/Atom"
    xmlns:app="http://www.w3.org/2007/app"
    xmlns:bs="http://www.packtpub.com/a3ws/samples/bookshop">
<title>${categoryDesc?xml}</title>
<link href="${absurl(url.full)?xml}"/>
<updated>${updated?string("yyyy-MM-dd'T'HH:mm:ssZ")}</updated>
<id>${absurl(url.full)?xml}</id>
<@generator/>
<#list books as book>
<@bookToAtomEntry book />
</#list>
</feed>
```

A couple of things to note about this template:

- You need to make sure that all values emitted do not break the well-formedness of the output XML document. In order to do this, use the FreeMarker XML built-in.

- The `url` variable that is passed to templates by the Alfresco runtime is a relative URL that does not contain the protocol, hostname, and port. To convert it to an absolute URL, use the FreeMarker `absurl` function.

The following code snippet shows the contents of the `atomlib.ftl` file:

```
<#macro optelem elemname value="">
    <#if value != "">
      <${elemname}>${value?xml}</${elemname}>
    </#if>
</#macro>

<#macro bookToAtomEntry book>
  <entry
    xmlns="http://www.w3.org/2005/Atom"
    xmlns:app="http://www.w3.org/2007/app"
    xmlns:bs="http://www.packtpub.com/a3ws/samples/bookshop">
    <id>${book.id}</id>
    <link rel="self"
    href="${absurl(url.serviceContext + '/books/' +
    book.properties['bs:isbn'])}"/>
    <#if book.mimetype??>
    <link rel="alternate" type="${book.mimetype?xml}"
    href="${absurl(url.context + book.url)}"/>
    </#if>
    <link rel="edit-media"
    href="${absurl(url.serviceContext + '/books/' +

    book.properties['bs:isbn'] + '/content')}"/>
    <updated>${book.properties.modified?string("yyyy-MM-
dd'T'HH:mm:ssZ")}</updated>
    <@optelem "title" book.properties.title/>
    <@optelem "summary" book.properties.description/>
    <#list book.properties["bs:author"] as author>
    <author><name>${author?xml}</name></author>
    </#list>
    <#list book.properties.categories as cat>
    <category term="${cat.name?xml}"
    scheme="http://www.packtpub.com/a3ws/bookshop/categories" />
```

```
        </#list>
        <bs:isbn>${book.properties["bs:isbn"]?xml}</bs:isbn>
        <bs:publisher>${book.properties["bs:publisher"]?xml}
        </bs:publisher>
        <bs:price>${book.properties["bs:price"]?xml}</bs:price>
    </entry>
</#macro>

<#macro generator>
    <generator version="${server.version?xml}">Alfresco
    (${server.edition?xml})</generator>
</#macro>
```

Notice that each entry element we output can contain up to three child link elements, each one specifying a different type of relationship by means of standardized values for the `rel` attribute:

- `link rel="self"`: This link points to a URI that returns the representation of this entry alone. It is possible for Atom servers to return feeds that only contain an abridged representation of entries, with a link to a more complete representation. Although we are not using this possibility in our implementation, having this link is recommended.

- `link rel="alternate"`: This link points to a URI that returns the contents of the document represented by this entry.

- `link rel="edit-media"`: This link points to a URI that accepts a byte stream containing the updated contents of the media entry associated with this entry. Clients can put a PDF (or other format) file to this URI to update a document's contents.

Testing the service

Once you have deployed the Web Script, you might want to test it. We are going to first do some basic verification, then proceed to write a Java client to fetch and parse the feed.

Using curl

A simple check using `curl` can be made to ensure that the service works as expected:

```
curl -v http://localhost:8080/alfresco/service/books/category/fiction -u
admin:admin
```

If you don't have `curl` installed, you can always use your browser to access the service. Mozilla Firefox, for instance, will recognize the response as an Atom feed and offer you an opportunity to subscribe to it.

A simple Java client

In order to write some Java client code that can retrieve the Atom feed served by our Web Script and parse it, we could use the core Java classes contained in the `java.net` and `javax.xml` packages.

However, one of the reasons why we chose a standardized format like Atom for our service is that this choice allows us to leverage existing libraries that provide much of the code needed to interact with Atom-based services. We can concentrate on writing application-specific code and avoid the more tedious and error-prone tasks, as somebody else has already done them for us.

Moreover, if we are able to select an Open Source library, we get all of this for free! One such toolkit is indeed already available, and it is the one delivered by the **Apache Abdera** project, which you can find at `http://abdera.apache.org`.

Using Abdera, we can write a program that retrieves the Atom feed produced by our service and prints out the titles of all entries in a handful of lines of code:

```java
package com.packtpub.a3ws.samples.bookshop.rest.client;

import org.apache.abdera.model.Document;
import org.apache.abdera.model.Entry;
import org.apache.abdera.model.Feed;
import org.apache.abdera.protocol.client.AbderaClient;
import org.apache.abdera.protocol.client.ClientResponse;
import org.apache.commons.httpclient.UsernamePasswordCredentials;

public class RESTClient {

    public static void main(String[] args) throws Exception {
        String serviceURL = args[0];
        AbderaClient client = new AbderaClient();
        client.addCredentials(serviceURL, null, null,
            new UsernamePasswordCredentials
                ("admin", "admin"));
        ClientResponse response = client.get(serviceURL);
        Document<Feed> doc = response.getDocument();
        Feed feed = doc.getRoot();
        for (Entry entry : feed.getEntries()) {
            System.out.println(entry.getTitle());
        }
        response.release();
    }

}
```

Installing Abdera

Instructions for downloading and installing the Abdera toolkit can be found at the project's website. As Abdera has quite a number of dependencies that you would have to download and add to the Java `classpath`, we recommend using **Apache Maven** to manage the dependencies for you. This way, you don't even need to download Abdera, as Maven will download it, together with all needed dependencies, automatically for you.

All you have to do is create a POM file like the following which we used for the examples in this chapter:

```xml
<?xml version="1.0"?>
<project xmlns=http://maven.apache.org/POM/4.0.0
  xmlns:xsi="http://www.w3.org/2001/XMLSchema-instance"
  xsi:schemaLocation="http://maven.apache.org/POM/4.0.0
  http://maven.apache.org/maven-v4_0_0.xsd">

<modelVersion>4.0.0</modelVersion>
<groupId>com.packtpub.a3ws.samples.bookshop.rest</groupId>
<artifactId>client</artifactId>
<packaging>jar</packaging>
<version>1.0-SNAPSHOT</version>
<name>A3WS REST Bookshop Client</name>
<url>http://www.packtpub.com</url>

<repositories>
  <repository>
  <id>apache-incubating</id>
  <name>Apache Incubating Repository</name>
  <url>http://people.apache.org/repo/m2-incubating-
  repository/</url>
  </repository>
</repositories>

<dependencies>
  <dependency>
    <groupId>junit</groupId>
    <artifactId>junit</artifactId>
    <version>4.7</version>
    <scope>test</scope>
  </dependency>
  <dependency>
      <groupId>log4j</groupId>
      <artifactId>log4j</artifactId>
```

```
        <version>1.2.14</version>
        <scope>test</scope>
    </dependency>
    <dependency>
        <groupId>org.apache.abdera</groupId>
        <artifactId>abdera-client</artifactId>
        <version>0.4.0-incubating</version>
    </dependency>
  </dependencies>
</project>
```

Creating a new book

This service allows client applications to upload information about the content of a new book.

Service URI

The service will respond to POST requests directed to the /books/ URI. This URI represents the collection of all books existing in the repository.

Clients must send a request whose body must contain an Atom entry describing the new book. The server responds with a **201 Created** result code and a response body consisting of an Atom entry representing the newly created resource.

The actual contents of the book as a PDF document must be sent later, with a PUT request to the edit-media link contained in the entry sent as a response by the server.

This interaction is depicted in the sequence diagram, shown as follows:

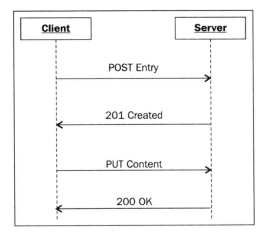

Request format

The client should send a request having a body similar to the one shown as follows:

```
<entry xmlns="http://www.w3.org/2005/Atom"
       xmlns:bs="http://www.packtpub.com/a3ws/samples/bookshop">
  <id>urn:isbn:978-0201616224</id>
  <updated>2010-01-14T14:20:24+0100</updated>
  <title>The Pragmatic Programmer</title>
  <author><name>David Thomas</name></author>
  <author><name>Andrew Hunt</name></author>
  <category term="computers"
  scheme="http://www.packtpub.com/a3ws/bookshop/categories" />
  <bs:isbn>978-0201616224</bs:isbn>
  <bs:publisher>Addison-Wesley Professional</bs:publisher>
  <bs:price>12.99</bs:price>
</entry>
```

As per the Atom Publishing Protocol specification, the entry document must have an id element, whose value must be a valid URI. What we used here is an "isbn" URN (defined in RFC 3187), but the actual value is not used by the service implementation, which will instead use the NodeRef assigned by Alfresco to generate a new identifier.

Implementing the service

As with the previous example, we will show the descriptor, the controller, and the template.

The descriptor

Here is the entire descriptor, book.post.desc.xml:

```
<webscript>
  <shortname>Create a book</shortname>
  <description>Creates a new book from an Atom entry</description>
  <url>/books/</url>
  <authentication>user</authentication>
  <transaction>required</transaction>
  <format default="atom">any</format>
</webscript>
```

The controller

The heart of the controller, stored in the file `book.post.atom.js`, is the `postBook` function:

```
function postBook() {
    if (entry != null) {
        var books = companyhome.childByNamePath("Books")
        var isbn = entry.getExtension(isbnQName).text
        var book = books.createNode(isbn + ".pdf", "bs:book",
            [], "cm:contains")
        book.addAspect("cm:generalclassifiable")
        book.addAspect("cm:versionable")
        book.properties.title = entry.title
        book.properties.description = entry.summary
        book.properties["bs:isbn"] = isbn

        var publisher = entry.getExtension(publisherQName)
        if (publisher != null) {
            book.properties["bs:publisher"] = publisher.text
        }

        var price = entry.getExtension(priceQName)
        if (price != null) {
            book.properties["bs:price"] = price.text
        }

        var authors = []
        for (var i = 0 ; i < entry.authors.size() ; ++i) {
            authors[i] = entry.authors.get(i).name
        }
        book.properties["bs:author"] = authors

        var categories = []
        for (var i = 0 ; i < entry.categories.size() ; ++i) {
            var category =
                findBookCategory(entry.categories.get(i).term)
            if (category != null) {
                categories.push(category)
            }
        }
        book.properties["cm:categories"] = categories
```

```
            book.save()
            model.book = book
            status.code = 201 // Created
            status.location = url.server + url.serviceContext +
                "/books/" + isbn + ".atom"
            status.redirect = true
        } else {
            status.code = 400 // Bad Request
            status.message = "Format of request not recognized"
            status.redirect = true
        }
    }
```

This function basically creates an Alfresco node of type `bs:book` and fills its properties with values taken from various elements of the Atom entry.

No content is created yet, as the client hasn't sent any files, but will do so in a subsequent request.

Notice that we make the document to be automatically versioned by Alfresco by adding the `cm:versionable` aspect to it. This will become useful when we deal with concurrent updates later.

The template

Upon a successful creation of a new book, as previously mentioned, the response of the server consists of a **201 Created** response whose body is an Atom entry representing the book. To obtain this in our Web Script, we need to create a template file called `book.post.atom.201.ftl` with the following content:

```
<#include "atomlib.ftl">
<?xml version="1.0" ?>


<@bookToAtomEntry book />
```

As you can see, the template just invokes the `bookToAtomEntry` user macro that was defined in our template library.

Uploading content

As previously mentioned, the client has to send the actual file contents in a subsequent request directed at the `edit-media` URI. Therefore, we need to implement a service to respond to such a request, which we will do with another Web Script named `bookcontent`.

The descriptor

We want the client to use the PUT command to upload the file, so we save the descriptor as bookcontent.put.desc.xml. The URI template of this service, of course, matches the format of the edit-media link, as previously shown:

```
<webscript>
  <shortname>PUT a book's contents</shortname>
  <description>Accepts the contents of a book as a PDF
  file</description>
  <url>/books/{isbn}/content</url>
  <authentication>user</authentication>
  <transaction>required</transaction>
  <format default="atom">any</format>
</webscript>
```

The controller

The controller, bookcontent.put.js, is quite short:

```
var isbn = url.templateArgs.isbn
var results = search.luceneSearch("@bs\\:isbn:" + isbn)
if (results.length <= 0) {
    status.code = 404 // Not Found
    status.message = "No book with ISBN " + isbn + " found."
    status.redirect = true
} else {
    var book = results[0]
    book.properties.content.mimetype = requestbody.mimetype
    book.properties.content.write(requestbody)
}
```

Here we are using a type of JavaScript object that we haven't introduced yet, the ScriptContent. For every Alfresco node, such as a document, that has some content associated to it, typically via the cm:content property, the corresponding ScriptNode object in JavaScript has a property, named content, whose type is indeed ScriptContent.

Therefore, to access the ScriptContent associated with a ScriptNode named book, we just have to write book.properties.content.

In a Web Script, there is another object of type ScriptContent available, called requestbody, which contains the body of the HTTP request.

Objects of type `ScriptContent` allow direct manipulation of the content using code such as the one previously shown, which copies the body of the request to a document's content in a very simple and straightforward way:

```
book.properties.content.mimetype = requestbody.mimetype
book.properties.content.write(requestbody)
```

The template

The service doesn't provide any output in reply to an upload request, so we just have to create an empty FreeMarker file called `bookcontent.put.atom.ftl`.

Testing the service

The two Web Scripts that we have just introduced make up the interface of our service. Let's now test them. As with the previous example, we will first do a basic smoke test using `curl`, then move on to write a Java client application.

Using curl

To test the service using `curl`, first create a file containing a copy of the entry previously displayed or create a new one using information for your favorite title. Save it as `newbook.xml`, and then submit it to the server with the following command:

```
curl -v -u admin:admin -d @newbook.xml -H 'Content-Type:application/
atom+xml;type=entry' http://localhost:8080/alfresco/service/books/
```

The server should respond with something similar to the following:

```
HTTP/1.1 201 Created
Server: Apache-Coyote/1.1
Cache-Control: no-cache
Pragma: no-cache
Location: http://localhost:8080/alfresco/service/books/978-0201616224.
atom
Content-Type: application/atom+xml;charset=UTF-8
Content-Length: 850
Date: Sun, 17 Jan 2010 12:48:45 GMT

<?xml version="1.0" ?>
```

```
<entry
    xmlns="http://www.w3.org/2005/Atom"
    xmlns:app="http://www.w3.org/2007/app"
    xmlns:bs="http://www.packtpub.com/a3ws/samples/bookshop">
<id>988a7615-3d96-4612-b260-a6929c5d71d8</id>
<link rel="self"
      href="http://localhost:8080/alfresco/service/books/978-
0201616224"/>
<link rel="edit-media" href="http://localhost:8080/alfresco/service/
books/978-0316769174/content"/>
<updated>2010-01-17T13:48:45+0100</updated>
<title>The Pragmatic Programmer</title>
    <author><name>David Thomas</name></author>
    <author><name>Andrew Hunt</name></author>
    <category term="computers"
    scheme="http://www.packtpub.com/a3ws/bookshop/categories" />
    <bs:isbn>978-0201616224</bs:isbn>
    <bs:publisher>Addison-Wesley Professional</bs:publisher>
<bs:price>12.99</bs:price>
</entry>
```

Take note of the value of the `href` attribute of the `link` element having `rel="edit-media"`. In this case, it is:

```
http://localhost:8080/alfresco/service/books/978-0316769174/content
```

You can supply any random PDF file for this test, which uses `curl`'s `-T` switch to upload a file using the PUT method, as required by our service:

```
curl -v -u admin:admin -T book.pdf -H 'Content-Type:application/pdf'
'http://localhost:8080/alfresco/service/books/978-0201616224/content'
```

If everything went as expected, the server will respond with the following:

```
HTTP/1.1 100 Continue
HTTP/1.1 200 OK
Server: Apache-Coyote/1.1
Cache-Control: no-cache
Pragma: no-cache
Content-Type: application/atom+xml;charset=UTF-8
Content-Length: 0
Date: Sun, 17 Jan 2010 13:57:51 GMT
```

You can now use the Alfresco Explorer to examine the document you just created, which will be inside the **Books** space.

A simple Java client

Our Java client for creating a new book also uses the Abdera toolkit. This time, we are not showing the full code of the class that you can find in the accompanying source code, but we will be including some relevant snippets and commenting on them.

Initial set-up

In the following snippet, we define a constant for the bookshop domain model namespace and create a handful of objects that we will use later. We have already encountered the `AbderaClient` class. This time we will use the `Abdera` class for creating a new entry from scratch as follows:

```
final String BOOKSHOP_NS_URI =
  "http://www.packtpub.com/a3ws/samples/bookshop";
String serviceURL = args[0];
```

```
Abdera abdera = new Abdera();
AbderaClient client = new AbderaClient(abdera);
client.addCredentials(serviceURL, null, null,
new UsernamePasswordCredentials("admin", "admin"));
```

Generating a random ISBN

This is just an example, so we are not using real data for it. For the ISBN, we generate a random value, so you can run the example again without getting errors due to duplicate filenames.

```
int rnd = new Random().nextInt(1000000000);
String rnds = String.format("%010d", rnd);
String isbn = "999-" + rnds;
```

Setting up the entry

Here we create a new Atom entry, represented by the Entry class in Abdera. Once again, we fill it with some sample data.

Notice that we use the Entry.addExtension method to add Atom extension elements to our entry for indicating the ISBN, publisher's name, and price.

```
Entry bookEntry = abdera.newEntry();
bookEntry.setId("urn:isbn:" + isbn);
bookEntry.setUpdated(new Date());
bookEntry.setTitle("Book " + isbn);
bookEntry.addAuthor("Anonymous");
bookEntry.addCategory(BOOKSHOP_NS_URI + "/categories" ,
 "fiction", null);
ExtensibleElement e1 = bookEntry.addExtension(BOOKSHOP_NS_URI,
"isbn", "bs");
e1.setText(isbn);
ExtensibleElement e2 = bookEntry.addExtension(BOOKSHOP_NS_URI,
"publisher", "bs");
e2.setText("PACKT");
ExtensibleElement e3 = bookEntry.addExtension(BOOKSHOP_NS_URI,
"price", "bs");
```

The entry created by this code would appear, when serialized as XML, as follows:

```
<entry xmlns=http://www.w3.org/2005/Atom
xmlns:bs="http://www.packtpub.com/a3ws/samples/bookshop">
  <id>urn:isbn:999-0271668006</id>
  <updated>2010-01-17T15:49:08.127Z</updated>
  <title type="text">Book 999-0271668006</title>
  <author><name>Anonymous</name></author>
```

```
   <category term="fiction"
scheme="http://www.packtpub.com/a3ws/samples/bookshop/categories" />
   <bs:isbn>999-0271668006</bs:isbn>
   <bs:publisher>PACKT</bs:publisher>
   <bs:price>12.99</bs:price>
</entry>
```

Submitting the entry

The following code sends the entry to the server, using the POST command:

```
ClientResponse response = client.post(serviceURL, bookEntry);
response.release();
```

A realistic application would, at this time, check the response status code and verify that it is 201 as expected. For brevity, we are omitting all error checking in this sample.

[Remember to always call response.release() after you have finished using the response, in order to free any connections held up by the client.]

Uploading the content

In order to upload the content, we must read the server's response to the previous request and retrieve the destination URI for the edit-media link. Once we have it, we can upload the content of the local file named book.pdf:

```
Document<Entry> doc = response.getDocument();
Entry entry = doc.getRoot();
String link = entry.getLink("edit-media")
.getHref().toString();
InputStream in = new FileInputStream("book.pdf");
RequestOptions options = new RequestOptions();
options.setContentType("application/pdf");
response = client.put(link, in, options);
response.release();
```

This concludes our sample, which you can run from the command line or from within your IDE such as with the previous one. Once you have executed it, use the Alfresco Explorer to check that a new document, with the desired metadata and content, has been created in the **Books** space.

Updating an existing book

When thinking of updating a book, there are two aspects that we must consider separately: updating the book's content by submitting a new PDF file, and updating the information about the book (the metadata). For the former case, we don't have to implement anything new with respect to the service that was presented in the previous section, as that works the same way regardless of whether we are uploading new or updated content.

For updating metadata, we need to send a PUT request to the book's URI, containing an updated Atom entry. Before they do that, clients should perform a GET request in order to retrieve the most recent representation of the book, modify it, and send it back to the server.

The implementation

The controller is very similar to the one used for the POST case. We just have to search for a book based on the ISBN, instead of creating a new one. Here's the portion that differs; everything else stays pretty much the same:

```
var isbn = url.templateArgs.isbn
var results = search.luceneSearch("@bs\\:isbn:" + isbn)
if (results.length <= 0) {
    status.code = 404 // Not Found
    status.message = "No book with ISBN " + isbn + " found."
    status.redirect = true
    return
}
var book = results[0]
```

Another difference is that, in case of success, as per the Atom Publishing Protocol specification, we respond with a status of **200 OK** and no response body. To achieve this, just create an empty template, and name it book.put.atom.ftl.

As we want our updating service to respond to the /books/{isbn} URI, we need to provide an appropriate descriptor in the file book.put.desc.xml:

```
<webscript>
  <shortname>Update an existing book</shortname>
  <description>Updates an existing book from an Atom
  entry</description>
  <url>/books/{isbn}</url>
  <authentication>user</authentication>
  <transaction>required</transaction>
  <format default="atom">any</format>
</webscript>
```

Testing with curl

You can use the `curl` command to fetch one of the entries that we created previously and save it to a file as follows:

```
curl -v -u admin:admin -o updated.xml 'http://localhost:8080/alfresco/
service/books/978-0201616224'
```

Open the `updated.xml` file in an editor and perform some changes, for example changing the price tag:

```
<bs:price>15.99</bs:price>
```

Save the file and submit it back to the server with PUT:

```
curl -v -u admin:admin -T updated.xml -H 'Content-Type:application/
atom+xml' 'http://localhost:8080/alfresco/service/books/978-0201616224'
```

The server should respond with a **200 OK** status. Use the Alfresco Explorer to verify that the metadata has actually changed.

Dealing with concurrent edits

What would happen if two users decided to retrieve and update the same entry at roughly the same time? How do you deal, in a REST scenario, with concurrent edits and how do you avoid losing updates because of this?

A possible solution is to adopt the so-called *optimistic locking* method. In order to implement optimistic locking, you need to identify each version of a resource and return this version identifier together with the representation of the resource. Clients must submit a possibly modified version of the same representation, together with the original version identifier. The server checks that the current version identifier is identical to the one submitted by the client; if it isn't, the server should not perform the update and return a suitable error to the client. If it is, the server should assign a new version identifier to the resource.

Using this protocol, a client cannot overwrite changes made by another client between the time it retrieved the original resource and the time it tried to submit its modifications. Once the second client successfully makes some changes, the version identifier will change and render the representation held by the first client invalid.

The following diagram depicts this scenario. The update requested by the first client will fail.

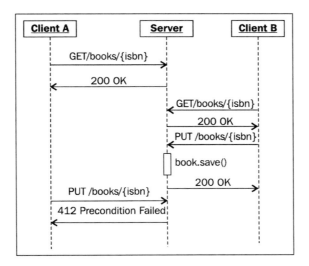

We can use Alfresco's own versioning support for this, which automatically increments a document's version number when the document is modified. When we introduced the script used for processing the POST request, did you notice that it added the cm:versionable aspect to the created node? Now we are going to benefit from this.

Implementation

In order to implement optimistic locking, we need to establish how to represent versions and how the server and the client are going to inform each other about them.

We will use the node's UUID, followed by the version label assigned by Alfresco, to identify a specific version of a specific document. In this way, we can be sure that the version identifier will change every time a new version of the document is created, and also if the document is deleted and then created anew with the same ISBN.

For client-server communication, we are going to rely on HTTP's *conditional update* mechanism, which is similar to the conditional GET that was described in *Chapter 5* .

The way this works is that the server, when requested for a resource's representation (a book in our case), emits an ETag response header, whose content is the version identifier described.

A client wishing to perform an update must first retrieve a representation of the current version of the resource, read the value of the ETag response header, and store it somewhere.

When the client is ready to submit an updated representation of the header, it must emit an If-Match request header, whose value is equal to the ETag previously received.

In other words, the client is telling the server to modify the resource *only if* the version it holds matches the one held by the client. The server must not perform the update if the received If-Match header does not match the identifier of the current version of the resource. It must also return a suitable HTTP result code such as **412 Precondition Failed**.

To implement this protocol, we need to modify the script that retrieves a single book, book.get.js, in this way:

```
var isbn = url.templateArgs.isbn
var results = search.luceneSearch("@bs\\:isbn:" + isbn)
if (results.length <= 0) {
    status.code = 404 // Not Found
    status.message = "No book with ISBN " + isbn + " found."
    status.redirect = true
} else {
    model.book = results[0]
    var etag = model.book.id
    if (model.book.versionHistory != undefined) {
        etag += " [" + model.book.versionHistory[0].label + "]"
    }
    cache.ETag = etag
}
```

If you look at the headers of a response to a GET request, using curl -v for instance, you should see a header similar to this one:

ETag: "2231d10c-274f-4bdc-987c-e8f583149260 [1.6]"

The script used for updating a book's data, book.put.atom.js, must have the following snippet added:

```
var currentVersion = '"' + book.id + ' [' +
 book.versionHistory[0].label + ']"'
var requestedVersion = headers["If-Match"]
if (currentVersion != requestedVersion) {
    status.code = 412 // Precondition failed
    status.redirect = true
    return
}
```

When submitting an updated book, remember to add the `If-Match` header:

```
curl -v -u admin:admin -T updated.xml -H 'Content-Type:application/
atom+xml' -H 'If-Match:2231d10c-274f-4bdc-987c-e8f583149260 [1.6]'
'http://localhost:8080/alfresco/service/books/978-0385333849'
```

The Java client

The Java code for updating an entry with annotations is shown as follows. As with previous samples, no error checking is performed. In real code, you should check HTTP response codes and catch exceptions.

We first set up a few constants and the client:

```
final String BOOKSHOP_NS_URI = "http://www.packtpub.com/a3ws/samples/
bookshop";
final QName BOOKSHOP_PRICE_QNAME = new QName(BOOKSHOP_NS_URI,
"price");

Abdera abdera = new Abdera();
AbderaClient client = new AbderaClient(abdera);
client.addCredentials(serviceURL, null, null,
new UsernamePasswordCredentials("admin", "admin"));
```

Then we fetch a feed of the fiction category, and we select its first entry for updating.

```
ClientResponse response = client.get(serviceURL +
"category/fiction");
Document<Feed> doc = response.getDocument();
Feed feed = doc.getRoot();
Entry entry = feed.getEntries().get(0);
response.release();
```

We now get the complete entry. We cannot reuse the one contained in the feed, since it might be incomplete, and we wouldn't get the `ETag` header. We store the value of the latter in a variable.

```
response =
client.get(entry.getSelfLink().getHref().toString());
Document<Entry> entryDoc = response.getDocument();
entry = entryDoc.getRoot();
String etag = response.getHeader("ETag");
```

We modify the entry somehow, for instance, by changing the price.

```
Element priceEl = entry.getExtension(BOOKSHOP_PRICE_QNAME);
priceEl.setText("15.99");
```

We need to know the URL to where the updated entry must be sent. This URL is the target of the link having a relationship of `edit`. In case this link is missing, we use the one with a relationship of `self`.

```
Link editLink = entry.getEditLink();
if (editLink == null) {
    editLink = entry.getSelfLink();
}
response.release();
```

Finally, we put the modified entry, after having added an `If-Match` header to the request, using the `ETag` previously obtained as follows:

```
RequestOptions options = client.getDefaultRequestOptions();
options.setHeader("If-Match", etag);
response = client.put(editLink.getHref().toString(), entry,
options);
response.release();
```

At the end of this process, you can check the return value of `response.getStatus()`; it should be `200`.

You can also try inserting a delay of several seconds before the update is performed. Use that time to go to the Alfresco Explorer and generate a new version of the document. When the program tries to submit the update, the server should respond with a status of `412`.

Deleting a book

To delete a book, we must send an HTTP DELETE command to the book's edit URI.

The service that handles deletions of existing books is the simplest one to implement. It consists of a typical descriptor, `book.delete.desc.xml`:

```
<webscript>
  <shortname>Delete an existing book</shortname>
  <description>Deleted an existing book given its ISBN</description>
  <url>/books/{isbn}</url>
  <authentication>user</authentication>
  <transaction>required</transaction>
  <format default="atom">any</format>
</webscript>
```

The controller, `book.delete.js`, is also very simple:

```
var isbn = url.templateArgs.isbn
var results = search.luceneSearch("@bs\\:isbn:" + isbn)
if (results.length <= 0) {
    status.code = 404 // Not Found
    status.message = "No book with ISBN " + isbn + " found."
    status.redirect = true
} else {
    book = results[0]
    book.remove()
}
```

As we don't expect any output from this operation, the template, `book.delete.atom.ftl`, is an empty file.

Testing deletion

You can test the deletion service using `curl` in this way:

```
curl -v -u admin:admin -X DELETE 'http://localhost:8080/alfresco/service/
books/999-0552997858'
```

The server will respond with:

```
HTTP/1.1 200 OK
Server: Apache-Coyote/1.1
Cache-Control: no-cache
Pragma: no-cache
Content-Type: application/atom+xml;charset=UTF-8
Content-Length: 0
Date: Sat, 23 Jan 2010 11:51:42 GMT
```

Use the Alfresco Explorer to check that the document was deleted as expected.

This concludes the implementation of the last operation made available by our Web Service, which is now complete.

Summary

In this chapter, we have demonstrated:

- How easy it is to implement a RESTful Web Service for the CRUD-like manipulation of Alfresco documents.

- That the number of lines of code we have to write, compared to other approaches is small, and the scripting nature of the environment makes the edit-deploy-test cycle tight, saving precious developers' time.

- That the resulting service also exhibits a number of useful properties of REST interfaces, namely, statelessness, loose coupling, the adoption of well-known representation formats, and using hyperlinks to drive the application state.

- That the Atom Publishing Protocol can be used as the basis for designing RESTful Web Services, without reinventing the wheel.

In the next chapter, we will introduce the **Content Management Interoperability Services (CMIS)** draft standard—a RESTful protocol for content management that, in the version currently supported by Alfresco, is implemented using Web Scripts.

10
Overview of CMIS

The **Content Management Interoperability Services (CMIS)** is a specification that aims to define a standardized method for accessing content repositories independent of vendor, platform, and programming language.

Alfresco has been one of the most prominent proponents of CMIS and started distributing an implementation of draft versions of the specification as early as version 3.0 Labs. This chapter and the following five will provide an overview of the main CMIS concepts, a look at the Alfresco implementation, and plenty of examples of real-world usage.

This chapter will provide a basic introduction to CMIS and will cover the following topics:

- A short history of CMIS
- What are the objectives of CMIS
- The main concepts underlying its object model
- What protocols can be used to talk to CMIS servers
- The state of the art regarding CMIS server and client implementations

A bit of history

A small, but influential, group of content management systems vendors took the world by surprise when they announced, in 2008, that they were going to submit a new specification, called the Content Management Interoperability Services, or CMIS for short, to the OASIS Consortium for review and approval.

The joint press release by EMC, IBM, and Microsoft, the original members of the group, was soon followed by announcements from a number of other ECM vendors (initially Alfresco, OpenText, Oracle, and SAP, and then many others) that they were immediately joining the standardization effort.

At the time this book was written, the Content Management Interoperability Services (CMIS) Version 1.0 was ratified by OASIS, and implementations of it are starting to be offered as part of the products of the major vendors. Alfresco started its implementation work when the specification was at a very preliminary stage, but they have continued refining the code and updating it rapidly with each new draft version. Now, with version Community 3.3, Alfresco claims to provide a CMIS service that is compliant with the CMIS 1.0 specification. Of course, their implementation is fully open source, which means you are free to fix it, if it turns out to be not perfectly compliant because of bugs or missing bits.

The full text of the CMIS specification is available at `http://docs.oasis-open.org/cmis/CMIS/v1.0/os/cmis-spec-v1.0.pdf`.

A word of warning

CMIS is a young standard. While every name that counts in the ECM world has rallied behind it and promises full support of it in the upcoming versions of their offerings, it remains to be seen whether CMIS will really be successful in the long term.

Moreover, version 1.0 of the specification was intentionally designed with a very limited scope. There are a number of areas that were left out because the members of the Technical Committee wanted to finish their job in a reasonable amount of time and to give software vendors a chance to implement it quickly. If you start using CMIS earnestly, you will soon discover that there are a number of things that you cannot do with CMIS alone.

With this caveat in mind, let us explore what kind of problems CMIS is designed to solve and how you can use it to implement real-world applications.

Objectives of CMIS

CMIS, as the specification text says,

> *"CMIS is intended to define a generic/universal set of capabilities provided by a CM system and a set of services for working with those capabilities."*

The word "universal" here is what matters the most. The main objective of CMIS is to describe the capabilities that every content management system can provide, at least in theory. Therefore, there aren't different levels of compliance with CMIS such as a "core" level and one or more "advanced" levels. An implementation is either fully compliant or it isn't compliant at all.

Even so, there are a number of features that implementers are not obliged to provide. Look out for words like "MAY" and "SHOULD" in the text of the standards if you want to know what these are. However, a server must always describe explicitly which capabilities it supports or not. For instance, some repositories are capable of performing full-text searches, whereas others aren't. Any client can ask any server about which capabilities it supports and act accordingly, for instance, by degrading its functionalities or refusing to work altogether with a server that doesn't support all the capabilities required by a specific application.

With this in mind, let's take a look at what CMIS does specify:

- An extensible domain model that describes the types of objects that a repository can contain and their relationships
- A query language for performing searches
- A set of protocol bindings for clients to interact with a server over the network
- A number of services and collections of methods, where clients can call upon a server to perform operations on the repository

The CMIS-defined services are designed to allow clients to:

- Manipulate content by creating, reading, updating, deleting it, and filing it inside the folders
- Describe content by means of properties (metadata)
- Follow and manipulate the relationships between items of content
- Navigate content using the classic filesystem metaphor based on a hierarchy of folders
- Search the repository using properties or the content itself
- Perform collaborative operations such as check-in and check-out
- Version content
- Manipulate policies and access rights associated with items of content

What CMIS does not include

As we mentioned before, CMIS was designed without including some features that maybe only a few CMS implement, or that would be too hard to specify in a vendor-independent way. Here are some of them:

- The ability to modify the domain model
- **Digital Asset Management (DAM)** features such as streaming
- Records Management features such as retention schedules

- Subscription services, notifications, and triggers
- Web Content Management features, such as templating, staging, and deployment
- A fully SQL-compliant query language

It is possible that a future version of CMIS will address those, and possibly others, but at this time, we're not aware of any intention to reconvene a Technical Committee in order to draft CMIS 2.0.

CMIS vs. JCR

Before CMIS, there was another specification which attempted to define a *lingua franca* for interoperability between content management systems, and that was the **Java** API for **Content Repositories (JCR** for short). JCR is a much more mature specification than CMIS, having been released as far back as 2005, as JSR-170, and recently updated to a much more comprehensive version 2.0 by the expert group behind JSR-283. So, if JCR is mature and has a rich set of features, one has to wonder what the purpose of CMIS might be. One of the possible answers is that JCR is a Java-only API, whereas CMIS aims to be completely language-and platform-agnostic. JCR was also designed to be essentially an in-process API, meaning that client and server need to reside in the same Java Virtual Machine. CMIS, on the contrary, was only ever meant to be used over the Web.

Actually, there exist implementations of JCR that provide access to JCR repositories over the Web such as the **WebDAV** protocol support that is included in Apache Jackrabbit.

The fact remains, though, that JCR has only been adopted by vendors of Java-based content management systems, including Day Software, Hippo, eXo to name a few, but not all of them. Alfresco has offered a JCR API for a long time but, as far as we know, there are no plans to upgrade it to JCR 2.0. As a consequence of this, if you want to develop an application that connects over the Web to an Alfresco server, you basically have three options:

- Use the proprietary Alfresco Web Services APIs
- Roll your own APIs using Web Scripts
- Use CMIS

The third option should give you a certain amount of portability and let you use your client, in theory at least, with other servers than Alfresco.

The CMIS domain model

The domain model defined by the CMIS specification describes the types of objects that make up the domain of a typical content management system: **documents, folders, relationships,** and **policies**. A CMIS type is identified by its name and defined by its properties, which themselves have an identifier, a type, a display name, and attributes, such as whether they are required, or can have multiple values, and so on.

Besides the types included in the CMIS specification, implementers are free to extend the domain model with their own custom types, derived from the base ones. If you are familiar with the Alfresco domain model and its extension mechanism, all of this should sound familiar to you.

Objects

Every object in a CMIS repository has a unique, immutable identifier that should never change during the lifetime of the object. It is recommended that repositories do not reuse object identifiers, even after the original objects have been deleted. Object types, besides having an opaque identifier, also have a so-called `queryName` that is used in queries and filters. They also have a `displayName` that can be used by applications as a field label, or as a column header in reports.

Every object belongs to one of the four types described as follows: `Document`, `Folder`, `Relationship`, and `Policy`, or to a type derived from one of those. Objects in CMIS are strongly typed; if a client specifies a value for a property that is not in the list of properties supported by a type, the server must report an error.

Documents

The `Document` type, obviously, represents the documents managed by our CMS. Documents can have content. They are, in fact, the only type of object that can have content. A document's content can optionally be rendered in multiple ways such as through different resolutions of an image or a PDF version of a Microsoft Word file. CMIS documents use the concept of **renditions** to represent this fact.

Documents are also the only type of object that can be versioned. They can also be **file-able**, that is, contained in one or more folders, **query-able** by using the **Discovery Services**, and finally **controllable** by policies and **Access Control Lists (ACLs)**.

Content streams

The binary content associated with a `document` object is called a **content stream**. A content stream can have properties, such as its MIME type, which are defined within the associated `document` object. Operations that retrieve or manipulate the content stream, do so by using the identifier of the containing `document` object. CMIS repositories are not required to support the updatability of the content streams.

Folders

Folders are similar to documents and pretty self-explanatory. Folders, unlike documents, cannot have content, nor can they be versioned, but they can have zero or more renditions. They can have child folders and documents, of course.

Every repository must have exactly one **root folder**. The root folder does not have any parent, whereas all the other folders must have exactly one parent. Objects which are not folders can instead have more than one parent (if the repository has the **multi-filing** capability). There cannot be any cyclic relationships in a tree of folders. In other words, a folder cannot be a descendant of itself. Only folders can have children.

Relationships

Relationships are used to define some kind of association or link between objects. They have a type, a source object, and a target object, much like associations in Alfresco. Relationships are managed as objects separate from the ones they link together and creating or removing a relationship should not affect the related objects, which remain independent. Indeed, it is possible for a repository to allow manipulation of relationships even if it does not allow us to update other objects.

Policies

According to the text of the specification,

> *"A policy object represents an administrative policy that can be enforced by a repository such as a retention management policy"*.

The way policies are managed in CMIS is via a textual description of the policy. While policies can be applied to and removed from objects (and objects that can have policies applied to them are said to be **controllable**), they are treated as opaque objects by the specification. Whichever effect applying a policy can have to an object is totally repository-specific. Policies can be created, updated, and deleted via CMIS.

Custom object types

Servers are free to define more object types, in addition to the basic four that we have just described. Each custom object type extends one of the basic ones or another custom type, thus adding new properties to those that it inherits from its parent. There is no support in CMIS for aspects, a-la Alfresco, or for mixins. This makes it hard for Alfresco applications, which typically make use of a lot of aspects to expose all of their domain models via CMIS.

Clients have no means to manipulate a server's domain model, by adding new types, but they can only interrogate the server about its existing domain model.

Properties

Every object type in CMIS is defined by the set of properties it can have. Each property is a named, typed container for zero, one, or more values. A property that has no value is said to be in a "value not set" state. There is no notion, in CMIS, of a `null` value.

Multi-valued properties are possible, but they must be in either the "value set" or "value not set" state as a whole. It is not possible for a single value in a multi-valued list to be unset. Property types defined by CMIS include `string`, `boolean`, `decimal`, `integer`, `datetime`, `uri`, `id`, and `html`. Properties, similar to objects, must have a `queryName`, which will be used in queries.

Services

The operations that a CMIS server exposes through the network protocols it supports are bundled together in a small number of **services**. These are described in the following sections:

Repository Services

The Repository Services (`getRepositories`, `getRepositoryInfo`, `getTypeChildren`, `getTypeDescendants`, and `getTypeDefinition`) are used to discover information about the repository, including information about the object types defined for it.

Navigation Services

The Navigation Services (`getDescendants`, `getChildren`, `getFolderParent`, `getObjectParents`, and `getCheckedoutDocs`) are used to traverse the folder hierarchy in a CMIS Repository and to locate documents that are checked out.

Object Services

The Object Services (`createDocument`, `createFolder`, `createRelationship`, `getProperties`, `getContentStream`, `updateProperties`, `setContentStream`, and others) provide methods for creating, updating, and deleting objects, reading and updating their properties and content, and more.

Multi-filing Services

The Multi-filing Services (`addObjectToFolder`, `removeObjectFromFolder`) are used to file and un-file objects into and from folders. They are available only if the repository supports the multi-filing or the unfiling optional capabilities.

Discovery Services

The Discovery Services (`query`) are used to search for objects within the repository.

Versioning Services

The Versioning Services (`checkOut`, `cancelCheckOut`, `getPropertiesOfLatestVersion`, `getAllVersions`, and `deleteAllVersions`) are used to navigate or update the versions of a document.

Relationship Services

The Relationship Services (`getObjectRelationships`) are used to retrieve the dependent `Relationship` objects associated with an object.

Policy Services

The Policy Services (`applyPolicy`, `removePolicy`, and `getAppliedPolicies`) are used to apply or remove policy objects to a controllable object.

ACL Services

The ACL Services (`getACL`, `applyACL`) are used to get the ACL currently applied to a `document` or `folder` object or to apply a new ACL to it.

Capabilities

As previously mentioned, a CMIS repository is not obliged to implement all the possible features described in the standard, so some of them are defined as optional in the specification. In any instance, clients wishing to work against a specific server implementation must have a way of knowing which features are supported and which are not.

In order to let clients discover which features a given service supports, the standard defines a way for servers to describe their **capabilities**. Capabilities are named properties that can take a boolean value (`true` if the server has that capability, `false` if it doesn't) or one of a list of possible values. The following tables list all of the optional capabilities defined by CMIS, grouped according to the relevant service.

Navigation capabilities

Capability	Description	Possible values
getDescendants	Ability of an application to enumerate the descendants of a folder	• `true` • `false`
getFolderTree	Ability of an application to retrieve the folder tree	• `true` • `false`

Object capabilities

Capability	Description	Possible values
contentStreamUpdatability	Indicates the support a repository has for updating a document's content stream	• `none`: The content stream may never be updated • `anytime`: The content stream may be updated at any time • `pwconly`: The content stream may be updated only when checked out

Capability	Description	Possible values
changes	Indicates what level of changes (if any) the repository exposes via the "change log" service	• none: The repository does not support the change log feature • objectidsonly: The change log can return only the object IDs for changed objects in the repository and an indication of the type of change, not details of the actual change. • properties: The change log can return properties and the Object IDs for the changed objects • all: The change log can return the Object IDs for changed objects in the repository and more information about the actual change
renditions	Indicates whether or not the repository exposes renditions of document objects	• none: The repository does not expose renditions at all. • read: Renditions are provided by the repository and readable by the client.

Filing capabilities

Capability	Description	Possible values
multiFiling	Ability of an application to file a document or some other file-able object in more than one folder	• true • false
unfiling	Ability of an application to leave a document or some other file-able object not filed in any folder	• true • false
versionSpecificFiling	Ability of an application to file individual versions (that is, not all versions) of a document in a folder	• true • false

Versioning capabilities

Capability	Description	Possible values
`PWC Updatable`	Ability of an application to update the "Private Working Copy" of a checked-out document	• `true` • `false`
`PWC Searchable`	Ability of the repository to include the "Private Working Copy" of checked-out documents in query search scope; otherwise PWCs are not searchable	• `true` • `false`
`allVersionsSearchable`	Ability of the repository to include non-latest versions of a document in the query search scope; otherwise only the latest version of each document is searchable	• `true` • `false`

Query capabilities

Capability	Description	Possible values
`query`	Indicates the types of queries that the repository has the ability to fulfill.	• `none`: No queries of any kind can be fulfilled. • `metadataonly`: Only queries that filter based on object properties can be fulfilled. Specifically, the `CONTAINS()` predicate function is not supported. • `fulltextonly`: Only queries that filter based on the full-text content of documents can be fulfilled. Specifically, only the `CONTAINS()` predicate function can be included in the `WHERE` clause. • `bothseparate`: The repository can fulfill queries that filter either on the full-text content of documents or on their properties, but not if both types of filters are included in the same query. • `bothcombined`: The repository can fulfill queries that filter on both the full-text content of documents and their properties in the same query.

Capability	Description	Possible values
join	Indicates the types of JOIN keywords that the repository can fulfill in queries.	• none: The repository cannot fulfill any queries that include any JOIN clauses. • inneronly: The repository can fulfill queries that include an INNER JOIN clause, but cannot fulfill queries that include other types of JOIN clauses. • innerandouter: The repository can fulfill queries that include any type of JOIN clause defined by the CMIS query grammar.

ACL capabilities

Capability	Description	Possible values
ACL	Indicates the level of support for ACLs by the repository	• none: The repository does not support ACL services • discover: The repository supports discovery of ACLs • manage: The repository supports discovery of ACLs and applying ACLs

Capabilities supported by Alfresco

Here is the list of capabilities that Alfresco, as of version Community 3.3 supports. This list can be obtained by examining the AtomPub Service Document, generally available at the following address:

`http://localhost:8080/alfresco/service/api/cmis`

Capability	Value
ACL	manage
allVersionsSearcheable	false
changes	objectidsonly
contentStreamUpdatability	anytime
getDescendants	true
getFolderTree	true
multifiling	true
PWC-Searchable	true
PWC-Updatable	true
query	bothcombined

Capability	Value
renditions	read
unfiling	false
versionSpecificFiling	false
join	none

Protocol bindings

In the ongoing "war" between proponents of traditional, SOAP-based Web Services and those who prefer the REST approach, the CMIS Technical Committee decided not to take sides and mandate that server implementers support both kinds of clients. They did so by defining the semantics of CMIS as a set of protocol-independent services that can be exposed using one of the two **protocol bindings**, namely, the *RESTful Atom* binding and the *Web Services* binding.

The first one is based on the Atom Publishing Protocol, which will be the subject of the next chapter, together with a number of CMIS-specific extensions. The second one uses SOAP.

The AtomPub binding

As with any AtomPub-based service, there is a single URL that clients need to know before they can start using the service. All of the other URLs can be derived from the document, called a **Service Document**, which can be retrieved at that URL. The Service Document contains references to **collections** that represent views into different parts of the repository, such as documents and folders, types, relationships, and permissions.

Collections are represented by Atom feeds, which clients can retrieve, for instance, to list the documents contained in a folder. Clients should post Atom entry documents to a collection's URL to create new entries such as new documents in a folder.

The Web Services binding

The services exposed through the Web Services binding are, naturally, described in a **Web Services Definition Language (WSDL)** document and the associated XML Schema documents. There are two schema documents: the first one defines elements for the primary data types of documents, folders, relationships, and policies as well as collections of these types of objects. The second schema files defines the message formats for each of the CMIS services.

The WSDL document basically describes a one-to-one mapping of the services and operations that are described in Part I of the specification and which have been summarized previously to SOAP methods.

CMIS in action

CMIS is a relatively new specification that was not even finalized at the time we were writing this chapter, but it has already seen wide adoption, both in server products and in client toolkits for various languages. The next sections attempt to present a reasonably up to date picture of the status of available implementations. Keep in mind that this is a quickly moving landscape, so new products will have certainly emerged, and existing products will have been updated by the time you read this.

CMIS-enabled servers

Content management products that have announced for some support for CMIS at present include Alfresco, Drupal, Nuxeo, eXo, KnowledgeTree, and Sense/Net.

Alfresco

Alfresco has always been at the forefront of CMIS, having announced a draft-compliant implementation as early as less than one month after the initial CMIS announcement, in October 2008.

The current version of Alfresco Community, 3.3, implements the CMIS 1.0 Committee Specification 01. This is the version that has been approved by OASIS and that we will be using in the upcoming chapters.

Progress towards keeping Alfresco conformant with newer versions of the specification is underway under the lead of David Caruana. If you build Alfresco from the most recent version of its source code (the *svn HEAD branch*), you will undoubtedly find that something new has been added. You are also welcome to submit patches if you like.

Alfresco also provides a publicly accessible test server, at `http://cmis.alfresco.com`, that you can use to test your client code for conformance. Use the user name `admin`, with the password `admin`, as the credentials for this server and feel free to create new content in it as you please.

Alfresco has also included CMIS support in Enterprise versions of the product, but new features in Enterprise versions tend to be released with much more care and oversight than in Community versions. Moreover, the CMIS implementation in Alfresco Enterprise is not included in the official support agreement. All things considered, if you want to experiment with CMIS, you'll be better served by using the Community version or the one hosted at `cmis.alfresco.com`.

Hosted CMIS AtomPub TCK

The same server that hosts the Alfresco publicly accessible CMIS server also includes a CMIS **Test Compatibility Kit (TCK)** for AtomPub bindings.

If you go to `http://cmis.alfresco.com`, you will find a form where you can input the URL of your CMIS server and have a comprehensive suite of compatibility tests executed against it. You need to provide the URL of the Service Document for AtomPub, as there is no TCK for Web Services bindings available as of now.

The CMIS implementation in Alfresco

Alfresco supports both CMIS protocol binding—both, the AtomPub one as well as the Web Services one. Implementation of the former is based on a set of Web Scripts that use the Apache Abdera library, with some CMIS-specific extensions to parse and generate Atom documents and leverage a Java API layer, whereas the latter uses the Apache CXF toolkit to make the same Java APIs available via SOAP messages. The following diagram illustrates the building blocks of the two implementations:

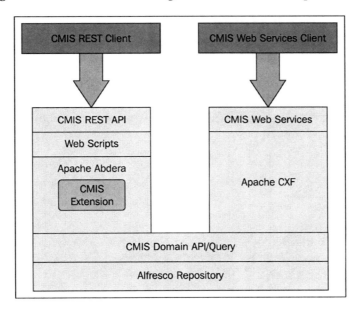

The Service Document for the AtomPub binding can be found at:

`http://localhost:8080/alfresco/service/api/cmis`

The WSDLs for the Web Services binding are listed at:

`http://localhost:8080/alfresco/cmis`

A peculiarity of the Alfresco CMIS implementation is that it supports the Alfresco full-text search language inside the CONTAINS predicate of CMIS-SQL queries. This allows you to run queries such as the following one, which finds all FreeMarker templates (extension ftl) that contain the phrase "alfresco" in their text:

```
SELECT * FROM cmis:document WHERE CONTAINS('TEXT:alfresco AND cm_
name:*ftl')
```

Of course, if you do this, your client application stops being portable between different CMIS servers.

The Alfresco implementation also provides a limited support for aspects. You can use aspects in queries by joining them with object tables on the objectid field as follows:

```
select d.*, o.* from cmis:document as d join cm:ownable as o on
d.cmis:objectid = o.cmis:objectid
```

Some of these implementation details will certainly change in future versions of Alfresco. If you want to keep an eye on updates, you should closely monitor the wiki page at `http://wiki.alfresco.com/wiki/CMIS`.

Nuxeo

Nuxeo is a popular, open source, Enterprise Content Management product. On February 4, 2010, Nuxeo announced the availability of version 1.0 of its **Digital Asset Management (DAM)** application, featuring support for the "currently available draft" of CMIS.

More information about Nuxeo DAM can be found at:
`http://nuxeo.com/en/products/dam`.

eXo

The **eXo Platform** is an open source suite of products that provide services such as Enterprise Content Management, Web Content Management, collaboration, portals, and Knowledge Management.

On February 11, 2010, eXo announced the availability of **xCMIS**, a Java implementation of CMIS 1.0 Committee Draft 06 that leverages eXo's JCR-based content repository.

The xCMIS project is hosted on Google Code at `http://code.google.com/p/xcmis/` and includes a **Google Web Toolkit (GWT)** client that can be used to develop gadgets to include in portals and gadget containers.

xCMIS is advertised as supporting both the AtomPub and the Web Services bindings.

KnowledgeTree

KnowledgeTree is a PHP-based open source document management software, available as a GPL-licensed Community Edition and as a more feature-rich commercial edition.

At the time of writing this, there is a CMIS server-side implementation for KnowledgeTree available at `http://wiki.knowledgetree.com/CMIS`. It is advertised as supporting draft 0.61c AtomPub bindings. Unfortunately, there doesn't seem to be any activity on it at the moment.

Sense/Net

Sense/Net is an open source platform for developing Enterprise Content Management and portal solutions on the .NET platform.

Sense/Net 6.0, which is only available in beta form at the moment, is both a CMIS server and a client that is able to aggregate content from other CMIS providers.

No information about which version of CMIS is implemented by Sense/Net could be gleaned from the website (`www.sensenet.com`) only.

The closed-source world

IBM distributes a "technology preview" that provides a CMIS AtomPub binding for the IBM FileNet and IBM Content Manager products. You can find more information at `http://www.ibm.com/developerworks/data/downloads/cmistechpreview/`.

As that page has last been updated in September, 2009, it is unlikely that the preview implements a recent version of the specification, but we have been unable to ascertain exactly which version it supports.

EMC, a long-established company that specializes in all forms of content storage and management, is one of the founding members of the CMIS committee. They recently acquired Documentum, one of the world's most prominent ECM vendors.

EMC distributes to registered users a CMIS Early Access product that is currently at release 3. Not being registered ECM users, we weren't able to find more details about it. More information is available at `https://community.emc.com/community/labs/cmis`.

Microsoft, apparently, has never officially announced support for CMIS in the upcoming 2010 version of its **SharePoint** product, which is currently available as a beta release, but rumors about it are widespread. A search on the official SharePoint website and assorted Microsoft developers' blogs didn't turn up any confirmation.

For SharePoint 2007, you can download and install a copy of an open source component called **CMIS4SharePoint** from `http://cmis4sharepoint.codeplex.com/`. This only covers draft version 0.5 and only the Web Services binding.

In April 2010, **Day Software** announced the availability of version 2.1 of their **CRX** platform for content applications, with support for CMIS 1.0, in addition to JCR 2.0.

Client toolkits

At the time we were writing this, there were only a handful of open source CMIS client toolkits that seem to have an appreciable amount of activity and traction among developers. These include ApacheChemistry, OpenCMIS, and the PHP CMIS client API for Drupal.

Apache Chemistry and OpenCMIS

OpenCMIS and Apache Chemistry have recently announced that the two projects have officially fused, with the donation of the OpenCMIS code to Chemistry. Therefore, the latter seems to be the place to look, if you want to develop CMIS clients using Java.

In the next few chapters, we are going to explain extensively how to develop CMIS applications using Apache Chemistry.

Drupal

Drupal has an optional CMIS module that, according to the description available at http://drupal.org/project/cmis, *"primarily provides an API for connecting to CMIS-compliant systems to bi-directionally synchronize content between the CMIS ECM system and Drupal. In addition to the API, this package provides a range of basic functionality for creating, updating, browsing, and searching content in the CMIS ECM system via the Drupal interface. The overall goal of the modules is to provide an easy-to-use, WCM frontend in Drupal for ECM systems that are often unfamiliar to web content managers."*

Undoubtedly, closed-source vendors that endorse CMIS, such as IBM, EMC, and Microsoft, will eventually provide libraries for letting developers interact with their server offerings using CMIS.

Summary

This chapter provided a high-level introduction to the CMIS specification, and we hope to have given you a sense of what CMIS is and where it is going, even though it might be too early to tell.

In the following chapters, we are going to take a deeper look at CMIS, by providing detailed instructions for how to perform complex tasks with it, using either of the two mandated protocol bindings, starting with AtomPub.

11
The CMIS AtomPub Binding

In this chapter, you will learn how the CMIS services can be accessed over the network using one of the two protocol bindings included in the specification, namely, the AtomPub binding.

We will investigate, using concrete examples, how AtomPub is used in practice by CMIS to perform operations such as:

- Authentication
- Retrieval of the Service Document
- Repository navigation
- Reading and manipulating entries
- Performing searches

For an in-depth discussion about AtomPub, turn to *Chapter 9, Putting it All Together*.

 All the samples contained in this chapter have been tested using Alfresco Community Edition 3.3, as this was the version having the most up-to-date support for CMIS at the time of writing of this chapter.

The CMIS AtomPub binding

The designers of CMIS choose to include two different protocol bindings in the specification. One is the Web Services binding, which will be described in the next chapter. The other one is the so-called RESTful Atom binding, which is based on the Atom Publishing Protocol, and which is the subject of this chapter.

The upcoming sections will describe how clients can use AtomPub to:

- authenticate against a CMIS server
- retrieve a description of the services that it provides
- obtain information about supported types
- navigate the tree of objects
- create, update, and delete objects
- perform searches

Authenticating

All CMIS-compliant servers must, at the very least, support client authentication using the HTTP Basic authentication schema. This is what we will, therefore, use in the following examples.

The alternative, if the server is Alfresco, is to use the Alfresco login service that was described in *Chapter 6, Introducing the Web Scripts Framework*. As this is not supported by other servers, we will stick with HTTP Basic authentication, which is portable.

If you use `curl`, as we did in the previous chapters, remember to include appropriate credentials in the command line, using the `-u` switch:

```
curl -u admin:admin
```

Getting the Service Document

The URL for the CMIS Service Document in Alfresco is

```
http://host:port/alfresco/service/cmis
```

Reading this document, you might notice that it's rather longer and more complicated than the simplified example that we showed in the previous chapter.

The extra stuff should start to be evident just by looking at the root element, which includes a handful of namespaces in addition to the standard Atom and AtomPub ones:

```
<service xmlns=http://www.w3.org/2007/app
  xmlns:atom=http://www.w3.org/2005/Atom
  xmlns:cmisra=http://docs.oasis-open.org/ns/cmis/restatom/200908/
  xmlns:cmis="http://docs.oasis-open.org/ns/cmis/core/200908/"
  xmlns:alf="http://www.alfresco.org">
```

The `cmis` namespace (URI `http://docs.oasis-open.org/ns/cmis/core/200908/`) includes elements that the CMIS specification defines as extensions to Atom. These are not dependent on a specific protocol binding. The `cmisra` namespace (URI `http://docs.oasis-open.org/ns/cmis/restatom/200908/`) includes CMIS extension elements that are specific to the AtomPub binding (`ra` stands for "REST Atom"). The `alf` namespace (URI `http://www.alfresco.org`) includes Alfresco-specific extension elements.

Collections

The Service Document served by Alfresco lists one workspace, having five collections, which are described in the following table:

Title	Description
Root collection	The collection of objects (documents and folders) that are children of the root folder. In Alfresco, this contains the children of the **Company Home** space.
Type collection	Contains all existing object type definitions.
Checkedout collection	Post a document here to perform a check-out operation.
Unfiled collection	The collection of all unfiled (that is, not belonging to any folder) documents.
Query collection	Post a query document here to perform a search.

All of the `collection` elements have a `cmisra:collectionType` child element that names the type of collection that it refers to. Different types of collections have different semantics in CMIS and clients can read the collection type to determine which collection to use in order to perform specific operations, such as filing, unfiling, doing check-ins and check-outs, and searching.

Other CMIS servers might have more than one workspace, corresponding to more than one repository, but Alfresco has only one workspace which is called the *Main Repository*.

Repository info and URI templates

The `cmisra:repositoryInfo` element provides clients with information about the repository such as the vendor name and the server product name and version.

It also includes a child `cmis:capabilities` element that provides values for all the CMIS capabilities that were listed in the previous chapter. Clients can use this information to determine whether the server supports any capabilities they might be interested in.

The cmisra:uritemplate, finally, lists a number of URI templates that clients can use to build URIs that give direct access to some repository features. By building a URI on the basis of the template with a cmisra:type of query, clients can quickly perform a query and obtain a feed of search results in reply.

Navigating the repository

The easiest way to navigate the repository is to start at the root collection. Let's take a look at a real Service Document:

```
<collection href="http://localhost:8080/alfresco/s/cmis/s/workspace:
SpacesStore/i/aeac2f09-f1e8-4e56-82d9-de929ba38004/children">
    <atom:title>root collection</atom:title>
    <cmisra:collectionType>root</cmisra:collectionType>
</collection>
```

We need to request the feed corresponding to the root collection by getting its URI:

```
curl -u admin:admin 'http://localhost:8080/alfresco/s/cmis/s/workspace:
SpacesStore/i/aeac2f09-f1e8-4e56-82d9-de929ba38004/children'
```

If you do this, you will obtain a feed listing the children of the root space (**Company Home**). The feed has one entry for every document and space found inside **Company Home**. In our case, there are four: **Sites**, **Data Dictionary**, **Guest Home**, and **User Homes**.

You can use those entries to drill down into the corresponding spaces by having a relationship of down and a type of application/atom+xml;type=feed as follows:

```
<entry>

    <link rel="down"
        href="http://localhost:8080/alfresco/.../children"
        type="application/atom+xml;type=feed"/>

    <title>Data Dictionary</title>

</entry>
```

Follow that link, and you get a feed listing all the children of the **Data Dictionary** space and so on. Following the link with a relationship type of up, naturally, gets you the parent folder.

Reading entries

The feed that we have just examined includes one entry for every member of the underlying collection. Each entry comes with an extensive set of properties describing the underlying resource. Even though entries are usually a complete representation of the resource, you should not rely on this as, in theory, the feed might only include a limited subset of properties.

To get a complete representation of each resource, especially if you intend to modify some properties, always get the entry's member URI, pointed to by the link having a relationship type of `edit`.

Reading type information

You can find out which types are defined for the repository by fetching the `types` collection. In Alfresco, the latter can be found at the URL `http://host:port/ alfresco/service/cmis/types`, and it is represented as a feed whose entries describe the existing root types, typically `folder`, `document`, `relationship`, and `policy`.

The types derived from one of the four base types can be listed by following the link, which is shown as follows, included in the corresponding entry:

```
<entry>
    <author>
        <name>admin</name>
    </author>
    <content>cmis:folder</content>
    <id>urn:uuid:type-cmis:folder</id>
    <link rel="down"
        href="http://localhost:8080/alfresco/…/children"
        type="application/atom+xml;type=feed"/>

</entry>
```

The properties of each type, such as its display name, query name, whether objects of this type can be created, filed, queried, and controlled, are listed inside the `cmisra: type` element:

```
<cmisra:type xmlns:xsi="http://www.w3.org/2001/XMLSchema-instance"
cmisra:id="cmis:folder" xsi:type="cmis:cmisTypeFolderDefinitionType">
  <cmis:id>cmis:folder</cmis:id>
  <cmis:localName>folder</cmis:localName>
  <cmis:localNamespace>http://www.alfresco.org/model/cmis/1.0/cd07</
cmis:localNamespace>
```

```
    <cmis:displayName>Folder</cmis:displayName>
    <cmis:queryName>cmis:folder</cmis:queryName>
    <cmis:description>Folder Type</cmis:description>
    <cmis:baseId>cmis:folder</cmis:baseId>
    <cmis:creatable>true</cmis:creatable>
    <cmis:fileable>false</cmis:fileable>
    <cmis:queryable>true</cmis:queryable>
    <cmis:fulltextIndexed>true</cmis:fulltextIndexed>
    <cmis:includedInSupertypeQuery>true</cmis:includedInSupertypeQuery>
    <cmis:controllablePolicy>false</cmis:controllablePolicy>
    <cmis:controllableACL>true</cmis:controllableACL>
</cmisra:type>
```

Creating new objects

With the information about the existing collections, repository capabilities, and the supported types that you can glean from reading the Service Documents and the other documents linked from it, you are now equipped to start creating new documents and folders in the repository.

Creating a new folder

Let's start by creating a new folder named **CMIS Demo** inside the **Company Home** space. As we did in the previous chapters, we are using the curl command for this.

First, we need to prepare an XML file containing the Atom entry that we will be posting. It should look like the following block of code:

```
<entry xmlns="http://www.w3.org/2005/Atom"
       xmlns:app="http://www.w3.org/2007/app"
       xmlns:cmisra="http://docs.oasis-open.org/ns/cmis/
restatom/200908/"
       xmlns:cmis="http://docs.oasis-open.org/ns/cmis/core/200908/">
  <author>
    <name>admin</name>
  </author>
  <id>ignored</id>
  <summary>Created via CMIS AtomPub</summary>
  <title>CMIS Demo</title>
  <updated>2010-02-27T15:30:39.767+01:00</updated>
  <cmisra:object>
    <cmis:properties>
      <cmis:propertyId
        propertyDefinitionId="cmis:objectTypeId">
```

```
        <cmis:value>cmis:folder</cmis:value>
      </cmis:propertyId>
      <cmis:propertyString propertyDefinitionId="cmis:name">
        <cmis:value>CMIS Demo</cmis:value>
      </cmis:propertyString>
    </cmis:properties>
  </cmisra:object>
</entry>
```

Save the previous code in a file named `newfolder.xml`, for instance. Then find the URL of the root collection in the Service Document:

```
<collection
href="http://localhost:8080/alfresco/service/cmis/s/workspace:
SpacesStore/i/c883295b-8610-4aa8-82fe-f6f3064769a3/children">

    <atom:title>root collection</atom:title>

    <cmisra:collectionType>root</cmisra:collectionType>

</collection>
```

The URL will likely be different on your system, so you need to copy it down for use with `curl`:

```
curl -v -u admin:admin -d @newfolder.xml -H 'Content-Type:application/
atom+xml;type=entry' 'http://localhost:8080/alfresco/service/cmis/s/
workspace:SpacesStore/i/c883295b-8610-4aa8-82fe-f6f3064769a3/children'
```

If everything went fine, the server will reply with something like the following response:

```
HTTP/1.1 201 Created

Server: Apache-Coyote/1.1

Cache-Control: no-cache

Pragma: no-cache

Location: http://localhost:8080/alfresco/s/cmis/s/workspace:SpacesStore/
i/37072466-0292-4986-8d7a-c01d523ddf70

Content-Type: application/atom+xml;type=entry;charset=UTF-8

Content-Length: 4941

Date: Sat, 27 Feb 2010 15:49:06 GMT
```

Copy down the value of the `href` attribute of the `<link rel="down">` element contained in the response body having `type="application/atom+xml;type=feed"`. We are going to use it later:

```
<link rel="down" href="http://localhost:8080/alfresco/service/cmis/s/
workspace:SpacesStore/i/a274de54-910d-4a4a-b500-543c13968602/children"
type="application/atom+xml;type=feed"/>
```

You can check with the Alfresco Explorer that **Company Home** now contains the new folder:

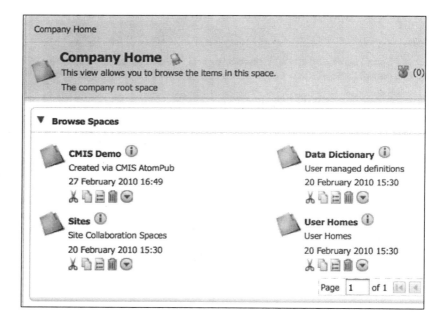

Creating a new document

To create a new document, we could upload a file first, thus creating the Media Resource, as previously described. Then we could update the Media Link Entry to specify more properties for the document. Unfortunately, Alfresco does not currently support this mode of operation. We must create the Media Link Entry first, then use the `edit-media` link to upload the binary content stream.

Therefore, we will start with an Entry document. Call it `newdoc.xml`:

```
<entry xmlns="http://www.w3.org/2005/Atom"
       xmlns:app="http://www.w3.org/2007/app"
       xmlns:cmisra="http://docs.oasis-open.org/ns/cmis/
restatom/200908/"
       xmlns:cmis="http://docs.oasis-open.org/ns/cmis/core/200908/">
```

```
<author>
  <name>admin</name>
</author>
<id>ignored</id>
<summary>A Picture</summary>
<title>image.jpg</title>
<updated>2010-02-27T17:18:01.134+01:00</updated>
<cmisra:object>
  <cmis:properties>
    <cmis:propertyId
      propertyDefinitionId="cmis:objectTypeId">
      <cmis:value>cmis:document</cmis:value>
    </cmis:propertyId>
    <cmis:propertyString propertyDefinitionId="cmis:name">
      <cmis:value>image.jpg</cmis:value>
    </cmis:propertyString>
  </cmis:properties>
</cmisra:object>
</entry>
```

Once you have saved this document, use curl to post it to the URL of the collection of children of the CMIS Demo folder that we created before, the one you should have copied somewhere:

```
curl -v -u admin:admin -d @newdoc.xml -H 'Cone:application/
atom+xml;type=entry' 'http://localhost:8080/alfresco/service/cmis/s/
workspace:SpacesStore/i/a274de54-910d-4a4a-b500-543c13968602/children'
```

If the operation is successful, you should receive a **201 Created** response. Look for the edit-media link in the returned entry:

```
<link rel="edit-media" href="http://localhost:8080/alfresco/service/cmis/
s/workspace:SpacesStore/i/5397a343-593c-45a9-b258-e755f568dd9d/content.
jpg" type="image/jpeg"/>
```

Also, copy the Member URI of the new entry somewhere, as you will need it later. This is the href of the edit link:

```
<link rel="edit" href="http://localhost:8080/alfresco/service/cmis/s/
workspace:SpacesStore/i/5397a343-593c-45a9-b258-e755f568dd9d"/>
```

If you are confused by all those links, keep this in mind: You use the edit link to operate on the Media Link Entry when you want to update the document's metadata or when you want to delete the document. You use the edit-media link when you want to operate on the Media Resource, which represents the contents of the document.

Now take a random file you have lying somewhere on your disk such as a JPEG picture called `image.jpg`. Upload it, using `curl`, to the `edit-media` URL. We must use the PUT command for this as follows:

```
curl -v -u admin:admin -T image.jpg 'http://localhost:8080/alfresco/
service/cmis/s/workspace:SpacesStore/i/5397a343-593c-45a9-b258-
e755f568dd9d/content.jpg'
```

The server should issue a response, as shown in the following response:

```
HTTP/1.1 100 Continue

HTTP/1.1 200 OK

Server: Apache-Coyote/1.1

Expires: Mon, 29 Mar 2010 16:35:59 GMT

Cache-Control: public

Content-Length: 0

Date: Sat, 27 Feb 2010 16:35:59 GMT
```

You can use the Alfresco Explorer to check that the image file was uploaded successfully:

Updating a document's metadata

To update a document's metadata, it is recommended that you start by retrieving its current representation by issuing a GET request against its member URI.

```
curl -v -u admin:admin -o entry.xml 'http://localhost:8080/alfresco/
service/cmis/s/workspace:SpacesStore/i/5397a343-593c-45a9-b258-
e755f568dd9d'
```

The previous command will save the body of the server's response in a file named `entry.xml`. You can edit that file to modify properties such as the document's title or summary, and then you can use the PUT command to submit the modified version of the entry. Remember to always specify the correct content type as follows:

```
curl -v -u admin:admin -T entry.xml -H 'Conteapplication/
atom+xml;type=entry' 'http://localhost:8080/alfresco/service/cmis/s/
workspace:SpacesStore/i/5397a343-593c-45a9-b258-e755f568dd9d'
```

For testing that this operation is working as expected, we changed the document's title and summary before submitting it. Then we checked the result in the explorer as follows:

Technically, you should always resubmit a complete copy of the possibly modified entry when performing an update. In Alfresco, if you submit an entry that contains only the properties that you want to modify and omit all the others, the update will work. However, this could fail with other servers.

Deleting a document

Now, that was one beautiful image you uploaded in the previous section. Luckily, you still have a copy of it on your hard disk, so we can safely remove it from Alfresco by sending a DELETE command to the entry's Member URI:

```
curl -v -u admin:admin -X DELETE 'http://localhost:8080/alfresco/service/
cmis/s/workspace:SpacesStore/i/5397a343-593c-45a9-b258-e755f568dd9d'
```

The server should reply with:

```
HTTP/1.1 204 No Content
Server: Apache-Coyote/1.1
Cache-Control: no-cache
Pragma: no-cache
Date: Sat, 27 Feb 2010 16:55:22 GMT
```

And your file should be gone. Of course, with Alfresco, it can still be recovered from the **Deleted Items** section of your user's profile.

Performing a search

If you look at the Service Document produced by the Alfresco CMIS service again, you will notice that there is a special collection listed there:

```
<collection
    href="http://localhost:8080/alfresco/service/cmis/queries">
    <atom:title>query collection</atom:title>
    <accept>application/cmisquery+xml</accept>
    <cmisra:collectionType>query</cmisra:collectionType>
</collection>
```

This is a collection that, instead of the usual Atom entry documents (MIME type `application/atom+xml;type=entry`), accepts documents of type `application/cmisquery+xml`.

By posting such a document to this collection, the client does not create any new resources. Instead, it asks the server to perform a search and return its results as an Atom feed.

A CMIS query document looks like the following:

```
<cmis:query
xmlns:cmis="http://docs.oasis-open.org/ns/cmis/core/200908/">
   <cmis:statement>
     <![CDATA[SELECT * FROM cmis:document]]>
   </cmis:statement>
</cmis:query>
```

To perform this search, post the query document to the query collection URI, and remember to specify the correct MIME type:

```
curl -v -u admin:admin -d @query.xml -H 'Content-Type: application/
cmisquery+xml' 'http://localhost:8080/alfresco/s/cmis/queries'
```

The server's reply will be a feed containing one entry for each document present in your repository. If you have many of them, the feed will be quite large, and it will take a long time for the server to generate all of it.

Paging search results

If you anticipate that searches could produce a huge number of hits, it can be convenient to ask the server to serve results in smaller batches or pages. You can do so by adding a couple more elements to the query document, as shown in the following example:

```
<cmis:query
xmlns:cmis="http://docs.oasis-open.org/ns/cmis/core/200908/">
  <cmis:statement>
    <![CDATA[SELECT * FROM cmis:document]]>
  </cmis:statement>
  <cmis:skipCount>0</cmis:skipCount>
  <cmis:maxItems>10</cmis:maxItems>
</cmis:query>
```

This commands the server to return up to 10 search results, skipping zero initial results.

When you want to fetch the next page, issue a request such as the following one:

```
<cmis:query
xmlns:cmis="http://docs.oasis-open.org/ns/cmis/core/200908/">
  <cmis:statement>
    <![CDATA[SELECT * FROM cmis:document]]>
  </cmis:statement>
  <cmis:skipCount>10</cmis:skipCount>
  <cmis:maxItems>10</cmis:maxItems>
</cmis:query>
```

When a request returns less than maxItems results, you know that you are at the last page.

Some servers, Alfresco included, might provide a feed enriched with OpenSearch information. This includes links to follow when you want to move to the next, previous, first, and last page of search results.

Let's have a look at what Alfresco includes in the feed, when we ask for the first 10 results:

```
<link rel="first" href="http://localhost:8080/alfresco/s/cmis/query?
q=SELECT%20*%20FROM%20cmis:document&amp;skipCount=0&amp;maxItems=10"
type="application/atom+xml;type=feed"/>

<link rel="next" href="http://localhost:8080/alfresco/s/cmis/query?q
=SELECT%20*%20FROM%20cmis:document&amp;skipCount=10&amp;maxItems=10"
type="application/atom+xml;type=feed"/>

<title>Result set for SELECT * FROM cmis:document</title>

<updated>2010-05-10T13:46:58.445+02:00</updated>

<opensearch:totalResults>11</opensearch:totalResults>

<opensearch:startIndex>0</opensearch:startIndex>

<opensearch:itemsPerPage>10</opensearch:itemsPerPage>
```

If we follow the `next` link (by using the `GET` method), we will receive the next 10 search results and so on.

Queries

We've seen, in the previous code, one example of a CMIS query:

```
SELECT * FROM cmis:document
```

This looks remarkably similar to SQL and indeed, the CMIS query language is a subset of SQL-92, with extensions for full-text search and folder membership. The authors of the CMIS specification probably reasoned that using a language that is familiar to many developers would facilitate the adoption of CMIS, so they chose to use SQL instead of inventing yet another query language.

Relational view

The domain model of CMIS is a set of trees, not a set of relational tables. So, in order to make SQL work over a CMIS repository, those trees must be made to appear somehow as relational tables. This operation is called **projection**. The result of the projection is a read-only relational view of the repository.

The relational view is created by taking all of the *query-able* object types in the domain model and defining a virtual table for each of them. The virtual table is named after the `queryName` property of the underlying object type.

The columns of the virtual table include all the properties defined for the object type and for any of its ancestor types. The names of the columns are taken from the `queryNames` of the corresponding properties.

Statement syntax

With the relational view in mind, you can now issue statements that adhere to the following general syntax:

SELECT *col1* [, *col2* ...] FROM *table1* [, *table2* ...] [WHERE *condition*] [ORDER BY *sort specification*]

The WHERE and ORDER BY clauses are optional, as indicated by the square brackets.

The CMIS query syntax also includes the possibility of performing relational joins (inner and outer) using the JOIN keyword. This is an optional capability, however, and at this time, Alfresco does not provide it, as indicated by the presence of the

```
<cmis:capabilityJoin>none</cmis:capabilityJoin>
```

element in the Service Document.

The WHERE clause supports all of the usual SQL operators, depending on the property types, as shown in the following table:

Property Type	Operators
String	=, <>, [NOT] LIKE, [NOT] IN
Decimal	=, <>, <, <=, >, >=, [NOT] IN
Integer	=, <>, <, <=, >, >=, [NOT] IN
Boolean	=
DateTime	=, <>, <, <=, >, >=, [NOT] IN
ID	=, <>, [NOT] IN
URI	=, <>, [NOT] LIKE, [NOT] IN

In addition to those, the CMIS query syntax also supports the ANY and IN/ANY predicates for multi-valued properties.

The ANY predicate can be used to filter rows where any one of the values of a multi-valued property is equal to a comparison value (here we are using the Bookshop model that was introduced in *Chapter 8, Writing a Web Script Controller in JavaScript and Java*):

```
SELECT * FROM  bs:book AS b WHERE ('Jerome D. Salinger' = ANY
b.author)
```

The previous statement will select all the books that have Jerome D. Salinger as one of their authors.

The IN/ANY predicate is an extension to SQL-92 and can be used to filter rows where any of the values of a multi-valued property are included in a list of comparison values:

```
SELECT * FROM  bs:book WHERE ANY author in ('Jerome D. Salinger',
'Kurt Vonnegut', 'Joseph Heller')
```

The previous statement will select all the books that have either Jerome D. Salinger, or Kurt Vonnegut, or Joseph Heller as one of their authors.

Full-text search

Another CMIS extension to SQL-92 is the CONTAINS predicate that is used to perform searches on the content of documents and not just on their properties. It works as follows:

```
SELECT cm:title FROM bs:book WHERE CONTAINS('Holden Caulfield')
```

The CONTAINS predicate can also specify a table name as follows:

```
SELECT cm:title FROM bs:book WHERE CONTAINS(bs:book, 'Holden
Caulfield')
```

This is only necessary (and mandatory) when doing joins, but, as we said earlier, Alfresco does not support joins yet. The search expression used in the CONTAINS predicate is a set of terms that are implicitly joined with AND and that can be joined with an OR, if needed. A '-' sign indicates negation. In a query that uses the CONTAINS predicate, the SCORE() function can be used in the SELECT clause to return a measure of relevance of each result with respect to the search phrase. This value returns a decimal number in the range 0 to 1.

There are other clauses and predicates that can be used in SQL queries. These are described in detail in *Appendix A, The CMIS Query Language*.

Summary

In this chapter, we have demonstrated how the CMIS AtomPub binding can be used in practice to:

- Retrieve information about a repository
- Browse the tree of folders and documents
- Create folder and documents, including binary data
- Modify a document's content and metadata
- Delete a document or a folder
- Perform searches

In the upcoming chapters, you will learn:

- About the Web Services protocol binding
- How to use the Apache Chemistry toolkit to develop CMIS client applications

We will also introduce a complete application as a sample of a Java-based CMIS client.

12
Developing a CMIS Client using Apache Chemistry

Now that you have learned almost everything there is to know about CMIS, and especially about its AtomPub protocol binding, you are prepared to start developing client applications that can talk to an Alfresco server using it; you might also want your client code to be portable across different vendors' servers.

One option is to roll your own toolkit for doing so, starting from the bare minimum that is included in the JDK — the java.net classes and the XML parsers that are included in **Java API for XML Processing (JAXP)**. But why bother when somebody else has already done much of the hard work of writing the code layer that understands CMIS and its peculiar protocol bindings?

Apache Chemistry is a project whose aim is to develop a comprehensive set of client and server implementations of the CMIS specification. Being open source, under the terms of the Apache License, you are free to grab its source code, use it in your applications, and modify it to suit your needs.

If, in doing so, you come across bugs and develop fixes for them, or you introduce some enhancements, it makes sense to contribute these as patches to the Chemistry projects. Otherwise, you would have to maintain your private, patched version, and synchronize your modifications with the public version of the code every time a new version comes out.

In this chapter, we will introduce the Java client side of Apache Chemistry and teach you how to:

- Download, install, and start using Chemistry
- Retrieve information about the repository
- List folders
- Create, modify, and delete folders, text, and binary documents
- Perform searches

Introducing Apache Chemistry

Following some discussions among people who wanted to develop an open source toolkit for developing CMIS client and server applications, in April 2009, the Chemistry project entered the **Apache Incubator**.

The Incubator of the **Apache Software Foundation (ASF)** is the home of projects that wish to be accepted under the umbrella of the ASF. New projects, either born within the foundation, originating from external developers, or from code donations from other organizations, go through an incubation process, where they are evaluated for adherence to the guiding principles of the ASF, the so-called *Apache Way*, which includes values such as meritocracy and diversity.

While it is still in the incubator, a project, affectionately called a *podling*, should grow under the supervision of a few mentors. Once it has attracted a sufficiently diverse set of contributors and it has demonstrated that it can stand on its own, it is usually promoted to a *top-level* project and is now officially part of the ASF. This process is called *graduation*.

As of today, Apache Chemistry is still incubating, but due to its liveness and through the constant addition of new contributors, it is to be expected that it will graduate soon. It should be noted that the incubation status of a project is not in any way a reflection of the maturity of its code base. Fully developed and tested code bases might never graduate from the incubator if they fail to attract other developers beyond the original ones.

The official Incubator page for Apache Chemistry is `http://incubator.apache.org/chemistry/`. As this is a fairly new and rapidly evolving project, it is advisable to keep an eye on the website and to subscribe to the project's mailing lists, if you want to be informed of everything that is happening around the Chemistry.

Chemistry, OpenCMIS, and the Alfresco TCK

A recent addition to Chemistry has been the code for the **OpenCMIS** project. OpenCMIS started at OpenText, with the subsequent contribution of developers from SAP and Alfresco. After some discussions, it was decided to donate the OpenCMIS code to the Apache Chemistry project. As a consequence, the committers of OpenCMIS became Chemistry committers and the original Chemistry Java client implementation was superceded by the OpenCMIS code.

The Alfresco **Test Compatibility Kit** (**TCK**) was also contributed to Chemistry recently. So now, basically, we have three Java client libraries in Chemistry, in addition to the Python `cmislib` library that was contributed by Jeff Potts.

In the following sections, we are going to show how to use the new Chemistry OpenCMIS client library to interact with a server, as a consensus was reached on using it as the official client-side implementation. Keep in mind that things are changing rapidly on the Chemistry front, so it is not easy to predict the direction in which it will evolve. Be prepared to adapt your client code if you decide to use a newer version of Chemistry.

Downloading and installing Chemistry

As of today, there hasn't yet been an official release of Apache Chemistry. This means that, in order to use it, you have to download the source code and build it yourself.

The best way to download an updated version of the Chemistry OpenCMIS source code is by using a **Subversion** client. The URL of the repository is `http://svn.apache.org/repos/asf/incubator/chemistry/opencmis/trunk`. Therefore, if you are accustomed to using the command-line Subversion client, you can fetch the whole source tree using the following command:

```
svn co -r942541 http://svn.apache.org/repos/asf/incubator/chemistry/
opencmis/trunk opencmis
```

The previous command will copy the source code into a folder called `opencmis`, under your current folder. If you prefer to use some other kind of Subversion client, or download the code directly from your IDE, follow the instructions provided for it and use the previous URL.

In Eclipse, for instance, you will have to install one of the existing Subversion plugins, such as **Subversive**, then open the **SVN Repository Browsing** perspective to connect to the Chemistry repository or use the **File | Import | Project from SVN** menu command.

Those readers with a good knowledge of the Subversion command-line tool will undoubtedly have noticed that we specified a specific revision number (942541) for checkout. As this is unreleased code, the only way to reliably refer to a specific version is to use its Subversion revision number.

Revision 942541 is the one that has been used to test the examples presented in this chapter. If you choose to use a more recent revision of the code, be warned that you might have to adapt them.

Building Chemistry

Once you have downloaded Chemistry, you need to compile the source code and package the JAR files that will be used by your application code. The recommended way to build Chemistry is by using **Apache Maven** (http://maven.apache.org).

If you haven't already done so, download and install Maven 2. You can also install a Maven plugin for your IDE of choice, such as **m2eclipse** for Eclipse, but we recommend using the mvn tool from the command line.

Compiling Chemistry and running all of its tests takes a bit of memory and time. Before you try to execute the build, therefore, it is necessary to increment the maximum heap size of the JVM. To do so, execute the following command (for Unix / Linux):

```
export MAVEN_OPTS=-Xmx512m
```

or the following one for Windows:

```
set MAVEN_OPTS=-Xmx512m
```

Then change to the opencmis folder and type:

```
mvn install
```

The first time you execute this command, it will take a while because Maven will go and download, from the public Maven repository, all the libraries that Chemistry depends on. This might be a good time to grab a cup of tea.

Hopefully, by the time you are in front of your PC again, you will be greeted by a message of:

```
[INFO] BUILD SUCCESSFUL
```

By now, Maven will have built all of the Chemistry modules and installed them in your local Maven repository, where they can be accessed by other projects as dependencies.

Importing Chemistry into Eclipse

If you are using Eclipse as your IDE of choice, you will be glad to know that Maven includes a plugin for generating Eclipse projects. It can be invoked as follows:

```
mvn eclipse:eclipse
```

This command will generate all the necessary .project and .classpath files for Eclipse. Before you import them into Eclipse, make sure that you have set the M2_REPO classpath variable to the path of the Maven repository (usually <your-home-directory>/.m2/repository) under the **Java | Build Path | Classpath Variables** section of Eclipse preferences, as shown in the following screenshot:

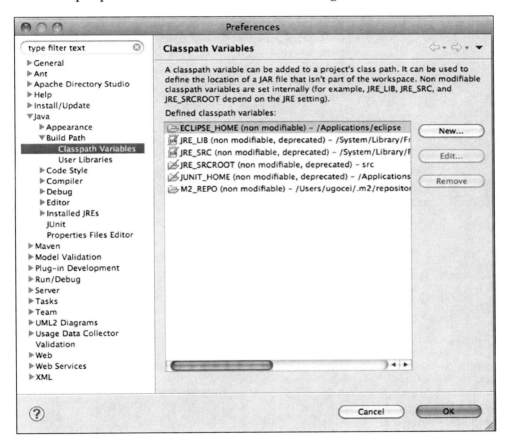

Once it has been completed, launch Eclipse, and from the **File** menu, choose **Import....** Then select **General | Existing Projects into Workspace**, and finally select the root directory, opencmis.

Confirm the selection of all projects shown in the **Import** dialog box, and your **Package Explorer** tab will appear, as shown in the following screenshot:

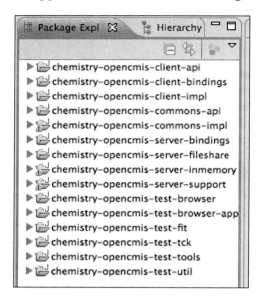

You can now start developing your client code in Eclipse by creating a new project and adding some of those projects as dependencies to your project. For a client application, you will need to at least add the following dependencies:

- chemistry-opencmis-client-api
- chemistry-opencmis-client-bindings
- chemistry-opencmis-client-impl
- chemistry-opencmis-commons-api
- chemistry-opencmis-commons-impl

The following screenshot displays the relevant configuration, as shown in the **Project Properties** dialog box:

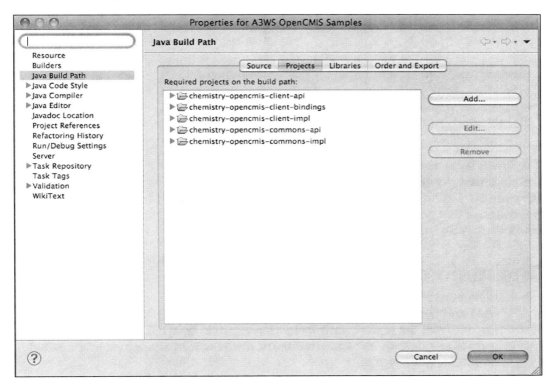

The modules of the Chemistry client API

As previously mentioned, the client APIs that are included with Chemistry were derived from OpenCMIS, therefore, the documentation, the package, and artifact names refer to OpenCMIS.

The client APIs are made up of two layers—the higher one, called the **OpenCMIS Client API**, is an object-oriented layer that client applications, including all the code presented in this chapter and in the next, typically will use.

This layer includes the following packages and artifacts:

Package	Artifact	Description
`org.apache.chemistry.opencmis.client.api`	chemistry-opencmis-client-api	Main interfaces of the client API
`org.apache.chemistry.opencmis.commons.api`	chemistry-opencmis-commons-api	Interfaces and classes shared by client and client bindings API
`org.apache.chemistry.opencmis.client.runtime`	chemistry-opencmis-client-impl	Implementation classes of client interfaces

The lower level makes up the **OpenCMIS Client Bindings API** and provides an interface that closely mirrors the CMIS domain model. It also hides the details of the protocol bindings, permitting the development of protocol-independent client applications that should work unchanged using either binding, except for the connection setup code.

The main client classes

- `SessionFactory`: This interface provides the entry point into the Client API and is responsible for creating a `Session` object. Additionally, it gives access to all the repository information exposed by the CMIS. The runtime provides a default implementation for the `SessionFactory` interface called `SessionFactoryImpl`.

- `Session`: This is the main interface an application has to work with. A session is attached to one and only one repository. Depending on the concrete implementation of the `Session` interface, all the data that is received through the Session interface can be cached in the session object.

- `Repository`: This interface wraps the CMIS `Repository` information service.

- `CmisObject`: The `CmisObject` interface represents a generic CMIS domain object.

- `ObjectType`: The base interface for all CMIS object types such as `FolderType`, `DocumentType`, `PolicyType`, and `RelationType`.

- `Folder`: This interface represents a CMIS `Folder` object.

- `Document`: This interface represents a CMIS `Document` object.

- `ContentStream`: This interface wraps the content stream of a CMIS document.

- `Policy`: This interface represents a CMIS `Policy` object.

- `Relation`: This interface represents a CMIS `Relation` object.

Setting up a connection

The code for setting up a connection with a CMIS Repository depends on the chosen protocol binding, even though the interfaces involved are the same — `SessionFactory` and `Session`. What changes are the values of the parameters passed to the `SessionFactory.createSession` method.

Setting up a connection with AtomPub

The following code creates an AtomPub Session by connecting to a CMIS repository called **Main Repository**, which is available at `http://host/alfresco/service/cmis`, authenticating as `admin` with the password `admin`.

```
SessionFactory f = SessionFactoryImpl.newInstance();
Map<String, String> params = new HashMap<String, String>();
params.put(SessionParameter.USER, "admin"); params.
put(SessionParameter.PASSWORD, "admin");
params.put(SessionParameter.ATOMPUB_URL,
  "http://host/alfresco/service/cmis");
params.put(SessionParameter.BINDING_TYPE, BindingType.ATOMPUB.
value()); parameter.put(SessionParameter.REPOSITORY_ID,
"Main Repository");
Session s = f.createSession(parameter);
```

In case the repository name is not known, it is possible to list all the available repositories using the following code:

```
List<Repository> repos =
  sessionFactory.getRepositories(params);
```

In this case, the `params` maps must not contain an entry for the repository ID. Once an instance of `Repository` has been obtained, a `Session` can be opened on it by using the `Repository.getSession` method.

Setting up a connection with Web Services

In order to set up a connection using the Web Services binding, the URLs of the WSDL files for the various services must be specified as parameters as follows:

```
SessionFactory f = SessionFactoryImpl.newInstance();
Map<String, String> params = new HashMap<String, String>();
params.put(SessionParameter.USER, "admin");
params. put(SessionParameter.PASSWORD, "admin");
params.put(SessionParameter.WEBSERVICES_ACL_SERVICE,
```

```
         "http://host/alfresco/cmis/ACLService?wsdl"); params.
    put(SessionParameter.WEBSERVICES_DISCOVERY_SERVICE,
         "http://host/alfresco/cmis/DiscoveryService?wsdl");
    params.put(SessionParameter.WEBSERVICES_MULTIFILING_SERVICE,
         "http://host/alfresco/cmis/MultiFilingService?wsdl");
    params.put(SessionParameter.WEBSERVICES_NAVIGATION_SERVICE,
         "http://host/alfresco/cmis/NavigationService?wsdl");
    params.put(SessionParameter.WEBSERVICES_OBJECT_SERVICE,
         "http://host/alfresco/cmis/ObjectService?wsdl");
    params.put(SessionParameter.WEBSERVICES_POLICY_SERVICE,
         "http://host/alfresco/cmis/PolicyService?wsdl");
    params.put(SessionParameter.WEBSERVICES_RELATIONSHIP_SERVICE,
         "http://host/alfresco/cmis/RelationshipService?wsdl");
    params.put(SessionParameter.WEBSERVICES_REPOSITORY_SERVICE,
         "http://host/alfresco/cmis/RepositoryService?wsdl");
    params.put(SessionParameter.WEBSERVICES_VERSIONING_SERVICE,
         "http://host/alfresco/cmis/VersioningService?wsdl");
    params.put(SessionParameter.BINDING_TYPE,
      BindingType.WEBSERVICES.value()); parameter.put(SessionParameter.
    REPOSITORY_ID,
         "Main Repository");
    Session s = f.createSession(parameter);
```

Once you have a session, its usage doesn't change depending on the protocol binding, as all the interfaces of the client API effectively hide all the details of the protocol.

Code samples

Each of the following sections contain a short example program that illustrate how to perform a single operation on a CMIS service, using the Chemistry OpenCMIS client library.

Listing the server's capabilities

The following sample illustrates a method for retrieving the list of all the CMIS capabilities and whether they are supported by the server. Refer to the tables contained in *Chapter 10, Overview of CMIS*, for a description of what each capability means.

```
package com.packtpub.a3ws.samples.chemistry;

import java.util.HashMap;
import java.util.List;
import java.util.Map;
```

```
import org.apache.chemistry.opencmis.client.api.Repository;
import org.apache.chemistry.opencmis.client.api.Session;
import org.apache.chemistry.opencmis.client.api.SessionFactory;
import org.apache.chemistry.opencmis.client.runtime.
SessionFactoryImpl;
import org.apache.chemistry.opencmis.commons.SessionParameter;
import org.apache.chemistry.opencmis.commons.api.
RepositoryCapabilities;
import org.apache.chemistry.opencmis.commons.api.RepositoryInfo;
import org.apache.chemistry.opencmis.commons.enums.BindingType;

public class ListServerCapabilities {

    private static Session getSession(String serverUrl, String
username, String password) {
        SessionFactory sessionFactory = SessionFactoryImpl.
newInstance();
        Map<String, String> params = new HashMap<String, String>();
        params.put(SessionParameter.USER, username);
        params.put(SessionParameter.PASSWORD, password);
        params.put(SessionParameter.ATOMPUB_URL, serverUrl);
        params.put(SessionParameter.BINDING_TYPE, BindingType.ATOMPUB.
value());
        List<Repository> repos = sessionFactory.
getRepositories(params);
        if (repos.isEmpty()) {
            throw new RuntimeException("Server has no repositories!");
        }
        return repos.get(0).createSession();
    }

    public static void main(String args[]) {
        String serverUrl = args[0];
        String username = args[1];
        String password = args[2];
        Session session = getSession(serverUrl, username, password);
        RepositoryInfo info = session.getRepositoryInfo();
        RepositoryCapabilities capabilities = info.getCapabilities();
        System.out.println("CAPABILITIES of " + info.getName());
        System.out.println("ACL:                       " +
capabilities.getAclCapability());
        System.out.println("Change:                    " +
capabilities.getChangesCapability());
        System.out.println("Join:                      " +
capabilities.getJoinCapability());
```

```
        System.out.println("Query:                         " +
capabilities.getQueryCapability());
        System.out.println("Rendition:                     " +
capabilities.getRenditionsCapability());
        System.out.println("GetDescendants:                " +
capabilities.isGetDescendantsSupported());
        System.out.println("GetFolderTree:                 " +
capabilities.isGetFolderTreeSupported());
        System.out.println("Multifiling:                   " +
capabilities.isMultifilingSupported());
        System.out.println("Unfiling:                      " +
capabilities.isUnfilingSupported());
        System.out.println("VersionSpecificFiling:         " +
capabilities.isVersionSpecificFilingSupported());
        System.out.println("AllVersionsSearchable:         " +
capabilities.isAllVersionsSearchableSupported());
        System.out.println("ContentStreamUpdatableAnytime: " +
capabilities.getContentStreamUpdatesCapability());
        System.out.println("PWCSearchable:                 " +
capabilities.isPwcSearchableSupported());
        System.out.println("PWCUpdatable:                  " +
capabilities.isPwcUpdatableSupported());
    }
}
```

The `getSession` method is a generic method for obtaining a CMIS session over AtomPub, using the values of Service Document URI, username, and password passed in as arguments, and connecting to the first available repository. All of the other samples presented in this chapter will use the same method again.

The values of the `serverUrl`, `username`, and `password` variables are taken from command-line arguments. Consequently, if you are running Alfresco on your local machine, you should invoke the program as follows:

```
java com.packtpub.a3ws.samples.chemistry.ListServerCapabilities http://
localhost:8080/alfresco/service/cmis admin admin
```

Of course, you need to set your CLASSPATH environment variable to the full list of Chemistry and dependent JARs, before running the command. Alternatively, if you copy the previous code in an Eclipse project, you just need to declare its dependencies, as illustrated before, and then use the **Run As | Java Application** menu command (you can configure the arguments to be passed on the command line by editing the **Run Configuration** created by Eclipse when you run the program for the first time). The code samples that you can download from the book's website are already configured as an Eclipse project that you can simply import alongside the Chemistry modules.

On the current version of Alfresco at the time of writing this (Community 3.3), the following is the output that you will get:

```
CAPABILITIES of Main Repository
ACL:                            MANAGE
Change:                         NONE
Join:                           NONE
Query:                          BOTHCOMBINED
Rendition:                      READ
GetDescendants:                 true
GetFolderTree:                  true
Multifiling:                    true
Unfiling:                       false
VersionSpecificFiling:          false
AllVersionsSearchable:          false
ContentStreamUpdatableAnytime:  ANYTIME
PWCSearchable:                  true
PWCUpdatable:                   true
```

By the time you are reading this, Alfresco will have probably published one or more updated releases, and you might get a wider set of supported capabilities if you run the previous code against a more recent one.

Listing repository types

The following sample lists all of the object types supported by the default repository. For each type, its identifier, display name, and parent type are printed. Here is the `main` method, which calls the same `getSession` method included with the previous sample:

```
public static void main(String args[]) {
    String serverUrl = args[0];
    String username = args[1];
    String password = args[2];
    Session session = getSession(serverUrl, username, password);
    RepositoryInfo info = session.getRepositoryInfo();
    System.out.println("Types of " + info.getName());
    List<Tree<ObjectType>> trees = session.getTypeDescendants(null,
-1, false);
    listTypes(trees, 1);
}
```

The `Session.getTypeDescendants` method returns a tree of all object types descended from the type passed as the first parameter (or of all object types, starting at the root, if `null` is passed).

The `listTypes` method, which is part of the sample, recurses over the tree of descendant types and prints their name, and they are indented according to their position in the tree:

```
private static void listTypes(List<Tree<ObjectType>> trees, int level)
{
    for (Tree<ObjectType> tree : trees) {
        for (int i = 0 ; i < level ; ++i) {
            System.out.print("\t");
        }
      System.out.println(tree.getItem().getId());
      listTypes(tree.getChildren(), level + 1);
    }
}
```

The output from this program is quite long, so we are only showing the first few lines:

```
Types of Main Repository
    cmis:folder
        F:cm:systemfolder
            F:act:savedactionfolder
            F:app:configurations
            F:bpm:package
        F:wcm:avmfolder
            F:wcm:avmplainfolder
            F:wca:webfolder
            F:wcm:avmlayeredfolder
        F:imap:imapFolder
        F:wca:formfolder
...
```

In our server, we also have deployed the Bookshop model that was developed in *Chapter 8, Writing a Web Script Controller in JavaScript and Java*. Therefore, it should not come as a surprise that the "book" and "review" types are listed here:

```
cmis:document
    ...
    D:bs:book
    ...
    D:bs:review
```

Getting a type definition

Once we have the identifier of an object type, we would like to know more about it; we might want to list its properties in order to create a data entry form, for instance. The following sample demonstrates how to do that by invoking the `Session.getTypeDefinition` method:

```
public static void main(String args[]) {
    String serverUrl = args[0];
    String username = args[1];
    String password = args[2];
    Session session = getSession(serverUrl, username, password);
    ObjectType type = session.getTypeDefinition("D:bs:book");
    System.out.println("Type " + type.getId() + ":");
    System.out.println("Display name: " + type.getDisplayName());
    System.out.println("Description: " + type.getDescription());
    System.out.println("Query name: " + type.getQueryName());
    System.out.println("Properties:");
    Map<String, PropertyDefinition<?>> properties = type.
getPropertyDefinitions();
    for (String propName : properties.keySet()) {
        PropertyDefinition<?> property = properties.get(propName);
    System.out.println("  " + property.getId() +
        " (" + property.getDisplayName() + "): " +
        property.getPropertyType().name());
    }
}
```

Here we take the "book" type (identified as `D:bs:book`) and display its name, description, and query name. In addition, for each of its properties, we print out the property's identifier, display name, and type name. Here is the output, which contains, as expected, a mix of locally-defined and inherited properties:

```
Type D:bs:book:
Display name: Book
Description:
Query name: bs:book
Properties:
  bs:price (Price): DECIMAL
  cmis:contentStreamLength (Content Stream Length): INTEGER
  cmis:versionSeriesCheckedOutBy (Version Series Checked Out By): STRING
  cmis:objectTypeId (Object Type Id): ID
```

```
cmis:versionSeriesCheckedOutId (Version Series Checked Out Id): ID
bs:isbn (ISBN): STRING
cmis:versionSeriesId (Version series id): ID
bs:author (Author): STRING
cmis:isLatestVersion (Is Latest Version): BOOLEAN
cmis:versionLabel (Version Label): STRING
cmis:isVersionSeriesCheckedOut (Is Version Series Checked Out): BOOLEAN
cmis:lastModifiedBy (Last Modified By): STRING
cmis:createdBy (Created by): STRING
bs:publisher (Publisher): STRING
cmis:isLatestMajorVersion (Is Latest Major Version): BOOLEAN
cmis:contentStreamId (Content Stream Id): ID
cmis:name (Name): STRING
cmis:contentStreamMimeType (Content Stream MIME Type): STRING
cmis:creationDate (Creation Date): DATETIME
cmis:changeToken (Change token): STRING
cmis:checkinComment (Checkin Comment): STRING
cmis:objectId (Object Id): ID
cmis:isImmutable (Is Immutable): BOOLEAN
cmis:isMajorVersion (Is Major Version): BOOLEAN
cmis:baseTypeId (Base Type Id): ID
cmis:lastModificationDate (Last Modified Date): DATETIME
cmis:contentStreamFileName (Content Stream Filename): STRING
```

Listing the root folder

In the previous samples, we have shown how to retrieve information about the repository configuration, its list of supported types, and information about a single type. We might call this kind of information *meta-metadata*, as it describes the metadata structure of the repository.

In the next samples, we will begin interacting with the actual repository content, folders, and documents, starting with illustrating how to list the contents of a folder.

```
public static void main(String args[]) {
    String serverUrl = args[0];
    String username = args[1];
    String password = args[2];
    Session session = getSession(serverUrl, username, password);
```

```
    Folder folder = session.getRootFolder();
    for (CmisObject child : folder.getChildren()) {
        System.out.println(child.getName() + " (" +
          child.getType().getDisplayName() + ")");
    }
}
```

In this sample, we list the contents of the root folder, as obtained by a call to the `Session.getRootFolder` command. With a default Alfresco installation, this should come out as follows:

```
Sites (Sites)
Data Dictionary (Folder)
Guest Home (Folder)
User Homes (Folder)
```

Creating a new folder

With this sample, we actually begin modifying the contents of the repository. We start with creating a new folder inside the root folder, corresponding to the **Company Home** space.

```
public static void main(String args[]) {
    String serverUrl = args[0];
    String username = args[1];
    String password = args[2];
    Session session = getSession(serverUrl, username, password);
    Folder root = session.getRootFolder();
    Map<String, Object> properties = new HashMap<String, Object>();
    properties.put(PropertyIds.OBJECT_TYPE_ID, BaseTypeId.CMIS_FOLDER.
value());
    String name = "New Folder (" + System.currentTimeMillis() + ")";
    properties.put(PropertyIds.NAME, name);
    List<Ace> addAces = new LinkedList<Ace>();
    List<Ace> removeAces = new LinkedList<Ace>();
    List<Policy> policies = new LinkedList<Policy>();
    Folder newFolder = root.createFolder(properties, policies, addAces,
removeAces, session.getDefaultContext());
    System.out.println(newFolder.getId());
}
```

To create a folder inside its parent object, we call the `createFolder` method on the parent object, passing in a number of arguments:

- A map of property values, including at least the name and the type of the new folder (`BaseTypeId.CMIS_FOLDER` for a plain folder)
- A list of policies (can be `null` if not needed)
- A list of **Access Control Entries (ACEs)** to add (can be `null` if not needed)
- A list of Access Control Entries to remove (can be `null` if not needed)
- An operation context for specifying extra details about the creation operation

Using the default values (`null` and `session.getDefaultContext()`) for all arguments, except the first, is all that is needed in most cases.

It would be nice if we could have a convenient method to create a folder, specifying only its type and name, in a single method call, but this is not the case with Chemistry right now.

 This example, and the following two, require at least Alfresco Community 3.3g to work properly and will fail on previous versions.

You can, however, test them against the public Alfresco CMIS server by using `http://cmis.alfresco.com/service/cmis` as the value for the Service Document URL.

Creating a new text document

In order to create a text document, we must use the `createDocument` method of the `folder` class. This method takes even more arguments than `createFolder`, due to the need to specify a content stream for the document. The arguments are as follows:

- A map of property values, including at least the name and the type of the new document (`BaseTypeId.CMIS_DOCUMENT` for a plain document)
- `ContentStream contentStream`: The contents of the document
- `VersioningState versioningState`: This specifies whether to create the document as a checked-out one or to create it as a major or minor version of a checked-in document
- A list of policies (can be `null` if not needed)
- A list of Access Control Entries (ACEs) to add (can be `null` if not needed)
- A list of Access Control Entries to remove (can be `null` if not needed)
- An operation context for specifying extra details about the creation operation

For specifying the content stream, we use the ContentStreamImpl class, which allows us to create a content stream from a java.io.InputStream method. The constructor for ContentStreamImpl takes the following arguments:

- String filename: The name of the content stream
- BigInteger length: The length of the content stream
- String mimetype: The media type of the content stream
- InputStream stream: This is needed to initialize the contents of the stream

Here is the complete code of the main method:

```
public static void main(String args[]) {
    String serverUrl = args[0];
    String username = args[1];
    String password = args[2];
    Session session = getSession(serverUrl, username, password);
    Folder root = session.getRootFolder();
    Map<String, Object> properties = new HashMap<String, Object>();
    properties.put(PropertyIds.OBJECT_TYPE_ID, BaseTypeId.CMIS_
DOCUMENT.value());
    String name = "New Document (" + System.currentTimeMillis() +
").txt";
    properties.put(PropertyIds.NAME, name);
    List<Ace> addAces = new LinkedList<Ace>();
    List<Ace> removeAces = new LinkedList<Ace>();
    List<Policy> policies = new LinkedList<Policy>();
    String content = "The quick brown fox jumps over the lazy dog.";
    ContentStream contentStream = new ContentStreamImpl("text.txt",
BigInteger.valueOf(content.length()),
            "text/plain", new ByteArrayInputStream(content.
getBytes()));
    Document newDocument = root.createDocument(properties,
contentStream, VersioningState.MAJOR, policies, addAces, removeAces,
session.getDefaultContext());
    System.out.println(newDocument.getId());
}
```

Uploading a binary document

In *Chapter 11, The CMIS AtomPub Binding*, we explained that the most efficient method for uploading binary resources to an AtomPub Server is to create the Media Link Entry first, then use the `edit-media` link to upload the binary content stream.

Unfortunately, as of now, there doesn't seem to be a simple way to follow this method using the Chemistry client API only. You would have to first create a document with a null content stream, then fetch the corresponding entry and do the upload using lower-level libraries such as Abdera and Commons HttpClient.

However, it is still possible to create a document with a binary content stream in the same way as we did with the text document in the previous sample. The drawback is that the binary stream gets encoded as a Base64 string inside the XML message, which is not as efficient as a native binary upload.

The following sample, therefore, uses the exact same technique that we used to create a text document:

```java
public static void main(String args[]) throws FileNotFoundException {
    String serverUrl = args[0];
    String username = args[1];
    String password = args[2];
    Session session = getSession(serverUrl, username, password);
    Folder root = session.getRootFolder();
    Map<String, Object> properties = new HashMap<String, Object>();
    properties.put(PropertyIds.OBJECT_TYPE_ID, BaseTypeId.CMIS_
DOCUMENT.value());
    String name = "New Image (" + System.currentTimeMillis() + ").jpg";
    properties.put(PropertyIds.NAME, name);
    List<Ace> addAces = new LinkedList<Ace>();
    List<Ace> removeAces = new LinkedList<Ace>();
    List<Policy> policies = new LinkedList<Policy>();
    File image = new File("image.jpg");
    ContentStream contentStream = new ContentStreamImpl("content.jpg",
BigInteger.valueOf(image.length()),
        "image/jpeg", new FileInputStream(image));
    Document newDocument = root.createDocument(properties,
contentStream, VersioningState.MAJOR, policies, addAces, removeAces,
session.getDefaultContext());
    System.out.println(newDocument.getId());
}
```

To run this program, save a JPEG file as `image.jpg` in the folder from where you run the program. You can check with the Alfresco Explorer that the image has been uploaded correctly.

Reading a document's content

Now that you have learned how to create a new document, you might want to learn how to read it back. This is the purpose of the next sample, which creates a text document such as the one in the previous samples, then obtains it again from the repository in order to print out its contents.

Once we have an object, we can use the getContentStream method to obtain its content stream. This gives us access to its properties, such as the size and MIME type, and a pointer to an InputStream object from which we can read the actual document's content.

```java
public static void main(String args[]) {
    String serverUrl = args[0];
    String username = args[1];
    String password = args[2];
    Session session = getSession(serverUrl, username, password);
    Folder root = session.getRootFolder();
    Map<String, Object> properties = new HashMap<String, Object>();
    properties.put(PropertyIds.OBJECT_TYPE_ID, BaseTypeId.CMIS_
DOCUMENT.value());
    String name = "New Document (" + System.currentTimeMillis() +
").txt";
    properties.put(PropertyIds.NAME, name);
    List<Ace> addAces = new LinkedList<Ace>();
    List<Ace> removeAces = new LinkedList<Ace>();
    List<Policy> policies = new LinkedList<Policy>();
    String content = "The quick brown fox jumps over the lazy dog.";
    ContentStream contentStream = new ContentStreamImpl("text.txt",
BigInteger.valueOf(content.length()),
        "text/plain", new ByteArrayInputStream(content.getBytes()));
    Document newDocument = root.createDocument(properties,
contentStream, VersioningState.MAJOR, policies, addAces, removeAces,
session.getDefaultContext());
    try {
        ContentStream cs = newDocument.getContentStream();
        System.out.println("File type = " + cs.getMimeType());
        System.out.println("File size = " + cs.getLength());
        System.out.println("File contents:");
        byte[] buf = new byte[1024];
        InputStream in = cs.getStream();
        in.read(buf);
        System.out.write(buf);
        System.out.println();
    } catch (IOException e) {
        e.printStackTrace();
    }
}
```

This is the output you should see when you run the previous program:

```
File type = text/plain;charset=UTF-8
File size = 44
File contents:
The quick brown fox jumps over the lazy dog.
```

In a less-contrived example, we would have obtained a reference to a document by navigating the repository (using the `Folder.getChildren` method, for instance) or via searching, which will be demonstrated in a later sample.

Updating properties

To modify the properties of an existing object, you first need to retrieve it, using any of the methods previously described. Then you can call the `setProperty` method on the object itself, passing in the ID and the new value for each property that you intend to change. At the end, simply call the `updateProperties` method as follows:

```java
public static void main(String args[]) {
    String serverUrl = args[0];
    String username = args[1];
    String password = args[2];
    Session session = getSession(serverUrl, username, password);
    Folder root = session.getRootFolder();
    Map<String, Object> properties = new HashMap<String, Object>();
    properties.put(PropertyIds.OBJECT_TYPE_ID, BaseTypeId.CMIS_DOCUMENT.
value());
    String name = "New Document (" + System.currentTimeMillis() +
").txt";
    properties.put(PropertyIds.NAME, name);
    List<Ace> addAces = new LinkedList<Ace>();
    List<Ace> removeAces = new LinkedList<Ace>();
    List<Policy> policies = new LinkedList<Policy>();
    String content = "The quick brown fox jumps over the lazy dog.";
    ContentStream contentStream = new ContentStreamImpl("text.txt",
BigInteger.valueOf(content.length()),
        "text/plain", new ByteArrayInputStream(content.getBytes()));
    Document newDocument = root.createDocument(properties,
contentStream, VersioningState.MAJOR, policies, addAces, removeAces,
session.getDefaultContext());
    newDocument.setProperty(PropertyIds.NAME, "Modified document (" +
System.currentTimeMillis() + ").txt");
    newDocument.updateProperties();
    session.save();
}
```

Deleting a document

To delete an existing document, retrieve it in the same way as we did in the previous samples, and then call the `delete` method on it.

```
public static void main(String args[]) {
    String serverUrl = args[0];
    String username = args[1];
    String password = args[2];
    Session session = getSession(serverUrl, username, password);
    Folder root = session.getRootFolder();
    Map<String, Object> properties = new HashMap<String, Object>();
    properties.put(PropertyIds.OBJECT_TYPE_ID, BaseTypeId.CMIS_
DOCUMENT.value());
    String name = "New Document (" + System.currentTimeMillis() +
").txt";
    properties.put(PropertyIds.NAME, name);
    List<Ace> addAces = new LinkedList<Ace>();
    List<Ace> removeAces = new LinkedList<Ace>();
    List<Policy> policies = new LinkedList<Policy>();
    String content = "The quick brown fox jumps over the lazy dog.";
    ContentStream contentStream = new ContentStreamImpl("text.txt",
BigInteger.valueOf(content.length()),
            "text/plain", new ByteArrayInputStream(content.
getBytes()));
    Document newDocument = root.createDocument(properties,
contentStream, VersioningState.MAJOR, policies, addAces, removeAces,
session.getDefaultContext());
    newDocument.delete(true);
    session.save();
}
```

The `boolean` argument passed to the `delete` method is used to specify whether the operation should remove all versions of the document or only the most recent one.

After deletion, you can find the document in the **Manage deleted items** section of your user profile in Alfresco Explorer (it won't actually be shown unless you search for it or click the **Show All** button):

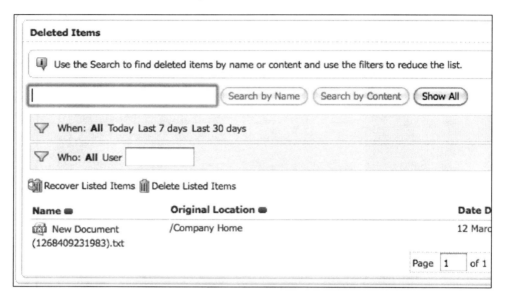

Searching

To search the repository, use the `query` method of the `Session` interface. The first argument is the CMIS-SQL query to execute. The second argument, if `true`, instructs the server to search all the previous versions of the objects and not only the most recent one.

As Alfresco does not support searching older versions of items, you should pass `false` to the method.

```
public static void main(String args[]) {
    String serverUrl = args[0];
    String username = args[1];
    String password = args[2];
    Session session = getSession(serverUrl, username, password);
    ItemIterable<QueryResult> results = session.query("SELECT * FROM
cmis:document WHERE CONTAINS('alfresco')", false);
    for (QueryResult result : results) {
    System.out.println(result.getPropertyValueById(PropertyIds.NAME));
    }
}
```

Listing relationships

In order to list the relationships of a given CMIS object, use the `CmisObject.` `getRelationships` method:

```
public static void main(String args[]) {
    String serverUrl = args[0];
    String username = args[1];
    String password = args[2];
    Session session = getSession(serverUrl, username, password);
    Folder folder = (Folder) session.getObjectByPath("/Wiki");
    ObjectType wikiLinkType = session.getTypeDefinition("R:wiki:
linkedPages");
    for (CmisObject child : folder.getChildren()) {
        System.out.println(child.getName());
        ItemIterable<Relationship> rels =            child.
getRelationships(false, RelationshipDirection.SOURCE, wikiLinkType,
session.getDefaultContext());
        for (Relationship rel : rels) {
          System.out.println("  --> " +
            rel.getTarget().getName());
        }
    }
}
```

The `CmisObject.getRelationships` method returns an iterable collection of `Relationship` objects and takes the following arguments:

- `boolean includeSubRelationshipTypes`: This specifies whether to include derived relationship types in the list

- `RelationshipDirection relationshipDirection`: Should be `RelationshipDirection.SOURCE` (for outgoing links) or `RelationshipDirection.TARGET` (for incoming links)

- `ObjectType type`: This specifies the type of relationship to list

- `OperationContext context`: This is used for specifying extra details about the creation operation

Summary

This chapter introduced the Apache Chemistry project and presented you with a number of code samples that illustrate how to perform the operations that are commonly required in a CMIS client application, including:

- Getting repository meta-metadata
- Creating objects
- Reading objects' metadata and contents
- Updating objects
- Searching for objects
- Listing an object's relationships

All of the code samples were tested using a recent build of Chemistry and Alfresco Community. As the level of CMIS support and compliance is rapidly evolving in both projects, you should closely follow the developments going on in both places and be prepared to update your client code, based on these samples, when new versions come out. A good way to keep in touch with the Chemistry community is by subscribing to its developers' mailing list.

The samples included in this chapter were designed with the AtomPub protocol binding in mind. The next chapter will describe the CMIS Web Services binding and how to write client applications that exploit it in order to talk to an Alfresco server.

In a later chapter, we will return to use the Chemistry AtomPub client classes in order to develop a complete application that uses Alfresco, via CMIS, as a backend storage.

13
The Web Services Binding

In this chapter, we will see how to implement a CMIS client application using the Web Services binding provided in Alfresco. All the samples attached with this chapter are based on the Java language and the client stub is implemented using Apache CXF, that is, the same implementation used in Alfresco for the CMIS Web Services server stub. We will start by discussing the CMIS services and how to retrieve each WSDL from Alfresco.

In the next section, you will learn some basic information about WS-Security and WS-I **Basic Security Profile (BSP)**, which are the two important directives used for the Web Services binding of the CMIS standard.

Then, we will describe how to set up a CMIS Web Services client stub using the Spring Framework, declaring all the needed services in the application context. Finally, we will show you how to implement different operations upon objects. You will learn how to:

- Get all the CMIS WSDLs exposed by Alfresco
- Implement your CMIS Web Services client stub
- Retrieve information about involved repositories
- Browse contents in a workspace
- Inspect objects and properties inside folders
- Perform CRUD operations upon objects
- Search objects

Getting at the WSDLs

In order to implement a CMIS Web Service client stub, you need to know where you can find all the exposed WSDLs. In this section, we are going to show all the details about the service descriptors.

Alfresco provides all the services dedicated to the CMIS Web Services binding using Apache CXF as the SOAP service framework. CXF is an Apache project dedicated to providing a complete implementation for Web Services.

 For more information about Apache CXF, you can visit the official project website available at this URL: `http://cxf.apache.org/`.

The main CXF servlet in Alfresco allows you to retrieve an HTML index of all the WSDLs that you can use to perform operations, and it is available at this URL in your Alfresco instance:

`http://localhost:8080/alfresco/cmis`.

Alfresco Community 3.3 provides the following available services:

Name	Description
DiscoveryService	Perform queries to find existing contents
MultiFilingService	Retrieve and manage associations between contents
NavigationService	Browse folders and all the related contents
ObjectService	Perform all the CRUD operations on contents
PolicyService	Manage policies (it is exposed, but it is not implemented yet in Alfresco)
RelationshipService	Retrieve information about content associations
RepositoryService	Retrieve information about repositories and content types
VersioningService	Retrieve and manage versioning of contents

For each service, you can bind your client using the following WSDLs:

Name	WSDL
DiscoveryService	`http://localhost:8080/alfresco/cmis/DiscoveryService?wsdl`
MultiFilingService	`http://localhost:8080/alfresco/cmis/MultiFilingService?wsdl`
NavigationService	`http://localhost:8080/alfresco/cmis/NavigationService?wsdl`

Name	WSDL
ObjectService	http://localhost:8080/alfresco/cmis/ObjectService?wsdl
PolicyService	http://localhost:8080/alfresco/cmis/PolicyService?wsdl
RelationshipService	http://localhost:8080/alfresco/cmis/RelationshipService?wsdl
RepositoryService	http://localhost:8080/alfresco/cmis/RepositoryService?wsdl
VersioningService	http://localhost:8080/alfresco/cmis/VersioningService?wsdl

At the moment, not all the services are completely implemented, and some of the exposed methods could not be implemented yet. Anyway, you have the availability of all the source code of Alfresco that allows you to take a look into the code by browsing all the services of the server stub. In this way, you can view the state of the implementation for a specific service or a specific method.

You'll find a dedicated Spring context in Alfresco for the Web Services binding of CMIS in this file:

```
HEAD/projects/Remote API/config/alfresco/cmis-ws-context.xml.
```

From this file, you can browse the Alfresco source code to find the related implementation for a specific service.

Setting up the client project

Now we are going to show you all the details about the sample application attached with this chapter that is based on the Spring Framework. The Spring Framework is a J2EE application framework used to manage all the Java resources. This is the same framework used in Alfresco to manage all the resource dependencies for services and components.

Before explaining the Spring context, we need to show you how to manage the project dependencies using Apache Maven.

Apache Maven is an open source project provided by the Apache Software Foundation that helps you in every aspect related to the **Application Lifecycle Management (ALM)**. This means that, by using Maven, you can manage your development process for many goals such as building, continuous integration, testing, and releasing. You can find more information about Maven at its official website at http://maven.apache.org/

This means that you have to run the following command from the root of the project, in order to correctly import the Maven project in Eclipse:

```
mvn eclipse:eclipse
```

The client stub project is based on the following components:

- The project descriptor of Maven (`pom.xml`)
- The Spring Framework beans definitions (`application-context.xml`)
- The Java stub client, generated from WSDLs (source folder: `target/generated/src/main/java`)
- Sample custom actions (source folder: `src/main/java`)

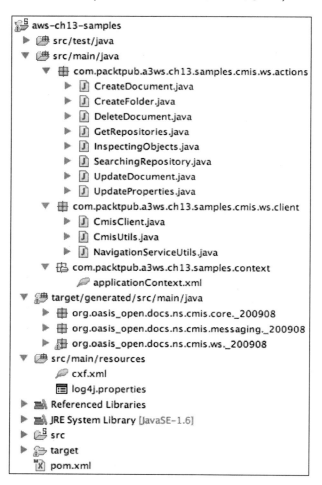

The pom.xml is the **Project Object Model (POM)** of the application, and you can find it in the root folder of the project. In this file, you will find the following declaration to define all the libraries used to implement the client actions:

```xml
<dependency>
    <groupId>log4j</groupId>
    <artifactId>log4j</artifactId>
    <version>1.2.15</version>
</dependency>
<dependency>
    <groupId>org.springframework</groupId>
    <artifactId>spring</artifactId>
    <version>2.5.6</version>
</dependency>
<dependency>
    <groupId>org.apache.cxf</groupId>
    <artifactId>cxf-rt-frontend-jaxws</artifactId>
    <version>${cxf.version}</version>
</dependency>
<dependency>
    <groupId>org.apache.cxf</groupId>
    <artifactId>cxf-rt-transports-http</artifactId>
    <version>${cxf.version}</version>
</dependency>
<dependency>
    <groupId>org.apache.cxf</groupId>
    <artifactId>cxf-rt-transports-http-jetty</artifactId>
    <version>${cxf.version}</version>
</dependency>
<dependency>
    <groupId>org.apache.cxf</groupId>
    <artifactId>cxf-rt-ws-security</artifactId>
    <version>2.2.5</version>
</dependency>
<dependency>
    <groupId>org.apache.ws.security</groupId>
    <artifactId>wss4j</artifactId>
    <version>1.5.4</version>
</dependency>
```

When you have a look at the `groupId` element in the previous snippet, you can see that the sample client application is implemented using the following frameworks:

- `Log4j` is the service framework used for logging
- `Spring` is the application framework
- Apache CXF is the service framework used for the SOAP implementation
- Apache `Wss4j` is the service library used for the WS-Security implementation

Once you declare all the dependencies in the `pom.xml` file, Maven allows you to use all these packages in your application, and it will download the artifacts, only if you don't have one of these in your local Maven repository. By default, the local Maven repository is stored in a special folder called `.m2`, inside the user folder of your operating system.

As a standard Web Service Client, you need to generate the client stub from one or more WSDLs. Using Maven and CXF, you can use the `cxf-codegen-plugin` to generate all the client stub code. You can declare the following snippet to bind the client stub code generation to the `generate-sources` goal of Maven:

```
<plugin>
    <groupId>org.apache.cxf</groupId>
    <artifactId>cxf-codegen-plugin</artifactId>
    <version>${cxf.version}</version>
    <executions>
        <execution>
            <id>generate-sources</id>
            <phase>generate-sources</phase>
            <configuration>
<sourceRoot>${basedir}/target/generated/src/main/java
</sourceRoot>
                <wsdlOptions>
                    <wsdlOption>
<wsdl>${basedir}/src/main/wsdl/CMISWS-Service.wsdl</wsdl>
                        <extraargs>
                            <extraarg>-client</extraarg>
                        </extraargs>
                    </wsdlOption>
                </wsdlOptions>
            </configuration>
            <goals>
                <goal>wsdl2java</goal>
            </goals>
        </execution>
    </executions>
</plugin>
```

This plugin will generate all the client stub code in a dedicated source folder in the project: `target/generated/src/main/java`. The WSDL used to generate all the service binding is `CMISWS-Service.wsdl` — it was taken from the OASIS official website, and it consists of the all the definitions of services for the Web Services binding. You will find the WSDL and the related XSD files in this folder: `src/main/wsdl`. WSDL and XSD files are also located in your Alfresco installation at the following path:

`Alfresco/tomcat/webapps/alfresco/wsdl.`

The CMIS specification will provide you with the main WSDL and with the following two XSD definitions:

XSD	Description
`CMIS-Core.xsd`	Definitions of all the data types involved
`CMIS-Messaging.xsd`	Definitions of all the message formats used for each service

Anyway, if you don't want to generate the code for all the available services, you can download the single WSDL of the specific service, and then you can declare it in the `wsdlOption` element in the previous snippet. For this sample application, we decided to bind all the services to show you how to implement some of the most used operations for each exposed service.

To regenerate the client stub code, you need to invoke the `generate-sources` goal of Maven using one of the Eclipse plugins (for example, m2Eclipse) in this way:

* Right-click on `pom.xml` or in the root folder of the project
* Click on **Run As | Maven generate-sources**

Or you can execute the following command from the root of the project (the same folder where you find the `pom.xml` file):

`mvn generate-sources`

Declaring the CMIS client bean

For this project, we used the Spring Framework, and this means that we need to declare Spring beans in the `application-context.xml` to create our beans with all the related dependencies to wire all the needed resources.

Using CXF with JAX-WS, you can declare a Web Service client stub in the Spring application context for each service exposed in a WSDL in this way:

```xml
<?xml version="1.0" encoding="UTF-8"?>
<beans xmlns="http://www.springframework.org/schema/beans"
    xmlns:xsi="http://www.w3.org/2001/XMLSchema-instance" xmlns:
jaxws="http://cxf.apache.org/jaxws"
    xsi:schemaLocation="http://www.springframework.org/schema/beans
http://www.springframework.org/schema/beans/spring-beans-2.5.xsd
http://cxf.apache.org/jaxws http://cxf.apache.org/schemas/jaxws.xsd">

    <jaxws:client id="repositoryService"
serviceClass="org.oasis_open.docs.ns.cmis.ws._200908.
RepositoryServicePort"
 address="http://localhost:8080/alfresco/cmis/RepositoryService" />

    <jaxws:client id="discoveryService"
serviceClass="org.oasis_open.docs.ns.cmis.ws._200908.
DiscoveryServicePort"
 address="http://localhost:8080/alfresco/cmis/DiscoveryService" />

    <jaxws:client id="multiFilingService"
serviceClass="org.oasis_open.docs.ns.cmis.ws._200908.
MultiFilingServicePort"
 address="http://localhost:8080/alfresco/cmis/MultiFilingService" />

    <jaxws:client id="navigationService"
serviceClass="org.oasis_open.docs.ns.cmis.ws._200908.
NavigationServicePort" address="http://localhost:8080/alfresco/cmis/
NavigationService" />

    <jaxws:client id="objectService"
serviceClass="org.oasis_open.docs.ns.cmis.ws._200908.
ObjectServicePort" address="http://localhost:8080/alfresco/cmis/
ObjectService" />

    <jaxws:client id="policyService"
serviceClass="org.oasis_open.docs.ns.cmis.ws._200908.
PolicyServicePort" address="http://localhost:8080/alfresco/cmis/
PolicyService" />

    <jaxws:client id="relationshipService"
serviceClass="org.oasis_open.docs.ns.cmis.ws._200908.
RelationshipServicePort" address="http://localhost:8080/alfresco/cmis/
RelationshipService" />
```

```
    <jaxws:client id="versioningService"
        serviceClass="org.oasis_open.docs.ns.cmis.ws._200908.
VersioningServicePort"
        address="http://localhost:8080/alfresco/cmis/VersioningService"
/>
```

Notice that you need to add the Apache CXF namespace in the beans definition, which allows you to declare the JAX-WS prefix. In this way, you can create the client stub for each service with a single Spring declaration with an element `jaxws:client`.

To declare each client, you need to provide the following information:

- The related implementation class for the interface, which is automatically generated by the plugin
- The endpoint address of the remote repository

If you need to change the endpoint dynamically, you can execute the same binding programmatically using Java. Once all the beans are configured, whenever this application is started, it will create all the instances as singletons by default. For the sample client, we provided you with a `CmisClient` bean as a service registry. In this way, you don't need to remember all the identifiers used in the Spring configuration for each service, as you can find useful public getter methods to retrieve service beans.

The `CmisClient` is defined in the following way:

```
<bean id="cmisClient" class=
"com.packtpub.a3ws.ch13.samples.cmis.ws.client.CmisClient">
    <property name="repositoryService">
        <ref bean="repositoryService"/>
    </property>
    <property name="discoveryService">
        <ref bean="discoveryService"/>
    </property>
    <property name="multiFilingService">
        <ref bean="multiFilingService"/>
    </property>
    <property name="navigationService">
        <ref bean="navigationService"/>
    </property>
    <property name="objectService">
        <ref bean="objectService"/>
    </property>
    <property name="policyService">
        <ref bean="policyService"/>
```

```
        </property>
        <property name="relationshipService">
           <ref bean="relationshipService"/>
        </property>
        <property name="versioningService">
           <ref bean="versioningService"/>
        </property>
    </bean>
```

In order to allow Spring to inject all the declared resources in the CmisClient instance, we have provided all the related public setter methods in the class for each private field in this way:

```
    private RepositoryServicePort repositoryService;
    private DiscoveryServicePort discoveryService;
    private MultiFilingServicePort multiFilingService;
    private NavigationServicePort navigationService;
    private ObjectServicePort objectService;
    private PolicyServicePort policyService;
    private RelationshipServicePort relationshipService;
    private VersioningServicePort versioningService;

    public void setRepositoryService(RepositoryServicePort
repositoryService) {
        this.repositoryService = repositoryService;
    }
    public void setDiscoveryService(DiscoveryServicePort
discoveryService) {
        this.discoveryService = discoveryService;
    }
    public void setMultiFilingService(MultiFilingServicePort
multiFilingService) {
        this.multiFilingService = multiFilingService;
    }
    public void setNavigationService(NavigationServicePort
navigationService) {
        this.navigationService = navigationService;
    }
    public void setObjectService(ObjectServicePort objectService) {
        this.objectService = objectService;
    }
    public void setPolicyService(PolicyServicePort policyService) {
        this.policyService = policyService;
    }
```

```
    public void setRelationshipService(RelationshipServicePort
relationshipService) {
        this.relationshipService = relationshipService;
    }
    public void setVersioningService(VersioningServicePort
versioningService) {
        this.versioningService = versioningService;
    }
```

Then we implemented all the getter methods to allow you to use this class as a service registry:

```
    public RepositoryServicePort getRepositoryService(String username,
String password){
        return CmisUtils.configureWss4jClient(repositoryService,
username, password);
    }

    public DiscoveryServicePort getDiscoveryService(String username,
String password){
        return CmisUtils.configureWss4jClient(discoveryService,
username, password);
    }

    public MultiFilingServicePort getMultiFilingService(String
username, String password){
        return CmisUtils.configureWss4jClient(multiFilingService,
username, password);
    }
    public ObjectServicePort getObjectService(String username, String
password){
        return CmisUtils.configureWss4jClient(objectService, username,
password);
    }

    public NavigationServicePort getNavigationService(String username,
String password){
        return CmisUtils.configureWss4jClient(navigationService,
username, password);
    }

    public PolicyServicePort getPolicyService(String username, String
password){
        return CmisUtils.configureWss4jClient(policyService, username,
password);
    }
```

```
    public RelationshipServicePort getRelationshipService(String
username, String password){
        return CmisUtils.configureWss4jClient(relationshipService,
username, password);
    }

    public VersioningServicePort getVersioningService(String username,
String password){
        return CmisUtils.configureWss4jClient(versioningService,
username, password);
    }
```

The method called `configureWss4JClient`, available in the `CmisUtils` class, has been provided with the attached code of this chapter. This method allows you to add the WS-Security layer needed to make this client completely compliant with the CMIS standard.

Whenever we need to invoke a service, we have to provide a username and a password for the related user session that we would like to use in the repository, and then we also need to configure SOAP header for WS-Security. A proxy class will be created at runtime for each service getter invocation to encapsulate security for each user session.

You need to follow the same mechanism sequence to perform operations with the `CmisClient`:

1. Bootstrap the application context using Spring.
2. Get the `CmisClient` bean.
3. Get one or more CMIS WS services.
4. Invoke service methods to perform operations on objects.

The first step allows you to create all the instances for beans declared in the application context with all the related wired resources. We will start Spring in the following way:

```
ClassPathXmlApplicationContext context =
new ClassPathXmlApplicationContext(
new String[] {CmisClient.APPLICATION_CONTEXT});
```

Now Spring has created all the Java resources declared in the application context. We can get the `CmisClient` instance as follows:

```
CmisClient cmisClient =
(CmisClient)context.getBean(CmisClient.CMIS_CLIENT_BEAN_NAME);
```

Now that we have the `CmisClient` instance, we can invoke a getter method of a specific service, and then we can invoke all the methods exposed by the service as follows:

```
RepositoryServicePort repositoryService = cmisClient.getRepositoryServ
ice(CmisClient.USERNAME, CmisClient.USER_PASSWORD);

    List<CmisRepositoryEntryType> repositories = repositoryService.
getRepositories(null);
```

For all the following actions, we will start the application context in a similar way, as you saw in the previous code.

Some necessary pieces: WS-Security and WS-I Basic Profile

The CMIS specification is strongly based on directives proposed by the **Web Services Interoperability Organization (WS-I)**. WS-I is an open industry organization, and the goal of their committees is to suggest best practices for Web Services to promote better interoperability. All the WS-I proposals are based on non-proprietary Web Services standards to ensure maximum transparency.

 For more information about the Web Services Interoperability Organization (WS-I), you can browse their official website at this address: `http://www.ws-i.org/`.

The CMIS Web Services binding must comply with two of the proposal directives suggested by the WS-I:

- WS-I Basic Profile
- WS-I Basic Security Profile

The WS-I Basic Profile consists of a set of directives dedicated to how the SOAP messages must be created. In this directive, you will find all the details about all the elements needed to create a correct SOAP message.

The WS-I Security Profile promotes a set of directives to help developers with the use of the WS-Security standard. WS-Security was defined and published by the OASIS organization to provide directives dedicated to add security features to Web Services.

WS-Security allows you to add a new messaging layer dedicated to security as a new security layer on top of the SOAP protocol. One of the most important features that a CMIS Web Services binding should support is the `UsernameToken` defined in the WS-I Security Profile. This directive, taken from the WS-Security standard, is dedicated to adding security during the authentication process using a specific XML schema definition and a specific digest for the exchanged password.

This mechanism allows you to define a secure method to exchange authentication data between client and server. For this specific case, the `UsernameToken` is the new security layer that consists of a snippet of XML data encapsulated in the SOAP header. For each SOAP-exchanged message between client and server, a new XML element will be added. This new XML element, called `UsernameToken`, will add security information in a unique SOAP XML element. You can take a look at the following SOAP message generated by a CMIS Web Service client to invoke the `getRepositories()` method exposed by the `RepositoryService`:

```
<soap:Envelope xmlns:soap="http://schemas.xmlsoap.org/soap/envelope/">

<soap:Header>

<wsse:Security xmlns:wsse="http://docs.oasis-open.org/wss/2004/01/
oasis-200401-wss-wssecurity-secext-1.0.xsd" soap:mustUnderstand="1">

<wsu:Timestamp xmlns:wsu="http://docs.oasis-open.org/wss/2004/01/
oasis-200401-wss-wssecurity-utility-1.0.xsd" wsu:Id="Timestamp-
2802048">
<wsu:Created xmlns:wsu="http://docs.oasis-open.org/wss/2004/01/oasis-
200401-wss-wssecurity-utility-1.0.xsd">yyyy-MM-ddTHH:mm:ss.fffZ</wsu:
Created>
<wsu:Expires xmlns:wsu="http://docs.oasis-open.org/wss/2004/01/oasis-
200401-wss-wssecurity-utility-1.0.xsd">yyyy-MM-ddTHH:mm:ss.fffZ</wsu:
Expires>
</wsu:Timestamp>

<wsse:UsernameToken xmlns:wsse=http://docs.oasis-open.org/wss/2004/01/
oasis-200401-wss-wssecurity-secext-1.0.xsd xmlns:wsu="http://docs.
oasis-open.org/wss/2004/01/oasis-200401-wss-wssecurity-utility-
1.0.xsd" wsu:Id="UsernameToken-826697">

<wsse:Username xmlns:wsse="http://docs.oasis-open.org/wss/2004/01/
oasis-200401-wss-wssecurity-secext-1.0.xsd">admin</wsse:Username>

<wsse:Password xmlns:wsse="http://docs.oasis-open.org/wss/2004/01/
oasis-200401-wss-wssecurity-secext-1.0.xsd"
```

```
Type="http://docs.oasis-open.org/wss/2004/01/oasis-200401-wss-
username-token-profile-1.0#PasswordDigest">YourCustomPasswordDigest</
wsse:Password>

<wsse:Nonce xmlns:wsse="http://docs.oasis-open.org/wss/2004/01/oasis-
200401-wss-wssecurity-secext-1.0.xsd">CustomAndUniqueNonceGeneratedVal
ue</wsse:Nonce>

<wsu:Created xmlns:wsu="http://docs.oasis-open.org/wss/2004/01/oasis-
200401-wss-wssecurity-utility-1.0.xsd">yyyy-MM-ddTHH:mm:ss.fffZ</wsu:
Created>
</wsse:UsernameToken>

</wsse:Security>

</soap:Header>

<soap:Body>
<ns1:getRepositories xmlns:ns1="http://www.cmis.org/2008/05" />
</soap:Body>

</soap:Envelope>
```

The previous highlighted code is the `UsernameToken` element, and it is added by the WS-Security framework, which is used to generate SOAP messages for the client. The **Apache Software Foundation (ASF)** provides you with a Java implementation of the WS-Security standard promoted by the OASIS organization, and it is called **Apache WSS4J (WS-Security for Java)**. This is the same implementation used in the sample that you can find in the source code attached with this chapter.

 For more information about Apache WSS4J, you can visit the related project website at this URL: `http://ws.apache.org/wss4j/`

The WS-Security elements in the CMIS WS client, provided by Alfresco, are the following:

- `Timestamp`: contains information about the creation time and when the request expires
- `UsernameToken`: contains information about the user session

As you can see, a `UsernameToken` element consists of the following children elements:

- `Username`: The username of the user who is requesting an operation
- `Password`: the digest for the user password
- `Nonce`: A unique ID generated to prevent the message from being intercepted
- `Created`: The request creation date in the ISO8601 format

Browsing the repository

Now we can start to discuss about client features, and specifically, how to browse the contents in the repository using the `CmisClient`, as shown in the previous section. In the `GetRepositories` action, you can see how to get information about all the repositories exposed by a single endpoint. In this sample, we used the `RepositoryService` to get the `rootFolderId` to start the navigation as follows:

```
ClassPathXmlApplicationContext context = new ClassPathXmlApplicationCo
ntext(new String[] {CmisClient.APPLICATION_CONTEXT});

    CmisClient cmisClient = (CmisClient)context.getBean(CmisClient.
CMIS_CLIENT_BEAN_NAME);

        RepositoryServicePort repositoryService = cmisClient.getReposito
ryService(CmisClient.USERNAME, CmisClient.USER_PASSWORD);

        List<CmisRepositoryEntryType> repositories = repositoryService.
getRepositories(null);

for (CmisRepositoryEntryType repository : repositories) {

CmisRepositoryInfoType repositoryInfo = repositoryService.
getRepositoryInfo(
repository.getRepositoryId(), null);

log.info("Repository Id: " + repository.getRepositoryId());
log.info("Repository Name: "+ repository.getRepositoryName());
log.info("RootFolder Id: " +repositoryInfo.getRootFolderId());
log.info("Cmis version supported: +repositoryInfo.
getCmisVersionSupported());
log.info("Vendor: " + repositoryInfo.getVendorName());
log.info(
"Product version:"+repositoryInfo.getProductVersion());
}
```

In the previous snippet, we were browsing all the repositories exposed by the endpoint and we were getting some useful information about each repository. Using the `rootFolderId`, we can start to browse the repository using the `getChildren` method, exposed by the `NavigationService`. The `rootFolderId` in Alfresco is the **Company Home** space, and you can see how to browse this space and one of the children called **Data Dictionary** as follows.

```
ClassPathXmlApplicationContext context = new ClassPathXmlApplicationContext(new String[] {CmisClient.APPLICATION_CONTEXT});

    CmisClient cmisClient = (CmisClient)context.getBean(CmisClient.CMIS_CLIENT_BEAN_NAME);
    RepositoryServicePort repositoryService = cmisClient.getRepositoryService(CmisClient.USERNAME, CmisClient.USER_PASSWORD);

    List<CmisRepositoryEntryType> repositories = repositoryService.getRepositories(null);

    String repositoryId = repositories.get(0).getRepositoryId();
    String rootFolderId = repositoryService.getRepositoryInfo(repositoryId, null).getRootFolderId();

    NavigationServicePort navigationService = cmisClient.getNavigationService(CmisClient.USERNAME, CmisClient.USER_PASSWORD);

    CmisObjectInFolderListType childrenList = navigationService.getChildren(repositoryId,
            rootFolderId , null, null, false, null, null, false, null, null, null);

    List<CmisObjectInFolderType> children = childrenList.getObjects();

    log.info("--- Inspecting Company Home ---");
    NavigationServiceUtils.logChildrenProperties(children);
    log.info("--- /Inspecting Company Home ---");

    //inspecting Data Dictionary
    String dataDictionaryFolderId = NavigationServiceUtils.getObjectIdFromProperties(children, "[Data Dictionary]");

    CmisObjectInFolderListType dataDictionaryChildrenList = navigationService.getChildren(repositoryId,
            dataDictionaryFolderId, null, null, false, null, null, false, null, null, null);
```

```
        List<CmisObjectInFolderType> dataDictionaryChildren =
dataDictionaryChildrenList.getObjects();

        log.info("--- Inspecting Data Dictionary ---");

NavigationServiceUtils.logChildrenProperties(dataDictionaryChildren);
        log.info("--- /Inspecting Data Dictionary ---");
```

In order to simplify this method, the navigation of children is implemented by a custom utility class called NavigationServiceUtils, which inspects objects using the logChildrenProperties method. The children list is provided by a specific CMIS object named CmisObjectInFolderListType. Each result in the list is a CmisObjectType that contains all the properties about the node.

Then you need to provide at least the repositoryId and the folderId to browse a repository. In the previous snippet, we have implemented a method called getObjectIdFromProperties to get the folderId from the specific name of the folder that is provided in the CMIS standard through a specific property named cmis:name:

```
    public static String getObjectIdFromProperties(List<CmisObjectInFolder
    Type> children, String name){

        String objectId = StringUtils.EMPTY;
        String objectName = StringUtils.EMPTY;

    for (CmisObjectInFolderType child : children) {

            CmisObjectType object = child.getObject();

        List<CmisProperty> properties = object.getProperties().
    getProperty();

            for (CmisProperty cmisProperty : properties) {
        if("cmis:name".equals(
    cmisProperty.getPropertyDefinitionId())){

                objectName = ((CmisPropertyString)cmisProperty).
    getValue().toString();

                if(objectName.equals(name)){
                    objectId = getObjectId(properties);
                        break;
                }
            }
```

```
        }
    }
    objectId = StringUtils.removeEnd(objectId, "]");
    objectId = StringUtils.removeStart(objectId, "[");
    return objectId;
}
```

Inspecting objects

In this section, we are going to see how to retrieve metadata information from nodes. In the previous section, we had discussed CMIS properties, and now we can discuss all the property types that we can find in a CMIS object.

Now, take a look at the `logChildrenProperties` method, available in the `NavigationServiceUtils` class, to learn how to get the different property types from a specific object:

```
for (CmisObjectInFolderType child : children) {

CmisObjectType object = child.getObject();

List<CmisProperty> properties = object.getProperties().getProperty();

String name = getName(properties);
        log.info("--- "+name+" ---");
        log.info("--- Properties ---");
        for (CmisProperty property : properties) {
        //inspecting properties for each node

    if("cmis:path".equals(property.getPropertyDefinitionId()))
            log.info("PATH: "+ ((CmisPropertyString)property).
getValue());
            else if("cmis:name".equals(property.
getPropertyDefinitionId()))
            log.info("Name: "+ ((CmisPropertyString)property).
getValue());
            else if("cmis:objectId".equals(property.
getPropertyDefinitionId()))
                log.info("Object Id: "+ ((CmisPropertyId)property).
getValue());
            else if("cmis:objectTypeId".equals(property.
getPropertyDefinitionId()))
                log.info("Object Type: "+ ((CmisPropertyId)property).
getValue());
```

```
                else if("cmis:baseTypeId".equals(property.
getPropertyDefinitionId()))
                    log.info("Base Type: "+ ((CmisPropertyId)property).
getValue());
                else if("cmis:lastModifiedBy".equals(property.
getPropertyDefinitionId()))
                    log.info("Last Modified By: "+ ((CmisPropertyString)pro
perty).getValue());
                else if("cmis:createdBy".equals(property.
getPropertyDefinitionId()))
                    log.info("Created By: "+ ((CmisPropertyString)property
).getValue());
                else if("cmis:creationDate".equals(property.
getPropertyDefinitionId()))
                    log.info("Creation Date: "+ ((CmisPropertyDateTime)prop
erty).getValue());
                else if("cmis:lastModificationDate".equals(property.
getPropertyDefinitionId()))
                    log.info("Last Modification Date: "+ ((CmisPropertyDate
Time)property).getValue());
                else if("cmis:parentId".equals(property.
getPropertyDefinitionId()))
log.info("Parent Id: "+ ((CmisPropertyId)property).getValue());
            }
```

In the previous snippet, you can find some of the properties with the related CMIS property types that are shown in the following table:

Property Definition ID	Description	CMIS Property Type
cmis:name	Name	CmisPropertyString
cmis:path	Content path	CmisPropertyString
cmis:objectId	Content ID(NodeRef)	CmisPropertyId
cmis:objectTypeId	Content Type	CmisPropertyId
cmis:baseTypeId	Root Type	CmisPropertyId
cmis:lastModifiedBy	Modifier username	CmisPropertyString
cmis:lastModificationDate	Last modification date	CmisPropertyDateTime
cmis:createdBy	Creator username	CmisPropertyString
cmis:creationDate	Creation date	CmisPropertyDateTime
cmis:parentId	Parent ID (NodeRef)	CmisPropertyId

For instance, taking the **Data Dictionary** space as one of the contents to inspect, the output for this method lists all the following values:

```
--- [Data Dictionary] ---
--- Properties ---
PATH: [/Data Dictionary]
Last Modified By: [System]
Object Type: [cmis:folder]
Created By: [System]
Name: [Data Dictionary]
Object Id: [workspace://SpacesStore/3cc8eded-5dc8-4591-98cf-25b6be34f70d]
Creation Date: [2010-02-22T19:04:57.200+01:00]
Base Type: [cmis:folder]
Parent Id: [workspace://SpacesStore/4b3d69ff-e435-4c9f-8e84-48ff2e4e90e2]
Last Modification Date: [2010-02-22T19:04:57.220+01:00]
--- /Properties ---
--- /[Data Dictionary] ---
```

Acting upon objects

In this section, we will see some sample actions that we can invoke upon nodes. We will learn how to perform some CRUD operations using CMIS. To run each sample from this chapter, you need only select the related class with a single click, and then you have to:

1. Right-click on the specific sample class.
2. Click on **Run As | Java Application**.

Creating a new text document

In order to create a new document, you need to use the createDocument method provided by the ObjectService. Before uploading new content, we need to get the information about the target repository and the target folder.

In this first step, we need to get the repositoryId and the rootFolderId, as we have seen in the previous section:

```
        RepositoryServicePort repositoryService = cmisClient.getReposito
    ryService(CmisClient.USERNAME, CmisClient.USER_PASSWORD);

    List<CmisRepositoryEntryType> repositories = repositoryService.
    getRepositories(null);
```

```
String repositoryId = repositories.get(0).getRepositoryId();

        String rootFolderId = repositoryService.getRepositoryInfo(reposi
toryId, null).getRootFolderId();
```

We need to get the `ObjectService`, that is, a bean defined in the Spring context as follows:

```
        ObjectServicePort objectService = cmisClient.getObjectService(Cm
isClient.USERNAME, CmisClient.USER_PASSWORD);
```

Now that we are defining the object properties, we need to use the `ObjectFactory` to create each type of property and the related value in a unique set in the `CmisPropertiesType` class. To create a standard document, we need to provide a `cmis:document` value for the `objectTypeId` property:

```
CmisPropertiesType newDocProperties =
new CmisPropertiesType();

ObjectFactory objectFactory = new ObjectFactory();

//creating the name property
CmisPropertyString nameDoc = objectFactory.createCmisPropertyString();

nameDoc.setPropertyDefinitionId("cmis:name");

nameDoc.getValue().add("CMIS WS API Sample Document "+System.
currentTimeMillis());

newDocProperties.getProperty().add(nameDoc);

//creating the type property
CmisPropertyId typeDoc = objectFactory.createCmisPropertyId();
typeDoc.setPropertyDefinitionId("cmis:objectTypeId");
typeDoc.getValue().add("cmis:document");
newDocProperties.getProperty().add(typeDoc);
```

In the next snippet, we are going to create a new content stream. For this sample, we are using a simple text file—we need to use the `DataHandler` class for providing the `content` and the related `mime` type:

```
//creating the content
String content =
"This is the content sample from CMIS Web Service API";
```

```
DataHandler dataHandler =
new DataHandler(content, "text/plain");

CmisContentStreamType stream = new CmisContentStreamType();
stream.setMimeType("text/plain");
stream.setStream(dataHandler);
```

Finally, we invoke the `createDocument()` method to upload the new content in the `rootFolderId`, that is, the parent folder:

```
Holder<String> idHolder = new Holder<String>();

objectService.createDocument(
        repositoryId, newDocProperties, rootFolderId, stream,
null, null, null, null, null, idHolder);

    log.info("Document created. Id: "+idHolder.value);
```

The required parameters needed to invoke the `createDocument` method are as follows:

- `repositoryId`
- `object` properties
- `rootFolderId`
- content `stream`

Optionally, you can use a `Holder<String>` class to return the new node reference created for the new content created in the repository.

Creating a new folder

In order to create a new folder, you need to use the `createFolder` method available from the `ObjectService`. As you can see, we need to create properties in the same way as that of the previous sample, but invoking a different method from the service:

```
CmisPropertyString folderName = objectFactory.
createCmisPropertyString();

folderName.setPropertyDefinitionId("cmis:name");
folderName.getValue().add("CMIS WS API Sample Folder "+System.
currentTimeMillis());

newFolderProperties.getProperty().add(folderName);
```

```
//creating the type property
CmisPropertyId folderType = objectFactory.createCmisPropertyId();

folderType.setPropertyDefinitionId("cmis:objectTypeId");
folderType.getValue().add("cmis:folder");
newFolderProperties.getProperty().add(folderType);

Holder<String> idHolder = new Holder<String>();

objectService.createFolder(repositoryId, newFolderProperties,
rootFolderId, null, null, null, null, idHolder);


log.info("Folder created. Id: "+idHolder.value);
```

Note that in this sample, we created a new folder and we need to set a `cmis:folder` value for the `objectTypeId` property. Then we need to set a `cmis:name` value for the new folder.

Updating a text document

When you store content for a node in the repository, you can update it using the `ObjectService`. The following example shows you how to update an existing document:

```
Holder<String> changeToken = new Holder<String>();
String contentUpdate = content + " - UPDATED";

DataHandler dataHandlerUpdate =
new DataHandler(contentUpdate, "text/plain");

CmisContentStreamType streamUpdate = new CmisContentStreamType();

streamUpdate.setMimeType("text/plain");
streamUpdate.setStream(dataHandlerUpdate);

objectService.setContentStream(repositoryId, idHolder, true,
changeToken, streamUpdate, null);

log.info("Content updated. Document Id: "+idHolder.value);
```

The most important method in the previous snippet is `setContentStream`, which you need to invoke using the `ObjectService`. The `idHolder` is referring at an existing content stored in the repository. Notice that you need to provide a `true` value for the third argument of the `setContentStream` method to set the overwrite flag in the repository for this specific node.

Updating properties

Using the `ObjectService`, you can update properties for content in the repository using the `updateProperties` method as follows:

```
CmisPropertiesType newUpdatedDocProperties = new CmisPropertiesType();

CmisPropertyString nameUpdatedDoc = objectFactory.
createCmisPropertyString();

nameUpdatedDoc.setPropertyDefinitionId("cmis:name");
nameUpdatedDoc.getValue().add("CMIS WS API Sample Document - UPDATED
- " + System.currentTimeMillis());

newUpdatedDocProperties.getProperty().add(nameUpdatedDoc);

objectService.updateProperties(repositoryId, idHolder, changeToken,
newUpdatedDocProperties, null);

log.info("Properties updated. Document Id: "+idHolder.value);
```

`idHolder` is the node reference of an existing object in the repository.

Deleting a document

In order to remove an existing document, you need to invoke the `deleteObject` method using the `ObjectService` providing the `repositoryId` and the `idHolder` in this way:

```
objectService.deleteObject(repositoryId, idHolder.value, true, null);

log.info("Document deleted. Id: "+idHolder.value);
```

Searching a document

You can search contents in the repository using `DiscoveryService`. This service allows you to execute queries using statements based on the CMIS SQL language. To execute a query in the repository, you need to provide a `Query` object by setting a `repositoryId` and a CMIS statement.

The result is returned in a `QueryResponse` object that contains objects and all the properties for each node. The following sample executes a full-text search, returning objects that contain a word that starts with the word `alfresc`:

```
DiscoveryServicePort discoveryService = cmisClient.getDiscoveryService
(CmisClient.USERNAME, CmisClient.USER_PASSWORD);

Query query = new Query();
query.setRepositoryId(repositoryId);

query.setStatement(
"SELECT * FROM cmis:document WHERE CONTAINS('alfresc*')");

QueryResponse results = discoveryService.query(query);

List<CmisObjectType> resultList = results.getObjects().getObjects();

for (CmisObjectType result : resultList) {

List<CmisProperty> properties = result.getProperties().getProperty();
    for (CmisProperty property : properties) {
                 if("cmis:name".equals(property.
getPropertyDefinitionId()))
                    log.info(((CmisPropertyString)property).getValue());

    }
}
```

The output returned by the execution of the previous code snippet is as follows:

```
[notify_user_email.ftl]
[invite_user_email.ftl]
[alfresco docs.js]
[readme.html]
[blogsearch.get.html.ftl]
[categorysearch.get.html.ftl]
[readme.html]
[blogsearch.get.atom.ftl]
[categorysearch.get.atom.ftl]
[RSS_2.0_recent_docs.ftl]
[invite-email.ftl]
[folder.get.atom.ftl]
[emailbody-texthtml.ftl]
```

Summary

This chapter discussed the CMIS Web Services binding. It started by explaining how to set up a standard client stub and how to configure all the services using the Spring Framework, Apache Maven, and Apache CXF. Then you learned some basic information about WS-Security and WS-I proposals promoted for the CMIS standard. Finally, you saw how to implement the basic operations on objects and how to their search contents. Specifically, you learned the following topics:

- Where all the WSDLs are located
- What WS-Security means and how it depends on the WS-I proposal
- How to start implementing your client stub
- How to get information about all the exposed repositories
- How to browse and inspect objects
- How to perform operations upon objects
- How to search contents in the repository

In the next chapter, you will see a complete example of an integration based on CMIS.

14
A Complete CMIS
Client Application

In the previous chapters, we saw how Apache Chemistry can be used to perform operations on a CMIS repository using a set of small, self-contained Java samples. In this chapter, we are going to leverage what we learned from those examples to build a complete, working application that showcases a typical use case for CMIS—managing content in a vendor-independent way.

CMISWiki—a CMIS-based wiki

The CMISWiki application is a web wiki that stores its content in a CMIS-compliant repository. If you don't know what a wiki is, it can be described as a web application for managing a set of pages that mainly consist of text. Page text is usually input not as HTML, but using a simplified syntax that allows users to have some limited amount of control over the layout and style of the text.

Central to a wiki is the use of nouns, or short phrases, to identify pages that are linked from other pages simply by naming them. Wikis tend to be self-organizing collections of pages that have very few controls on who is able to edit what.

Requirements

The CMISWiki application must let users easily and quickly create wiki pages. Users should be able to edit wiki pages using a well-known wiki syntax like the one used by **Textile**. It should be possible to create a new wiki page just by naming it in another page, and then clicking on its name to immediately go into the edit mode.

Wiki pages should be full-text searchable. It must be possible to upload images and insert them in wiki pages.

The user interface should be responsive. It should minimize unnecessary page reloads by using AJAX techniques wherever possible, but avoid breaking the behavior of the browser's back button.

Software building blocks

For building CMISWiki, it was decided to use the following software components, all of which are open source:

- The **Google Web Toolkit (GWT)** — for the Web user interface
- The Mylyn WikiText parser — for rendering wiki text
- Apache Chemistry — for interacting with the CMIS repository
- Alfresco Community — for the CMIS repository implementation

Apache Chemistry was described in *Chapter 12, Developing a CMIS client using Apache Chemistry*. Let's have a look at the other toolkits that we are going to use.

The Google Web Toolkit

The Google Web Toolkit (GWT for short) is a web application development environment. Its aim is to make it easy to write complex, highly interactive web applications, without requiring developers to be experts in HTML, CSS, JavaScript, and AJAX techniques.

Developers, using a familiar IDE such as Eclipse, write Java code, which the toolkit then translates to JavaScript for rendering the user interface. GWT also provides a mechanism whereby the client-side code can invoke methods to be executed on the server in the form of **Remote Procedure Calls (RPC)**. Having both client- and server-side code written in Java means that both sides can use the same Java interface that specifies which methods are exposed over RPC, thus reducing the possibility of communication errors and, at the same time, making the server-side methods easily unit-testable.

The Google Web Toolkit makes a number of widgets available, such as buttons, panels, lists, menus, a date picker, and a WYSIWYG rich-text editor, which make it possible to rapidly assemble powerful, in-browser user interfaces, all without touching a single line of HTML. More complex, custom widgets can also be created by application developers.

Information about GWT can be found at http://code.google.com/webtoolkit/.

The Mylyn WikiText parser

The **Mylyn WikiText** parser is a library for parsing and rendering wiki text into HTML and other formats. It is able to interpret wiki text in any of the MediaWiki, Textile, Confluence, TracWiki, and TWiki markups. For CMISWiki, the Textile markup was chosen.

Information about Mylyn WikiText can be found at `http://wiki.eclipse.org/Mylyn/Incubator/WikiText`. Information about the Textile markup language can be found at `http://textile.thresholdstate.com/`.

Building and running CMISWiki

The quickest way to get up and running with CMISWiki for a developer is to import the source code of the project in Eclipse. To do so, from Eclipse, select the **File | Import...** menu item, then select the **General | Existing Projects into Workspace** option and point to the folder where you have unpacked the source code for CMISWiki.

You must also have previously imported all the Apache Chemistry sub-projects in Eclipse, as explained in the previous chapter. This is how your Package Explorer tab should after a successful import:

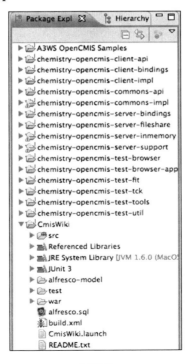

The project contains a run configuration that starts up the GWT engine in development mode, which includes the Jetty Web server, so you don't have to package the application as a WAR file for deployment into another application server.

To start it up, open the **Run Configurations** dialog box from the **Run** menu and run **CmisWiki**, as shown in the following screenshot:

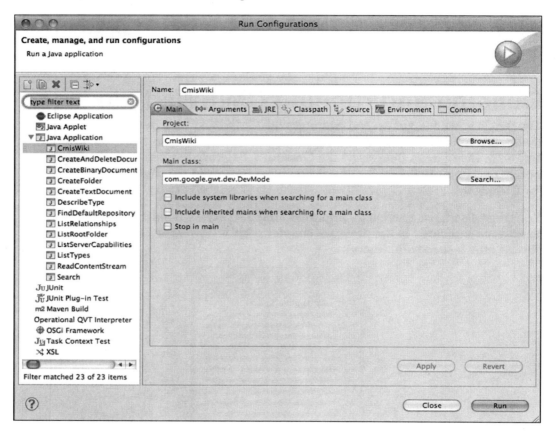

Before you do so, however, you must prepare your Alfresco installation, which involves two steps:

First, you have to load the custom model used by CMISWiki into Alfresco. The model definition file, which includes a custom `wiki:page` document type, and the corresponding Web Client configuration extension document can be found in the `alfresco-model` folder. Install them as you would normally install any customized Alfresco domain model. Step-by-step instructions for deploying a custom domain model are available at the following page: `http://wiki.alfresco.com/wiki/ Data_Dictionary_Guide#Step_by_Step_Model_Definition`.

The only other thing you must do is create a space named **Wiki** under the **Company Home** space and another space called **images** inside the former. Optionally, and only if your Alfresco installation is not listening on the default port, edit the value of the `serverUrl` variable in the `CMISClient` class. If necessary, also change the default `admin` password there. When you run CMISWiki at last, the GWT Development Mode console will pop up, allowing you to open the system's default browser to the starting page of CMISWiki, which corresponds to the following URL:

`http://127.0.0.1:8888/CmisWiki.html?gwt.codesvr=127.0.0.1:9997.`

When you will open that URL, it will automatically redirect you to a page called **Main**, which is the starting point of the Wiki. At this point, the page will not exist yet, so the **Edit** tab will be selected, allowing you to input the contents of the main page and save them.

The user interface

The user interface of CMISWiki is very simple. At the top of the page, a line displays the title of the current page. The central area of the page is taken up by a tabbed panel with three tabs: **View**, **Edit**, and **Search**. At the bottom of the page, we have a text input box with a **Search** button.

When the **View** tab is selected, it shows the contents of the current page, formatted as HTML. It can be shown as follows:

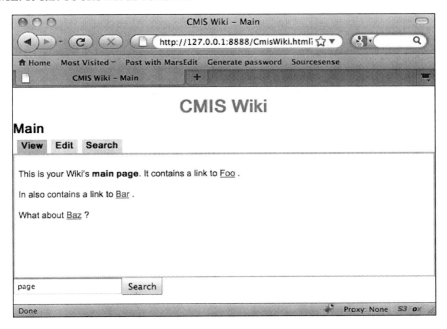

When the **Edit** tab is selected, users can edit the wiki text of the current page. It can be shown as follows:

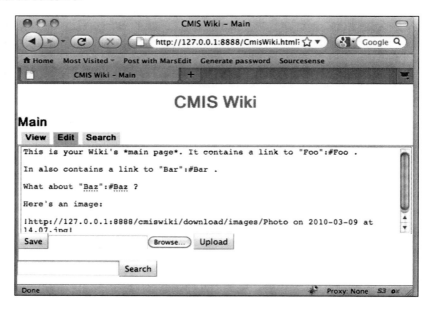

The **Edit** interface presents a file input field that can be used to upload images to the wiki. A link to the uploaded image is automatically inserted at the cursor position as follows:

When in **Edit** mode, users can type in the text area, and then click **Save** to save their modifications. The display will be returned to the **View** tab for an immediate verification of what was entered.

The **Search** tab is made visible when a user types a search phrase in the bottom text box and clicks on the **Search** button, as follows:

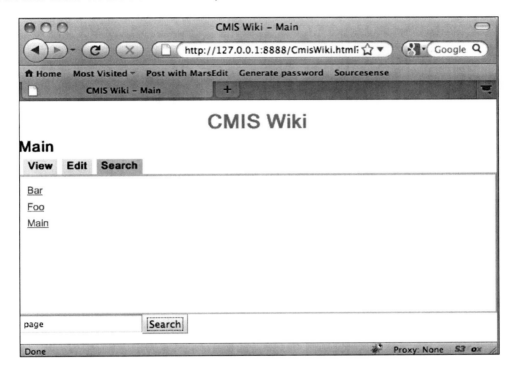

Implementation

The code of CMISWiki can be divided between client- and server-side code. This results in a three-tier system:

- The first tier is a JavaScript code, translated by GWT from Java code and running in the browser. It interacts with the second tier using the GWT-specific RPC mechanism.

- The second tier is the server-side application code. It acts as a client of the CMIS repository, which talks to it using the AtomPub binding.

- The third tier is the CMIS Repository (Alfresco in our case).

Client-side code

Client-side code is mostly contained in the `com.packtpub.a3ws.samples.cmis.wiki.client` package. This includes, among others, the `CmisWiki` class, which is the client code's entry point, and the `WikiPage` class, which defines the UI's behavior. It also contains the `WikiService` interface that is implemented by classes on the client and the server at the same time to provide the respective sides of the RPC mechanism.

The layout of the user interface is specified in the `WikiPage.ui.xml` file, which is a **GWT UiBinder** specification file.

The GWT UiBinder

The Google Web Toolkit lets you specify the layout of your application's user interface in two distinct ways. One way is by creating widgets programmatically and adding them to the page. Another option is to do it declaratively.

The latter method uses the `UiBinder` feature of GWT, and it is the one that has been used to develop CMISWiki. With `UiBinder`, you specify the layout of your interface using an XML description file, such as the following:

```
<ui:UiBinder xmlns:ui='urn:ui:com.google.gwt.uibinder'>
  <div>
    Hello, <span ui:field='nameSpan'/>.
  </div>
</ui:UiBinder>
```

In your Java code, you can declare variables that correspond to the elements of the user interface by using the `@UiField` annotation:

```
@UiField SpanElement nameSpan;
```

The `UiBinder` will automatically bind user interface elements that have a `ui:field` attribute to Java variables that are annotated with `@UiField` and whose name is equal to the value of the `ui:field` attribute. This lets you use those Java variables to access and manipulate the corresponding UI elements:

```
nameSpan.setInnerText(name);
```

You can find the `UiBinder` descriptor in the CMISWiki source code in the file `src/com/packtpub/a3ws/samples/cmis/wiki/client/WikiPage.ui.xml`.

Links and the browser history

GWT applications tend to be composed of a single web page. Changes to the application's state and to the UI are not normally accompanied by changes in the page's URL. But these are accomplished by means of AJAX calls and partial updates to the page content using Dynamic HTML (DHTML) techniques.

While this is a powerful system for building interactive, responsive Web applications, it has two main drawbacks. The first one is that it tends to break the functioning of the browser's back button.

The second—and more problematic for us—negative side-effect is that it breaks the assumption that every wiki page has a distinct URL. It effectively becomes impossible to link a specific wiki page that can be reused from outside the wiki.

Luckily, the GWT designers devised a solution to this problem that makes it possible to keep the history of an application state's changes in the browser's history, thus restoring the functionality of the back button and making every state addressable with a distinct URL.

This is accomplished via the `History` class. A developer that wants to record an application state in the browser's history only has to call:

```
History.newItem(name);
```

passing a name for the new state as an argument.

In the CMISWiki application, we decided to make application states correspond to wiki page names. Therefore, whenever a wiki page is loaded, the `History.newItem` method is called with the name of the page.

When this happens, GWT adds the new state name to the browser's URL as a fragment identifier, so the URL for the main page will look like the following:

```
http://server:port/CmisWiki.html#Main
```

When such a URL is requested again, a specific handler for history-change events is responsible for loading the corresponding page as follows:

```
History.addValueChangeHandler(
    new ValueChangeHandler<String>() {
    public void onValueChange
            (ValueChangeEvent<String> event) {
        String historyToken = event.getValue();
        if (historyToken != null) {
            wikiPage.loadPage(historyToken);
        }
    }
});
```

As the pages are identified with a URL fragment, inserting a link to a page in another page, using the Textile wiki markup, is as simple as writing:

```
"Pagename":#Pagename
```

Server-side code

Server-side code is contained in the `com.packtpub.a3ws.samples.cmis.wiki.server` package and includes the `WikiServiceImpl` class, which implements the RPC services and a couple of servlets used for uploading and downloading images.

The `CMISClient` class in the server package encapsulates the usage of the Chemistry library.

Implementation of use cases

The following sections detail how the most important use cases supported by CMISWiki — creating a new page, loading an existing page, uploading and displaying an image, searching — have been implemented.

Creating a new page

All you have to do to create a new page is to just name it. The recommended way to do this is to insert a link to a non-existing page into an existing page's text, save the latter, and click on the link. CMISWiki will interpret the link to a non-existing page as a request to create it, so it will go into edit mode and let you type the new page's text. When you click **Save**, the new page is created and linked from the starting page.

The relevant client-side method for creating a new page, or updating an existing one, is contained in the `savePage` method of the `WikiPage` class:

```
private void savePage() {
    AsyncCallback<CMISPage> callback = new AsyncCallback<CMISPage>() {
        public void onFailure(Throwable caught) {
            Window.alert(caught.getLocalizedMessage());
        }

        public void onSuccess(CMISPage result) {
            tabs.selectTab(VIEW_TAB);
            setPageText(result.getHtmlText(), result.getWikiText());
        }
    };

    wikiService.savePage(pageName.getInnerText(), editor.getText(),
callback);

}
```

With GWT, most operations that involve a client-server interaction are performed asynchronously—the client sets up an instance of an anonymous inner class implementing the AsyncCallback interface, then calls a method on the WikiServiceAsync interface. This method corresponds to a method of the same name, defined on the WikiService interface, but has one more argument, used for passing a reference to the callback class.

In the previous code, when the savePage method is invoked, GWT executes a remote call to the corresponding server method, using an asynchronous XMLHttpRequest (AJAX) invocation internally. When the remote call returns, either the onSuccess or the onFailure methods are called on the callback class, depending on the outcome (success or failure, respectively) of the call.

In our case, we pop up an alert box if there is an error and set the page text if successful.

On the server side, the corresponding savePage method is defined as follows:

```
public CMISPage savePage(String name, String text)
    throws IllegalArgumentException {
    // Verify that the input is valid.
    if (!FieldVerifier.isValidName(name)) {
        throw new IllegalArgumentException(
        "Name must be at least 3 characters long");
    }
    CMISClient client = CMISClient.getInstance();
    client.writeCMISDocument(name + ".txt", text);
    CMISPage page = new CMISPage();
    page.setName(name);
    page.setWikiText(text);
    page.setHtmlText(formatWikiText(text));
    return page;
}
```

After having validated the page name, we obtain an instance of the CMISClient class that provides access to the CMIS services and call its writeCMISDocument method to save the entered wiki text as a new document into the Alfresco Repository, having a name equal to the page title with a .txt extension appended.

The CMIS client code is similar to the one that was demonstrated in the `CreateTextDocument` class, which is contained in the samples for *Chapter 12*. It creates a new document of type `D:wiki:page`, whose content is the wiki text:

```
public void writeCMISDocument(String name, String content) {
    Session session = getSession();
    Folder wikiFolder = getWikiFolder();
    if (wikiFolder == null) {
        throw new RuntimeException
            ("Wiki folder missing. Create it under Company Home.");
    }
    Document page = getChild(wikiFolder, name);
    ContentStream contentStream = new ContentStreamImpl("content.txt",
        BigInteger.valueOf(content.length()),
        "text/plain", new ByteArrayInputStream(content.getBytes()));
    if (page == null) {
        Map<String, Object> properties = new HashMap<String, Object>();
        properties.put(PropertyIds.OBJECT_TYPE_ID, "D:wiki:page");
        properties.put(PropertyIds.NAME, name);
        page = wikiFolder.createDocument(properties, contentStream,
            VersioningState.MAJOR,
            null, null, null, session.getDefaultContext());
    } else {
        try {
            page.setContentStream(contentStream, true);
        } catch (Exception e) {
            throw new RuntimeException("While updating page: " +
                e.getLocalizedMessage());
        }
    }
}
```

The `getWikiFolder` utility method is shown as follows:

```
public Folder getWikiFolder() {
    try {
        return (Folder) getSession().getObjectByPath("/Wiki");
    } catch (CmisObjectNotFoundException e) {
        return null;
    }
}
```

We then create a `CMISPage` object that contains the page name, wiki text, and rendered HTML text, and return this to the caller. The `CMISPage` class is only used to group multiple, related values in a single object for relaying them back to the client.

The `formatWikiText` method is used to render the wiki text as HTML, using the Mylyn WikiText parser:

```
private String formatWikiText(String text) {
    StringWriter writer = new StringWriter();
    HtmlDocumentBuilder builder =
        new HtmlDocumentBuilder(writer);
    // avoid the <html> and <body> tags
    builder.setEmitAsDocument(false);
    MarkupParser markupParser = new MarkupParser(
        new TextileLanguage());
    markupParser.setBuilder(builder);
    markupParser.parse(text);
    return writer.toString();
}
```

Loading an existing page

Loading an existing page uses, once again, an asynchronous callback. Here is the client-side code:

```
public void loadPage(final String pageName) {
    setPageName(pageName);
    // Set up the callback object.
    AsyncCallback<CMISPage> callback = new AsyncCallback<CMISPage>() {
        public void onFailure(Throwable caught) {
            Window.alert(caught.getLocalizedMessage());
        }

        public void onSuccess(CMISPage result) {
            if (result != null) {
                setPageName(result.getName());
                setPageText(result.getHtmlText(), result.getWikiText());
                tabs.selectTab(VIEW_TAB);
            } else {
                // Switch to edit tab for new pages
                setPageText("", "");
                tabs.selectTab(EDIT_TAB);
            }
        }
    };

    wikiService.loadPage(pageName, callback);
}
```

If the wiki page already exists, the widgets on the web page will be filled with the values contained in the CMISPage object returned by the server. If the wiki page does not exist, the server returns null, in which case the web page widgets are left empty.

On the server side, the WikiServiceImpl class defines the loadPage method as follows:

```
public CMISPage loadPage(String name)
      throws IllegalArgumentException {
   CMISClient client = CMISClient.getInstance();
   String text = client.loadCMISDocument(name + ".txt");
   if (text != null) {
      CMISPage page = new CMISPage();
      page.setName(name);
      page.setWikiText(text);
      page.setHtmlText(formatWikiText(text));
      return page;
   }
   return null;
}
```

Apart from setting up a CMISPage instance to communicate data back to the client, the method delegates most of the work to the loadCMISDocument method of the CMISClient class. This one returns the contents of the CMIS document as a string:

```
public String loadCMISDocument(String name) {
   Folder wikiFolder = getWikiFolder();
   if (wikiFolder == null) {
   throw new RuntimeException
      ("Wiki folder missing. Create it under Company Home.");
   }
   Document page = getChild(wikiFolder, name);
   if (page == null) {
      return null;
   }
   try {
      ContentStream cs = page.getContentStream();
      InputStream in = cs.getStream();
      InputStreamReader reader = new InputStreamReader(in);
      StringWriter out = new StringWriter((int) cs.getLength());
      char[] buf = new char[1024];
      int n = 0;
      while ((n = reader.read(buf)) > 0) {
         out.write(buf, 0, n);
      }
      return new String(buf);
   } catch (IOException e) {
```

```
        throw new RuntimeException(e.getLocalizedMessage());
        }
    }
```

The `getChild` utility method is defined as follows:

```
public Document getChild(Folder parent, String name) {
    try {
        return (Document) getSession().
            getObjectByPath(parent.getPath() + "/" + name);
    } catch (CmisObjectNotFoundException e) {
        return null;
    }
}
```

Uploading an image

GWT provides support for uploading files in the background using AJAX with the `FileUpload` component. In order to receive the said files on the server, however, it is not possible to use the RPC framework that is normally employed for client-server communication. We must develop a custom servlet instead.

On the client side, the following `UiBinder` snippet sets up the form with the `FileUpload` field and an **Upload** button:

```
<g:FormPanel ui:field="uploadForm">
    <g:HTMLPanel>
        <g:FileUpload ui:field="fileUpload" />
        <g:Button ui:field="uploadButton">Upload</g:Button>
    </g:HTMLPanel>
</g:FormPanel>
```

In the `WikiPage` class, we need to set up the form attributes and an event handler to react to the event that is generated when the submission is completed. What we do, in this case, is insert a link to the image at the current cursor position in the text area. The upload servlet returns the path (relative to the `Wiki` folder) of the new file, which GWT includes in a `<pre>...</pre>` HTML element. Therefore, we need to substitute the extra HTML with the exclamation point symbol that is used in Textile markup to delimit image URLs. We also prepend the `"download"` path to the URL of the image in order to have it served by the download servlet that will be described in the next section:

```
fileUpload.setName("upload");
uploadForm.setEncoding(FormPanel.ENCODING_MULTIPART);
uploadForm.setMethod(FormPanel.METHOD_POST);
uploadForm.setAction(GWT.getModuleBaseURL() + "upload");
```

```
uploadForm.addSubmitCompleteHandler(new FormPanel.
SubmitCompleteHandler() {
    public void onSubmitComplete(SubmitCompleteEvent event) {
        String result = event.getResults();
        result = result.replace("<pre>", "!"+ GWT.getModuleBaseURL() +
"download/");
        result = result.replace("</pre>", "!");
        result = result.replaceAll("[\\r\\n]", "");
        // Insert a link to the image at the current cursor position
        int pos = editor.getCursorPos();
        String before = editor.getText().substring(0, pos);
        String after = editor.getText().substring(pos);
        StringBuffer newText = new StringBuffer(before);
        newText.append(result);
        newText.append(after);
        editor.setText(newText.toString());
    }
});
```

On the server side, the upload form submission is handled by the UploadServlet class, which uses the common FileUpload library to handle multipart/form-data requests. The doPost method is shown as follows:

```
protected void doPost(HttpServletRequest req, HttpServletResponse
resp)
        throws ServletException, IOException {
    boolean isMultipart = ServletFileUpload
            .isMultipartContent(new ServletRequestContext(req));
    if (isMultipart) {
        FileItem uploadItem = getFileItem(req);
        if (uploadItem != null) {
            CMISClient client = CMISClient.getInstance();
            client.writeImage(uploadItem.get(),
                uploadItem.getContentType(),
                uploadItem.getName());
            resp.setContentType("text/plain");
            PrintWriter out = resp.getWriter();
            out.println("images/" + uploadItem.getName());
            return;
        }
    }
    resp.setStatus(HttpServletResponse.SC_BAD_REQUEST);
}
```

This method obtains information about the uploaded file in the form of an instance of the `FileItem` class, part of commons-FileUpload. It then delegates sending it to the CMIS repository to the `CMISClient`'s class `writeImage` method:

```
public void writeImage(byte[] bytes, String contentType, String name)
{
    Session session = getSession();
    Folder wikiFolder = getImagesFolder();
    if (wikiFolder == null) {
        throw new RuntimeException
        ("Images folder missing. Create /Wiki/images under Company
Home.");
    }
    ContentStream contentStream = new ContentStreamImpl(
            "content.jpg",
            BigInteger.valueOf(bytes.length),
            "image/jpeg",
            new ByteArrayInputStream(bytes));
    Map<String, Object> properties = new HashMap<String, Object>();
    properties.put(PropertyIds.OBJECT_TYPE_ID,
            BaseTypeId.CMIS_DOCUMENT.value());
    properties.put(PropertyIds.NAME, name);
    wikiFolder.createDocument(properties, contentStream,
            VersioningState.MAJOR,
            null, null, null, session.getDefaultContext());
}
```

Displaying an image

An image that is found inside the `/Wiki/images` folder in the CMIS Repository can be inserted into a wiki page for display by using the following Textile markup, for example:

`!/download/images/filename.jpg.`

This URL is served by the download servlet, implemented by the `DownloadServlet` class. This servlet can actually serve any kind of content stored in the CMIS Repository, not just images. Its most important method is `streamCMISDocument`. It delegates finding the binary file to the `getChild` method of `CMISClient`. It then obtains a `ContentStream` from the file and streams it over HTTP:

```
private void streamCMISDocument(String path,
        HttpServletResponse resp) {
    CMISClient client = CMISClient.getInstance();
    int pos = path.lastIndexOf('/');
```

```
Folder folder = client.getWikiSubFolder(
   path.substring(0, pos));
if (folder == null) {
   throw new RuntimeException("Folder " + path +
   " missing. Create it under Company Home.");
}
CMISObject image = client.getChild(folder,
   path.substring(pos + 1));
if (image == null) {
   resp.setStatus(HttpServletResponse.SC_NOT_FOUND);
   return;
}
try {
   ContentStream cs = image.getContentStream(null);
   resp.setContentType(cs.getMimeType());
   resp.setContentLength((int) cs.getLength());
   OutputStream out = resp.getOutputStream();
   InputStream in = cs.getStream();
   byte[] buf = new byte[1024];
   int n = 0;
   while ((n = in.read(buf)) > 0) {
      out.write(buf, 0, n);
   }
} catch (IOException e) {
   throw new RuntimeException(e.getLocalizedMessage());
}
}
```

There is no corresponding client UI code for this use case, since the image is linked in text and streamed directly to the browser.

Searching

Searching is handled in the user-interface layer by the searchPages method. It asynchronously calls the search method on the WikiService interface, which in turn relays it to the corresponding server method.

The callback handler, in case of success, fills the rows of the table contained in the **Search** tab with links to the pages returned from the search. The code is as follows:

```
private void searchPages(String query) {
   AsyncCallback<List<String>> callback =
      new AsyncCallback<List<String>>() {
```

```
        @Override
        public void onFailure(Throwable caught) {
            Window.alert(caught.getLocalizedMessage());
        }

        @Override
        public void onSuccess(List<String> results) {
            searchResultsTable.removeAllRows();
            for (int i = 0 ; i < results.size(); ++i) {
                String name = results.get(i);
                int pos = name.lastIndexOf(".txt");
                if (pos > 0) {
                    name = name.substring(0, pos);
                    searchResultsTable.setWidget(i, 0,
                        new Hyperlink(name, name));
                }
            }
        }
    };

    wikiService.search(query, callback);
}
```

The server-side search method in the WikiServiceImpl class does nothing but delegate the operation to the CMISClient class:

```
public List<String> search(String query)
        throws IllegalArgumentException {
    CMISClient client = CMISClient.getInstance();
    return client.searchCMISDocuments(query);
}
```

Here is the latter:

```
public List<String> searchCMISDocuments(String query) {
    Session session = getSession();
    Folder wikiFolder = getWikiFolder();
    if (wikiFolder == null) {
        throw new RuntimeException
        ("Wiki folder missing. Create it under Company Home.");
    }
    String sql = "SELECT * FROM wiki:page WHERE IN_TREE('" +
        wikiFolder.getId() +
        "') AND CONTAINS('" + query + "')";
```

```
    ItemIterable<QueryResult> results = session.query(sql, false);
    List<String> pages = new ArrayList<String>((int) results.
getTotalNumItems());
    for (QueryResult result : results) {
        pages.add((String) result.getPropertyValueById(PropertyIds.
NAME));
    }
    return pages;
}
```

As you can see, it builds a CMIS-SQL query using the IN_TREE predicate function to restrict the search to the Wiki folder only and the CONTAINS predicate function to do a full-text search.

Summary

This concludes the description of the CMISWiki application and is the last chapter on CMIS. In this chapter, we have put together our knowledge about CMIS and the Apache Chemistry toolkit in order to create a working application that is quite simple, yet complete enough to be able to demonstrate how to accomplish the following operations on documents contained in a CMIS Repository:

- Create
- Update
- Read
- Search

CMISWiki has been tested with Alfresco Community 3.3g, but should be portable to other CMSs with little or no modification.

As an exercise for the reader, it would be useful to enrich CMISWiki by adding the following features and possibly more:

- Deleting pages
- Representing links between pages as CMIS relationships and discovering them
- Federating several CMIS Repositories in a single wiki

The CMIS Query Language

The **Content Management Interoperability Services (CMIS)** standard specifies a query service for finding objects of given types that match specific criteria, using a subset of the SQL-92 language with extensions, by defining a read-only projection of the CMIS data model onto a **relational view**. This appendix details the syntax and semantics of the CMIS query language with references to the Alfresco implementation, where it differs from the standard or where it does not implement some optional features.

The relational view projection

The relational view projection is composed of a set of **virtual tables** that are defined on top of the CMIS data model. For every CMIS object type that is `queryable`, the projection defines a corresponding virtual table whose name is the `queryName` attribute of the object type. Object types that are not `queryable` are not included in the projection.

Each virtual table includes all the properties defined for the object type itself as **virtual columns**, plus all the properties of ancestor types that are not defined in the object type definition itself. The names of the virtual columns are equal to the value of the `queryName` attribute of the corresponding properties.

For example, on a repository configured with the custom domain model defined for the Alfresco bookshop application introduced in *Chapter 4, A Complete Example*, the `bs:book` virtual table includes the following columns, added to the `bs:book` type:

- `bs:price`
- `bs:isbn`
- `bs:author`
- `bs:publisher`

in addition to the following, taken from the definition of `cmis:document`:

- `cmis:contentStreamLength`
- `cmis:objectTypeId`
- `cmis:lastModifiedBy`
- `cmis:createdBy`
- `cmis:name`
- `cmis:contentStreamMimeType`
- `cmis:creationDate`
- `cmis:objectId`
- `cmis:contentStreamFileName`
- `cmis:lastModificationDate`

 Object properties that are not set will cause the corresponding virtual column to have the SQL NULL value.

Hierarchy of types and the relational view

Object types that have the `includedInSuperTypeQuery` attribute set to `true` will be included in the virtual table for any of their ancestor types. Therefore, a query like:

```
SELECT * from cmis:document
```

will return not only rows corresponding to objects of type `cmis:document`, but also of all types derived from `cmis:document` that have `includedInSuperTypeQuery` equal to `true`.

In Alfresco Community 3.3, all object types, either built-in or custom-defined, have `includedInSuperTypeQuery` set to `true`.

Results of queries

When a query is executed, the repository must return a set of pseudo CMIS objects comprised of the properties defined in the `SELECT` clause of the query statement.

For every property of each object in the result set, the repository must include the property definition ID as well as the query name or alias used in the query.

Grammar of queries

The basic form of a CMIS SQL query is as follows:

```
SELECT <virtual columns> FROM <virtual tables> [WHERE <conditions>]
[ORDER BY <sort specification>]
```

The SELECT clause

The SELECT clause must either specify a comma-separated list of virtual column names or the '*' token. All column names must be valid queryNames of properties defined for the object types listed in the FROM clause.

In addition to column names, it is also possible to use the SCORE() predicate function as a column name. The SCORE() predicate returns the relevance value of the search made in the CONTAINS predicate. The value is between 0 and 1, with 0 it means that the text was not found in the document and 1 indicates a perfect match. You cannot use the SCORE() function in a query that does not use the CONTAINS predicate.

 Content streams are not part of the relational view. Therefore, they cannot be included in the SELECT clauses.

As with SQL-92, aliases can be defined for column names using the AS keyword as follows:

```
SELECT book.bs:price AS price, book.bs:isbn AS isbn, book.bs:author AS
author, book.bs:publisher AS publisher FROM bs:book AS book
```

The FROM clause

The FROM clause lists the queryNames of the virtual tables that are included in the query.

Joins

Repositories that support joins provide the capability of performing inner-or possibly outer-joins in queries, using the standard SQL-92 syntax. Only the equality predicate can be used on join conditions and single-valued properties.

Implicit joins as parts of the WHERE clause are not allowed in CMIS SQL. Only explicit joins as part of the FROM clause can be used, as follows:

```
SELECT b.cmis:name FROM bs:book AS b JOIN bs:review AS r ON r.cmis:
name = b.cmis:name
```

The WHERE clause

The WHERE clause defines the constraints that the rows, resulting from the join of all the virtual tables listed in the FROM clause, must satisfy in order to be included in the result set of a query.

All the column names used in the WHERE clause must be valid queryNames of properties, defined for the object types included in the FROM clause, or their aliases, as defined by the SELECT clause.

Comparison operators

The comparison operators, shown in the following table, can be used depending on the types of the columns involved in the comparison. These can only be used on single-valued properties.

Property Type	Operators
String	=, <>, [NOT] LIKE, [NOT] IN
Decimal	=, <>, <, <=, >, >=, [NOT] IN
Integer	=, <>, <, <=, >, >=, [NOT] IN
Boolean	=
DateTime	=, <>, <, <=, >, >=, [NOT] IN
ID	=, <>, [NOT] IN
URI	=, <>, [NOT] LIKE, [NOT] IN

Testing multi-valued properties

The ANY quantified comparison predicate can be used to filter rows where any one of the values of a multi-valued property is equal to a reference value:

```
SELECT * FROM  bs:book AS b WHERE ('Jerome D. Salinger' = ANY b.bs:
author)
```

The IN/ANY predicate is an extension to SQL-92. It evaluates to true when any of the values of a multi-valued property are included in a list of reference values:

```
SELECT * FROM bs:book WHERE ANY bs:author IN ('Jerome D. Salinger',
'Kurt Vonnegut', 'Joseph Heller')
```

Full-text search using CONTAINS

If a repository provides full-text search, then document text can be queried for using the CONTAINS predicate. Its syntax is as follows:

```
CONTAINS([<qualifier>,] <text>)
```

The value of qualifier, if present, must be the name of one of the virtual tables listed in the FROM clause. It indicates which table the search applies to.

If the FROM clause lists more than one virtual table, then the qualifier must be present. Otherwise, it can be omitted, as the search is performed only on the single table named.

The value of text must be a string enclosed in quotes, specifying words and phrases to look for. Search terms can be made up of multiple words and must be enclosed in double quotes.

Terms can be negated by prefixing them with the '-' character. Separate terms are implicitly joined with the AND conjunction (which can be made explicit), unless they are explicitly joined by OR.

At most, one CONTAINS expression can be present in a WHERE clause, and, where it is present together with other predicates, it can only be joined through an AND clause. The return value of the CONTAINS function is a boolean: either true when the content is considered relevant with respect to the search text, or false otherwise. When the CONTAINS predicate is used, it is possible to use the SCORE function in the SELECT clause. Its value is a decimal number between 0 (minimum relevance) and 1 (maximum relevance).

The IN_FOLDER predicate

The IN_FOLDER predicate function, whose syntax is

```
IN_FOLDER([<qualifier>,]  <id>)
```

is used to test whether or not the candidate object is a direct child of the folder identified by id. If it is, the function returns true. The value of qualifier must be the name of one of the virtual tables listed in the FROM clause and must be present if there are more than one.

The IN_TREE predicate

The IN_TREE predicate function, whose syntax is:

```
IN_TREE([<qualifier>,]  <id>)
```

works much like the IN_FOLDER predicate. However, it only tests whether or not the candidate object is a descendant of the folder identified by id.

The ORDER BY clause

The ORDER BY clause lists one or more names of virtual columns (or their aliases), according to whose values the objects in the result set are ordered. All the columns listed in the ORDER BY clause must be listed in the SELECT clause and must identify orderable properties of object types listed in the FROM clause. The collation rules used for ordering are repository-specific.

Escaping special characters

All repositories must support the escaping of special characters using the backslash (\) character inside quoted strings. The following table lists the allowed escape sequences and their meaning:

\"	"
\'	'
\\	\
\% (in the right-hand side of a LIKE comparison)	%
_ (in the right-hand side of a LIKE comparison)	_

All other uses of the backslash are disallowed and considered as an error.

 The full text of the CMIS specification is available at http://docs. oasis-open.org/cmis/CMIS/v1.0/os/cmis-spec-v1.0.pdf.

Index

Symbols

.NET project
  authentication 141
  child associations, managing 152
  CRUD operations 142
  Lucene query, performing 140, 141
  operations, performing 141
  setting up 135
.NET sample 135
.NET sample client
  testing 138, 139

A

Abdera
  installing 260, 261
Abstract Web Scripts 235
Access Control Entry (ACE) 70
Access Control List (ACL) 70
ACL capabilities
  ACL 290
ACL Services
  about 286
  applyACL 286
  getACL 286
action
  about 76
  executing 77, 80
  getting 82
  managing 76
  removing 84
  saving 81
ActionItemDefinition object 79
addACEs() method 71
addChildAuthorities() method 71

Alfresco
  about 292
  aspects 41
  associations 38
  authentication 26
  categories 203
  CMIS implementation 293, 294
  CMIS support 293
  CML 21
  hosted CMIS AtomPub TCK 293
  repository, searching 42
  root-scoped objects 208
  scripting techniques 209
  versioning 40
  Web Scripts 155
Alfresco Bookshop application
  about 202
  Atom, using 230
  duplicate reviews, checking 232
  first version, implementing 221
  protocol 220
  representations 220
  requisites 219
Alfresco Community 3.2r2
  services 344
Alfresco Foundation APIs
  about 8
  constraints 8
Alfresco index 214
Alfresco repository
  about 8
  associated nodes, querying 46
  child nodes, querying 50, 51
  Lucene queries, performing 42-45
  Lucene searches 213
  methods 42

C

Envelope element
  about 10
  Body element 11
  Header element 11
executeActions() method 77, 80
executeImpl method 236
eXo 294
extensions, AtomPub 244

F

FileItem class 387
FileUpload component 385
filing capabilities
  multiFiling 288
  unfiling 288
  versionSpecificFiling 288
first version implementation, Alfresco
    Bookshop application
  about 221
  Alfresco Explorer, explorer 223
  book, searching 225
  content model, extending 221, 222
  controller, creating 225
  response, returning 226
  review, creating 226
  review properties, setting 226
  template, creating 228
  Web Script, testing 228, 229
  Web Script descriptor, creating 225
format element, Web Script 172
formatWikiText method 383
FreeMarker
  about 181
  benefits 181
  comments 196
  concepts 181, 182
  directives 192
  expressions 183
  URL 181
  using, in Web Scripts 197
FreeMarker, in Web Scripts
  example 199, 200
FreeMarker expressions
  about 183
  built-ins 190
  containers 185

  missing values 189
  operators 186
  scalars 183
FreeMarker templates 165
FROM clause
  about 393
  joins 393
FTP 8
full-text search, using CONTAINS
  about 395
  IN_FOLDER predicate function 395
  IN_TREE predicate function 396

G

getACLs() method 71
getActionDefinitions() method 77
getActionItemDefinition() method 77
getActions() method 77
getAllAuthorities() method 71
getAuthenticationDetails() method 26
getAuthorities() method 71
getCategories() method 67
getChildAuthorities() method 72
getChildCategories() method 67
getChild method 387
getChildren method 359
getChild utility method 385
getClassifications() method 67
getClassPermissions() method 71
getColumns() method 45
getConditionDefinitions() method 77
getContentStream method 337
getDestination() method 34
getIsMultiValue() method 45
getLockOwner() method 64
getLockStatus() method 54
getLockStatus method 64
getLockType() method 64
GET method 160
getName() method 45
getNode() method 45
getOwners() method 72
getParentAuthorities() method 71
getPermissions() method 71
getRules() method 86
getRuleType() method 86

getRuleTypes() method 86
getSession method 329
getStores method 11
getStoresResponse method 12
getTicket() method 26
getUser() method 90
getValue() method 45
getValues() method 45
getVersionHistory() method 54
getVersionHistory method 61
getWikiFolder utility method 382
Google Web Toolkit 372
Google Web Toolkit (GWT) client 295
graduation 318
GWT UiBinder 378

H

hashes 185
hash operators 188
hasPermissions() method 72
home page, bookshop website
   about 102
   features 102
HTTP methods
   DELETE 160
   GET 160
   POST 160
   PUT 160
hyperlinks
   using, for application state modification
      161

I

IBM 295
if directive 192
IMAP 8
IN/ANY predicate 394
IN_FOLDER predicate function 395
IN_TREE predicate function 396
inbound events 85
include directive 194
Internet Engineering Task Force (IETF) 242,
      243
IRIs 243
ISO9075 32

J

Java
   Web Script, writing 234
Java-backed Web Scripts
   about 235
   Abstract Web Scripts 235
   Declarative Web Scripts 235
   types 235
java.io.InputStream method 335
Java API for XML Processing (JAXP) 317
Java classpath, CML
   setting up 24
   setting up, precompiled client used 24
   setting up, third-party frameworks used 25
Java client, for book update 275
JavaScript controller
   providing, to Web Script 208
JavaScript debugger 212
Java version, Web Script 238-240
JCR 8, 282
JSON
   about 205
   advantages 205
   categories 206
   creating 206
   URL 205

K

key 185
KnowledgeTree 295

L

list directive
   about 193
   loop-variable_has_next 193
   loop-variable_index 193
listTypes method 330
loadCMISDocument method 384
loadPage method 384
lock() method 54
lockChildren 63
locking mechanism
   about 62
   lock status, checking 64
   managing 62

Thank you for buying
Alfresco 3 Web Services

About Packt Publishing

Packt, pronounced 'packed', published its first book "*Mastering phpMyAdmin for Effective MySQL Management*" in April 2004 and subsequently continued to specialize in publishing highly focused books on specific technologies and solutions.

Our books and publications share the experiences of your fellow IT professionals in adapting and customizing today's systems, applications, and frameworks. Our solution based books give you the knowledge and power to customize the software and technologies you're using to get the job done. Packt books are more specific and less general than the IT books you have seen in the past. Our unique business model allows us to bring you more focused information, giving you more of what you need to know, and less of what you don't.

Packt is a modern, yet unique publishing company, which focuses on producing quality, cutting-edge books for communities of developers, administrators, and newbies alike. For more information, please visit our website: www.packtpub.com.

About Packt Open Source

In 2010, Packt launched two new brands, Packt Open Source and Packt Enterprise, in order to continue its focus on specialization. This book is part of the Packt Open Source brand, home to books published on software built around Open Source licences, and offering information to anybody from advanced developers to budding web designers. The Open Source brand also runs Packt's Open Source Royalty Scheme, by which Packt gives a royalty to each Open Source project about whose software a book is sold.

Writing for Packt

We welcome all inquiries from people who are interested in authoring. Book proposals should be sent to author@packtpub.com. If your book idea is still at an early stage and you would like to discuss it first before writing a formal book proposal, contact us; one of our commissioning editors will get in touch with you.

We're not just looking for published authors; if you have strong technical skills but no writing experience, our experienced editors can help you develop a writing career, or simply get some additional reward for your expertise.

Alfresco Enterprise Content Management Implementation

ISBN: 978-1-904811-11-4   Paperback: 356 pages

How to Install, use, and customize this powerful, free, Open Source Java-based Enterprise CMS

1. Manage your business documents: version control, library services, content organization, and search

2. Workflows and business rules: move and manipulate content automatically when events occur

3. Maintain, extend, and customize Alfresco: backups and other admin tasks, customizing and extending the content model, creating your own look and feel

Alfresco Developer Guide

ISBN: 978-1-847193-11-7   Paperback: 556 pages

Customizing Alfresco with actions, web scripts, web forms, workflows, and more

1. Learn to customize the entire Alfresco platform, including both Document Management and Web Content Management

2. Jam-packed with real-world, step-by-step examples to jump start your development

3. Content modeling, custom actions, Java API, RESTful web scripts, advanced workflow

4. This book covers Alfresco Enterprise Edition version 2.2

Please check **www.PacktPub.com** for information on our titles

Alfresco 3 Enterprise Content Management Implementation

ISBN: 978-1-847197-36-8   Paperback: 600 pages

How to customize, use, and administer this powerful, Open Source Java-based Enterprise CMS

1. Manage your business documents with version control, library services, content organization, and advanced search

2. Create collaborative web sites using document libraries, wikis, blogs, forums, calendars, discussions, and social tagging

3. Integrate with external applications such as Liferay Portal, Adobe Flex, iPhone, iGoogle, and Facebook

Choosing an Open Source CMS: Beginner's Guide

ISBN: 978-1-847196-22-4   Paperback: 340 pages

Building rigorously tested and bug-free Django applications

1. Understand different types of CMSs and select the one that best fits your needs

2. Install and customize a CMS with themes and plug-ins

3. Learn key concepts of Content Management Systems and how to systematically assess your requirements

4. Introduction to the major CMSs including Joomla!, Drupal, WordPress, Plone, Magento, Alfresco, and more

Please check **www.PacktPub.com** for information on our titles

Breinigsville, PA USA
27 September 2010
246189BV00004B/3/P